# A Good Life on a Finite Earth

STUDIES IN COMPARATIVE ENERGY
AND ENVIRONMENTAL POLITICS

Series editors: Todd A. Eisenstadt, American University,
and Joanna I. Lewis, Georgetown University

*Democracy in the Woods: Environmental Conservation
and Social Justice in India, Tanzania, and Mexico*
Prakash Kashwan

# A Good Life on a Finite Earth

*The Political Economy of Green Growth*

**DANIEL J. FIORINO**

# OXFORD

UNIVERSITY PRESS

Oxford University Press is a department of the University of Oxford. It furthers
the University's objective of excellence in research, scholarship, and education
by publishing worldwide. Oxford is a registered trade mark of Oxford University
Press in the UK and certain other countries.

Published in the United States of America by Oxford University Press
198 Madison Avenue, New York, NY 10016, United States of America.

Library of Congress Cataloging-in-Publication Data
Names: Fiorino, Daniel J., author.
Title: A good life on a finite earth : the political economy of green growth / Daniel J. Fiorino.
Description: New York, NY : Oxford University Press, 2018. |
Series: Studies of comparative energy and environmental politics |
Includes bibliographical references and index.
Identifiers: LCCN 2017020886 (print) | LCCN 2017047583 (ebook) |
ISBN 9780190605827 (Updf) | ISBN 9780190605834 (Epub) |
ISBN 9780190605803 (hardcover : acid-free paper) | ISBN 9780190605810 (pbk. : acid-free paper)
Subjects: LCSH: Environmental economics. | Environmentalism—Economic aspects. |
Economic development—Environmental aspects. | Environmental policy—Economic aspects.
Classification: LCC HC79.E5 (ebook) | LCC HC79.E5 F5147 2018 (print) | DDC 333.7—dc23
LC record available at https://lccn.loc.gov/2017020886

9 8 7 6 5 4 3 2 1

Paperback printed by Webcom, Inc., Canada
Hardback printed by Bridgeport National Bindery, Inc., United States of America

*To Beth Ann*

# CONTENTS

CONTENTS

# LIST OF TABLES, FIGURE, AND BOX

## TABLES

## FIGURE

## BOX

Desperate times call for desperate measures and creative thinking. The centrality of climate change and strong and proactive energy and environmental policies is under question, at least in the United States, where this new book series is being launched. Despite the bedrock consensus in the scientific community about the need to diversify the earth's sources of energy and find also other means of drastically cutting greenhouse gas emissions, important sectors of the public—and now political leadership—question these facts. This backdrop offers us a particularly auspicious moment to launch our new book series with Oxford University Press and to introduce the second title in the new series, "Studies in Comparative Energy and Environmental Politics." We are striving to launch the series at a moment of particular flux in US policies because we think that by focusing more concertedly on the advancements made in some parts of the world regarding energy and environmental policies, we can help showcase and compare for scholars, students, and practitioners everywhere the quickly emerging advances and best practices in empirical research, policymaking, and implementation. We can think of no better book to help us showcase the objectives of this new series than Dan Fiorino's empirically grounded and innovatively argued monograph, *A Good Life on a Finite Earth: The Political Economy of Green Growth.*

While the previous generation of global environmental politics research focused primarily on environmental treaty making, this new era of environmental governance has shifted, for a host of reasons, to a need to better understand the development and implementation of national and subnational policies. This requires both an in-depth understanding of domestic contexts as well as a complex understanding of the relationship between state actors across all levels of governance as well as nonstate actors. Our premise in the series is that few studies exist to systematically address the domestic energy and environmental policy strategies of the world's nations. National and subnational solutions also are increasingly being viewed as vital in the face of international negotiation stalemates. In addition, as developing and emerging economies play ever increasing roles in global energy and climate challenges and solutions, more focus on these regions is particularly important. Of course, as Professor Fiorino's book shows us, new forms of thinking about economic growth and development in industrial economies—where energy usage and environmental degradation disproportionately impact the rest of the world—are also central to creating a better future.

Seeking to reframe debates about sustainable growth away from the traditional dichotomy between growth and environmental protection, Fiorino provides an important argument that these two goals may be complementary rather than opposed. Indeed, he argues in the preface that "the business-as-usual brown [growth] scenario is irresponsible and ultimately a recipe for a fundamentally different and damaged world." At the same time, Fiorino warns that the opposite perspective, of "rejecting growth" is "politically unrealistic, economically risky, socially unfair, and undermines our ability to deal with the sources of ecological degradation and threats to our collective well-being."

*A Good Life on a Finite Earth* refutes the conventional argument that unqualified growth is beneficial for the environment, or even for the economy. In this era of policy polarization and an increasingly narrow focus on evaluations of environmental policies, Professor Fiorino steps back and takes a larger view and admonishes us that the discussion needs to be reformulated, as entrenched interests have gotten us stuck in the endless debate over whether economic growth requires a smaller role for government while environmental protection may need a larger one. The critique is an important one, which the author makes with compelling and well-stated claims; indeed, even this clear and cutting diagnosis of the problem would have constituted a successful book. But Professor Fiorino's contribution goes much further.

After discrediting the futility of much of the existing debate between either unrestrained and unguided or no growth, he picks up the pieces to structure a new and proactive approach for how to define green growth, understand policies which can lead us there, and to take stock of the progress already being made—mostly by subnational entities in the United States—when we dare to contemplate strong economic growth *with* responsible environmental stewardship. Indeed, a rich policy stream has emerged through which subnational actors, from city mayors and activists to supranational actors such as the World Bank and United Nations Environment Program, have recognized the "critical interactions among issues like energy and water, food and climate, or energy and health." These interactions can be (and are being) studied and addressed interactively and dynamically, rather than through the more static and unidimensional approaches taken separately to address each issue during "first generation" efforts to solve them. Using stream theory to convey how the agenda might be reset, and the Advocacy Coalition Framework model to consider concrete interest-group coalitions and how these might involve subnational actors, the author offers the beginning of a strategy for formulation of a green growth coalition in the United States.

Fiorino's far-reaching and ambitious book lays the groundwork for our series, along with the first book in the series, Prakash Kashwan's outstanding monograph, *Democracy in the Woods: Environmental Conservation and Social Justice in India, Tanzania, and Mexico*. Kashwan's book was in press when arrangements were finalized to launch the series, but the editors felt it would be an important cornerstone—along with *A Good Life on a Finite Earth*—to lay the foundation for our title list. Kashwan's book traces the effects of dominant political party intermediation of forest and land rights into policy on redistributive policies, be they inclusive (Mexico), or exclusive (Tanzania and India). *Democracy in the Woods* also sets the series on track with meticulous and explicit comparisons among the three countries' policy inputs (which vary according to impacts of party involvement in setting land policy) and divergent policy outcomes.

Taken together, the books offer an auspicious beginning to the series, which we hope will unearth new arguments, perspectives, and comparisons relating to how energy and environmental policies are being retooled and redirected to contribute to our collective well-being and ensure the continuance of *A Good Life on a Finite Earth*. This is an ambitious agenda for a book series, but in these times the stakes are high if we fall short. More importantly, Kashwan and Fiorino embraced this challenge, and we look forward to continuing to strive for excellence in forthcoming contributions to this series. We congratulate Dan Fiorino on his contribution, and thank our colleague Angela Chnapko of Oxford University Press for her steady guidance and leadership.

Todd A. Eisenstadt and Joanna I. Lewis
**Editorial Board**
Co-editor Todd A. Eisenstadt, American University (USA)
Co-editor Joanna I. Lewis, Georgetown University (USA)
Members:
Moises Arce, University of Missouri (USA)
Guri Bang, Center for International Climate Research (Norway)
Navroz K. Dubash, Centre for Policy Research (India)
Jennifer Hadden, University of Maryland (USA)

Kathryn Hochstetler, London School of Economics (Great Britain)
Llewellyn Hughes, Australian National University (Australia)
David Konisky, University of Indiana (USA)
Denise Mauzerall, Princeton University (USA)
Simone Pulver, University of California-Santa Barbara (USA)
Miranda Schreurs, Technical University of Munich (Germany)
Erika Weinthal, Duke University (USA)

Since the beginning of the 1970s, the United States and many other nations have been engaged in an effort to protect the environment and public health against a variety of threats: air and water pollution, harmful chemicals, loss of ecosystems, land degradation, habitat and species loss, and now climate change and its manifold consequences. There have been modest successes, to be sure. Especially in the United States, environmental conditions would be far worse without such innovations as the Clean Air Act, Clean Water Act, National Environmental Policy Act, and other laws and policies that, whatever their flaws, delivered a far better, healthier environment.

In my 2006 book on *The New Environmental Regulation*, I was concerned about the effects of a regulatory system that focused too narrowly on simple compliance, failed to distinguish among levels of performance by regulated firms, and prescribed solutions that constrained innovation and creativity in solving environmental problems. The challenge there was the limitations in environmental regulation given the changes that had occurred since the 1970s. Those issues still are relevant, but this book examines an even larger set of challenges: the growing pressures that economic growth and activity are placing on the planet. Despite the best efforts of critics of ecological protection to dismiss the threats to our ecological and thus to our economic and social well-being, the worlds of ecology and economy are on a collision course.

The case in this book is based on several assumptions. The first is that economies will grow, at least until external ecological (energy or water crises or mass climate migrations) or other events (global military conflict or major failures in the financial sector) stop or reverse growth. Like it or not, there are simply too many forces driving the global growth machine (discussed in Chapters 1 and 3) to expect leaders and institutions at many levels of government deliberately to shrink or constrain the scale of their economies. It makes sense to rethink the purpose and quality of economic growth—of a good life on a finite earth—and the effects it has on ecology and health, but focusing on stopping or reversing economic growth is a distraction from the need for greener growth.

As important, or perhaps even more important than growth itself, is a degree of fairness in distributing the benefits of that growth. Although economic equity and fairness have been a normative theme in the environmental policy field, I think there is a practical dimension to this issue as well, as examined in Chapter 5. More equitable societies may have an edge in achieving green or at least far greener growth.

Another assumption is that a transition to durable green growth is most likely to occur under a modified version of existing economic and political systems. Simply railing against capitalism or calling for a departure from democratic governance, in my view, will not address the conflicts between unabated growth and local, regional, and global ecological limits. Capitalism has been hard on ecosystems and resources, to be sure, but most other economic systems have been worse. The key to green growth is to restructure economic systems to account for the deficiencies in markets, institutions, and investments, and to link economic and ecological goals in positive ways. Although democratic governance is not the only way to accomplish this, and other models may work in some settings, it is the established and transitional democracies that may offer the best hope for effective ecological governance and green growth, as discussed in Chapter 4.

A third assumption is that a rich and varied set of policy solutions exists for advancing a green growth agenda, as presented in Chapter 6. Nearly half a century of experience with such issues as air and water pollution, habitat and species loss, and the like has generated a great number of policy solutions and evidence on their effectiveness, fairness, and feasibility. The challenge is not a lack of policy solutions; it is the inability to get political systems to get past short-term, narrow interests.

The final two chapters apply the analysis and evidence from the first six to the United States, specifically to its capacities for undergoing a durable transition to green growth. Viewed as a leader in the 1970s and in some respects into the 1990s, the United States has been evaluated less favorably for its ecological performance over time. Many reasons have been given for this trend—the many institutional veto points that make change difficult; the rise of a conservative political ideology, often captured in the term *neo-liberalism*; the power of brown sectors, like the fossil fuel industry; and a pluralist, fragmented, and adversarial policy style, to name a few. All of these should be taken into account in thinking about green growth politics and strategies.

Central to this book is the argument that a fundamental, long-term transition to a far greener growth path is necessary. Unguided growth that is insensitive to ecological limits is a path to disaster. Even a strategy of balancing trade-offs—of minimizing negative rather than seeking out positive ecology–economy relationships—will not get the job done in the next several decades. What follows is a path to a pragmatic way of responding to this challenge.

Although this book focuses at many points on the United States, it also is a book on comparative ecological politics. Indeed, the first five chapters are international and comparative in their review of research and issues related to green growth. Only the final two chapters are focused on the United States, where American institutions and politics are my main concern.

I am indebted to a number of people for their support and assistance on this book. I wish to thank Daniel Mazmanian, Manjyot Bhan, and the Oxford University Press reviewers for reading and providing valuable suggestions for the full manuscript. Riordan Frost provided expert research assistance and editorial support from the start to the end of this project. James Meadowcroft stimulated my interest in and appreciation of environmental concepts—green economy and green growth among them—and offered insights and perspective on this book in its early stages. I also wish to thank the entire team of authors from the *Conceptual Innovation in Environmental Policy* project (MIT Press, 2017) for their critical perspectives on my early drafts of a chapter on green economy, which greatly influenced my approach to this book. I learned a great deal from Pete Andrews, Michael Kraft, Philip Vergragt, Johannes Stripple, Karin Bäckstrand, Karen Baehler, Oluf Langhelle, Yrjo Haila, and the late Judy Layzer. Thanks also go to my classes in environmental and energy policy in the School of Public Affairs at American University for allowing me to test many ideas and to series editors Todd Eisenstadt and Joanna Lewis.

Chapter 2 is based in part on material from my chapter on "The Green Economy" in *Conceptual Innovation in Environmental Policy*, edited by James Meadowcroft and Daniel J. Fiorino and published by MIT Press.

I am indebted to Angela Chnapko of the Oxford University Press for her support and guidance in writing this book. Alexcee Bechthold and Alphonsa Prabakaran guided this book through the production process, and Carol Neiman served as an expert copy editor.

I want to thank Beth Ann Rabinovich for creating an ideal environment for thinking, writing, and flourishing. My debt to her is reflected in the dedication to this book. Thanks also to Matthew and Jacob for making it all fun and worthwhile.

Daniel J. Fiorino
Washington, DC
July 2017

A Good Life on a Finite Earth

# Two Worlds Colliding

In a book titled *Good Capitalism, Bad Capitalism, and the Economics of Growth and Prosperity*, three prominent economists set out to "explain and ultimately contribute to facilitating economic growth, traditionally measured by the increase in a country's output of goods and services (gross domestic product or GDP)" (Baumol, Litan, and Schramm 2007, 15). The book offers an insightful, accessible analysis of the causes of economic growth and ideas for promoting it. That economic growth is necessary, desirable, and essential for well-being is taken as a given. Indeed, the difference between *good* and *bad* capitalism in the book is that the former delivers consistent growth and the latter does not. Growth above all is good.

Still, is growth always an unalloyed good? Maybe not in all respects, the authors concede in the second chapter of the book. There are negatives, in the form of ecological and resource limits, the effects of globalization (rising inequality, for example), the likelihood that growth beyond a point does not necessarily bring happiness, and a potential mismatch between GDP and human well-being. These issues are not irrelevant, the authors concede, but they are manageable and pale next to the benefits of growth. They stand by their premise: "economic growth is good not only for rich countries like the United States, but for all countries, since it is only through growth that people's living standards, whatever they may now be, can improve" (25).

It is worth noting that in an otherwise thoughtful and well-argued 300-page book about economic growth, its effects on the planet garner only two pages of commentary. The authors recognize that growth means "societies will use up scarce resources and, at the same time, degrade the environment" (16). Between 1975 and their writing, world economic output increased seven-fold and per capita incomes five-fold. More growth occurred in the twentieth century than the last 1,000 years. Still, they view these as minor issues. After all, in the late 1790s Thomas Malthus predicted population would outgrow food production, leading to widespread starvation and malnutrition. That never happened, because technology and human ingenuity came to the rescue. Similarly, the "same process of technological advance that undermined Malthus's dire predictions may be able to quiet the concerns of the modern-day Malthusians who worry about disappearing energy, although more active involvement by governments may be necessary to address concerns about global warming" (17). As for energy, fossil fuel scarcity will push up prices; as a result consumers will use less energy or seek technological alternatives. Technology and markets will save the day.

Global warming, they admit, is a stickier issue. They accept the scientific consensus that the planet is warming and that this will have consequences. A solution is at hand, though, in "a mixture of rules and market-like incentives" that has come to be known as cap-and-trade. Of course, political and practical barriers may exist to such a scheme, but they do not consider that. "Thus pollu-  tion can be capped and growth can nevertheless continue" (18). In a wave of the hand, the problem is solved.

With this, the ecological case against continued, even exponential economic growth is dismissed. Planetary limits are swept aside in favor of the pursuit of faster growth. A wide range of serious, often irreversible problems go unmentioned. What about, for example, the alarming levels of air pollution in emerging economies, which cause millions of premature deaths each year? What of the many parts of the world that are running out of water needed to support not only the basics of life but the foundations of economies? Should the effects of rising levels of nutrient pollution around the world be ignored, even when it creates oxygen-deprived dead zones in the Gulf of Mexico or Chesapeake Bay? Are accelerating rates of species loss and habitat destruction not at least partly due to economic growth?

I start a book on green growth with this illustration not because the thesis of *Good Capitalism, Bad Capitalism* is particularly disturbing or one-sided, but because it is so common. Aside from national security, economic growth is probably the number one priority of modern governments. Political careers rise and fall on the ability to deliver rising GDP and incomes. Growth rates are a measure of success, a touchstone for progress, and a yardstick of national power and influence. Without growth, the standard thinking goes, people will  be unemployed, government revenues fall, life opportunities decline, the future darkens, children are worse off than their parents, and global social and political systems will erode. A society not growing is losing its way; it is on the way down in a state of material and even moral decline.

Everybody seems to agree on the need for growth. In the 2016 election, Vermont Senator Bernie Sanders was the most liberal serious contender for a major party nomination in decades and a self-declared socialist. When an economist from the University of Massachusetts concluded that Sanders' economic plan could generate GDP growth of more than 5% annually, his campaign rushed to embrace it (Timiraos and Meckler 2016). At the other end of the ideological divide, Republican contender and former Florida Governor Jeb Bush based his campaign on claims that he could deliver a 4% growth rate if elected to the presidency. Bernie Sanders and Jeb Bush may not agree on much, but they did agree on the need for and the political benefits of growth. And they had lots of company across the political spectrum.

Let me be clear from the start that this book does not make a case against growth in the abstract. Economic growth has delivered a better quality of life for much of the world (Sachs 2006). It has brought prosperity and security to billions of people globally. Among its many benefits are better health care, education, mobility, and comfort. Growth has led to dramatic gains in the status of women. It has enabled modern governments to provide, in various degrees, social safety nets and for retirement benefits later in life. Growth made possible the modern city and its role as an engine of prosperity. Economic growth also has promoted the spread of democracy around the world and supported expansions in civil liberties, freedom, and equality. In developed economies, growth has opened opportunities for a better quality of life, including what is known in happiness research as the capability *to flourish* (Jackson 2011).

Of course, there is a darker side to economic growth. One is the focus of this book: the effects of continued, exponential growth on the biophysical capacities of the planet. With all the benefits of growth come many kinds of ecological costs: the effects of fossil fuels; diets rich in meat; destruction and fragmentation of habitat; exploited fisheries; more synthetic chemicals; air and water pollution; species loss; and damage to ecosystems, to name a few. To be sure, contrary to the arguments of many growth critics, these costs do not rise linearly with growth. Indeed, economic growth tends to offset some of its negative effects as well as motivate and enable societies to respond to them. Still, it is fair to say that growth *as it has been practiced* so far has been rough on the planet and at some point undermines the foundations of human well-being.

These are what may be termed the *ecological costs* of growth. Growth critics cite a number of *social* costs as well. Although not my main focus, they are considered at many points because they relate to ecological aspects of growth. This social line of criticism is directed not at growth per se—few would argue against impoverished people being able to live a better quality of life—but at growth beyond some point. A fair amount of research suggests that, although people in affluent societies are happier than those in poor ones, some forms of happiness level off at a middle income range (Graham 2011). Economic growth begins to impose stress: in the competition for status; rising prices for housing and other goods; pressure to generate more income; hassles of long commutes and sprawl; and loss of a sense of place and community. Critics see growth in rich countries as a cause of rising inequality, social distance, and mistrust.

The complex interaction of ecology, politics, and economics, *the political economy of green growth*, is the subject of this book. This chapter presents the core dilemma—of the worlds of ecology and economy on a collision course. Whether or not they actually will collide and undermine the very basis of human progress is a matter of contention, it should be noted. For some people, mostly from the political right, aggressive economic growth solves all of the world's problems. Any ecological and resource limits that exist will be overcome through new technologies, higher incomes, and unfettered markets. Emphasizing economic growth over ecological and social concerns (which are greatly overblown, to this line of thinking) has worked perfectly well until now and will work in the future. In contrast, the ecological agenda, to these critics, constrains growth, lowers quality of life, and leads to less freedom and big government.

For others, evidence of ecological destruction is clear and demands a response. The most obvious sign is a changing climate and its consequences, but there are many other alarming signs as well—stresses on water resources, lost species and habitat, air and water pollution, and so on.

Whether or not economic growth in some form still is possible is an ongoing debate that is examined in this book. For many, mostly from the political left, anything resembling *business as usual* (a term used often in this debate) is a path to catastrophe. For some people expressing this point of view, growth has to stop or be scaled back, at least in rich countries. For others, the issue is not growth per se but how it occurs. Their issue is with dirty, brown, unsustainable growth, not incomes or GDP. In the United States, the main but not exclusive focus of this book, the fault line in political debate turns on the relationships of economic growth and the environment. Opponents of climate action, for example, base their case on claims of the economic costs of policy change, the potential for slower growth, and the asserted futility of the United States acting alone while other countries supposedly dawdle.

My view is that the business-as-usual, brown scenario is irresponsible and ultimately a recipe for a fundamentally different and damaged world. Whether the issue is climate, air and water pollution, lost habitat, or any number of other issues, unguided growth reflects a short-term, tunnel vision. On the other hand, rejecting growth in some form or actually reversing it, even if only in the more affluent countries, is politically unrealistic, economically risky, socially unfair, and undermines our ability to deal with the sources of ecological degradation and threats to our collective wellbeing. My goal is to attain a version of *ecologically guided, even ecologically driven, or green growth.*

The next section considers several terms, including *green growth*, and how they are used in this book. Following that are two sections introducing the protagonists in my story: ecological protection and economic growth. The final section of the chapter presents the plan for the book.

## THE CONCEPTUAL LANDSCAPE OF GREEN GROWTH

Before moving to the question of ecological limits, it will help to clarify some terms used in this book. *Economic growth* refers to increases in real incomes and GDP. The idea is that the economy will grow and incomes along with it, leading to an objectively better quality of life. As points of reference, the GDP of the United States at the start of 2016 was about $18 trillion and per capita income some $56,000 a year. This was among the highest in the world. For comparison, China's GDP was $11 trillion with a per capita income of about $8,000. The numbers for India were $2 trillion and $1600; for Germany $3.4 trillion and $48,000; and for Brazil $1.8 trillion and $8,500.[1] Richer countries, such as those in the Organization for Economic Cooperation and Development (OECD), are typically described as *developed* while others in the developing category may also be termed as *emerging, transitional*, or simply *poor* for those countries at the bottom of the income ladder. Growth critics often want to moderate or sharply reverse it in developed countries but encourage it in poor ones, for both normative and practical reasons. (An example is Cato 2009; for an overview of this issue, see Eriksson and Andersson 2010.)

Per capita incomes describe an average in a country and may disguise a great deal of inequality. A widely used measure of income inequality in a society is the Gini Index. A higher Gini means greater income inequality. If everyone has an identical income, the Gini is zero; if all the income is garnered by one person, the Gini is 1.0. In the United States, income inequality has increased in recent decades, and it has become a major political issue. It is also one with many implications for ecological problem solving. Another way to measure economic inequality is by the concentration of income or wealth; the Gini and wealth concentrations and what they mean for green growth are explored in Chapter 5.

Of course, it is the modifier *green* that distinguishes the growth considered here from the version envisioned in *Good Capitalism, Bad Capitalism* and much contemporary discourse. At the risk of oversimplifying the contrasts, it is safe to say there are two visions of economic growth in US politics—one that minimizes the significance of ecological issues and is focused entirely on the case for growth, and another that accepts ecological issues as highly relevant in deciding how to achieve growth. We see these most clearly in current debates on climate change.

Those who incorporate ecological issues into the economic landscape reflect many more specific viewpoints. Some see a direct conflict between continued growth and ecological well-being; others accept that a degree of economic growth (although variously defined) is inevitable, necessary, and/or desirable. At the far edge of this terrain is the de-growth movement, which calls for an immediate stabilization or reduction in GDP and incomes. Although this point of view is not influential in the United States, it appears often in the literature, especially in climate debates, as well as in this book. So, from the start, green growth has two sets of opponents: those rejecting the *green* part, because it makes us deal with ecological issues, and those who cannot accept the *growth* part, because that is what inevitably and irreversibly will doom the planet.

The concept of green growth accepts that economic growth in some form will continue to occur; not only is it inevitable, it is necessary and desirable. But the composition and trajectory of growth must change through the adoption of new investments, policies, technologies, and behavior. Simply continuing the growth model as it has been practiced in the past is not green growth. What distinguishes *green* from what may be termed *brown* growth? Many things do, and those distinctions are a central topic of this book. It is enough for the moment to say that green growth includes—at least within the time frame of the next three decades—such things as moving from fossil fuel to renewable energy; achieving aggressive water, energy, and materials efficiency; protecting much more land from development; adopting new models of urban design and development; promoting green infrastructure on a wide scale; and many other things. Brown growth means few of these: it assumes we do business as usual, even regressing to old practices, policies, and investments that pay little regard to ecological and health issues.

A kind of sibling concept to that of green growth is the *green economy.* In fact, it was the latter concept that first stimulated my own interest in issues of the economy and the environment. The green economy includes the core elements of green growth but in a more static conception. It less controversial for many growth critics; it at least implies an option for what ecological economist Herman Daly (1991) calls a *steady-state economy*—one that stabilizes at a level consistent with planetary capacities. I prefer green growth to green economy for two reasons. First, it accepts and confronts head-on the reality that growth is highly valued and sought after and will continue, whether we like it or not. Second, it is a far more dynamic conception of the economy–ecology relationship and thus a more valid way to approach the complex interactions among politics, economics, and ecology in the real world.

Another key distinction is between *growth* and *development*. Herman Daly provides a concise statement of the difference: growth is a "quantitative increase in physical dimensions" while development is a "qualitative improvement in physical characteristics" (1991, 224). In these terms, *growth* is a matter of accumulating more wealth, bigger incomes, a larger and more powerful economy, and higher levels of what economists call *welfare* or *utility maximization*. GDP and per capita income, as well as their rates of increase, are the standard indicators. The term *development* gets at something more nuanced: a better quality of life, self-fulfillment, fairer and more equitable societies, the previously mentioned capabilities for flourishing, and so on. Development means reasonable levels of nutrition, education, housing, health care, and social equity. Of course, economic growth could lead to all of these versions of well-being as well. Indeed, some growth—expanding GDP and rising incomes—is essential to human development.

Many people see no difference between growth and development. Growing economies and higher incomes bring a higher quality of life, to this point of view. Certainly rich countries provide their citizens in general with better education, health care, social safety nets, and material well-being than do poor ones. As we will see in Chapter 3, however, there is a point in the growth process where indicators of growth and development diverge, begin to *decouple* in the terms of ecological discourse. Measures of some forms of happiness level off, and perceptions of well-being may decline despite rising incomes (Graham 2011).

This growth versus development distinction is worth examining. It is the theme of Tim Jackson's book, *Prosperity without Growth* (2011), and a great deal of writing in the field. As will be clear in later chapters, part of my conception of green growth does involve a rethinking of our definitions of progress and well-being. Still, there is something unsatisfying about calling for a choice between a larger economy and higher incomes or better, more fulfilling lives. If you are poor and seeking a way out of poverty, growth is step to a better life. If you are rich, having more money and "stuff" may at some point become less than satisfying, to the extent that the search for meaning and self-fulfillment has become a recurring theme in post-industrial societies. There is evidence that many people in affluent societies are seeking something more than money. Still, simply saying that countries should stop growing and focus on development does not take us very far toward solutions and is not the kind of argument that could support political change.

Another distinction is between *environment* and *ecology*. As James Meadowcroft (2017) notes on the environment as a concept, its use for describing the interactions among humans and the physical world and their mutual interdependence is recent. Before the 1960s and the birth of modern environmentalism, it was common to speak of the political or the family environment, to name a few, but not of the ambient, physical environment. As issues of air and water pollution, toxic chemicals, loss of habitat and species, and others became visible in the 1960s, the concept of *the environment* emerged to describe them. It is standard practice to differentiate among two main types of environmental problems: human health, and ecological protection. Both played a role in the emergence of environmental issues in the 1960s and 1970s. Known as *focusing events* in the public policy field, worsening air pollution in southern California in the 1950s and 1960s, the Santa Barbara Oil spill in 1969, and revelations about effects of DDT (a pesticide) in Rachel Carson's *Silent Spring* (1962) made both types of problems relevant, although pollution programs focused initially on health more than ecology (Andrews 2006).

I use *ecology* rather than *environment* as my focus. One reason is that many of the direct conflicts with growth relate to ecology more than health. To be sure, growth does lead to adverse effects on health, such as higher levels of air and water pollution, exposures to larger amounts of pesticides and other synthetic chemicals, and contaminated drinking water in poor areas. Anyone doubting the effects of rapid growth on human health should examine the evidence on air quality in major cities in India and China. Economic growth also delivers improvement in human health through more pollution control (a phenomenon examined in Chapter 3), better health care and nutrition, and often more economic and social equity. Indeed, for many *health-related* indicators, rich countries actually perform better than poor ones; more affluent countries rank higher than lower-income ones in the Yale-Columbia *Environmental Performance Index* (Hsu 2016), an assessment of national environmental performance discussed in Chapter 7. For the indicators relating to ecosystem vitality, the effects of economic growth are mixed and often negative.

I find the ecology concept to be more precise and inclusive than that of the environment, and more suited to a discussion of global, regional, and local ecological limits. After all, humans are part of ecological systems at all levels. The health effects of urban air pollution and untreated sewage are as much an ecological failure as lost wetlands and polluted rivers. Moreover, much of the "limits to growth" debate is about sustaining the structural and functional integrity of critical ecosystems, including the global climate system, and about avoiding critical tipping points in ecosystems and resources that lead to irreversible damages. For my purposes, *ecology* captures the critical issues more completely and precisely than *environment*.

Another delicate issue in the conceptual landscape of green growth is *ecological limits*. For the advocates of unfettered growth, of course, limits either do not exist or may be overcome (Dryzek 2013). For determined growth critics, limits exist as firm, nonnegotiable constraints on economic activity (Cato 2009). The implications of these two positions are clear: If limits do not exist or matter, brown growth is perfectly acceptable and there is no need for change. If limits do exist as a kind of hard stop on growth, then either growth must end or contract, or its composition has to change fundamentally. This book is based on the premise that limits do exist, including health-based limits on air, water, and chemical exposure as well as ecosystems and resources.

Even among those accepting the existence of ecological (including health) limits in some form, there is debate over terminology. As is discussed later in the chapter, the notion of limits came out of the landmark study in the early 1970s, *The Limits to Growth* (Meadows et al. 1972). In a thirty-year update of the original study, the authors describe the physical limits to growth as "limits to the ability of planetary sources to provide materials and energy and to the ability of planetary sinks to absorb the pollution and waste" (Meadows et al. 2004, 9). At one point, the update refers to "global ecological *constraints*" [emphasis added] that "would have significant influence on global developments in the twenty-first century" (8). In the *Oxford Dictionary*, a limit is "a point beyond which something does not or may not extend or pass" or "a restriction on the amount of something that is permissible." A constraint is "a limitation or constriction," as in the statement that "the availability of water is the main constraint on food production."

A widely cited analysis published in 2009 used *boundaries* over the more standard *limits* terminology to delineate what may readily be seen as *constraints*. This collaboration of several experts set out to define "planetary boundaries within which we expect that humans can operate safely." They wanted to shift governance "away from the essentially sectoral analyses of limits to growth aimed at minimizing negative externalities, toward the estimation of the safe space for human development" (Rockstrom et al. 2009, abstract). In addition to relying on a softer approach than implied by the term *limits* to reflect the scientific uncertainty, the boundaries concept shifts our thinking from a negative of respecting limits to a positive of defining a safe operating space. It stresses where we may safely operate as opposed to the limits that should not be crossed (also see Boston 2011).

These are useful distinctions, and at times I may bring up *constraints* and *boundaries* as being relevant terms for examining green growth. Still, *limits* are my term for describing the point at which human activity (largely in the effects of population and economic growth) begins to cause long-term, irreversible effects on global, regional, and local ecosystems. The notion of limits is easy to grasp, and it suggests the existence of some line (or actually a series of lines with increasingly serious consequences) that should not be exceeded. As discussed next, limits are based on scientific analysis but involve a degree of uncertainty. Limits should be seen as a series of lines (rather than fixed black and white), each leading to more harm; and they exist at multiple governance levels and geographical scales in the form of global, regional, and local limits.

Part of the conceptual landscape of green growth are many terms that are similar. Indeed, the central ideas of green growth—that larger economies and rising incomes may be achieved without necessarily crossing ecological limits and that synergies exist among economic and ecological goals—is so appealing politically that it has been captured in a range of concepts used in the ecological policy field. A close sibling of green growth, of course, is the green economy, which I regard as similar in its essentials but less explicit on the issue of growth. At a local level in the United States, the notion of *smart growth* has gained currency. I regard it as one of the most effective and successful applications of green growth thinking. It refers to efforts in cities to redirect economic, ecological, and social policies to transition from simple "growth machines" to a more balanced vision of well-being (Portney 2013, 123–149; Fitzgerald 2010). Cities engaged in smart growth guide economic development, promote density and mixed uses of land, provide transportation options, protect air and water quality, stress energy and water efficiency, and take other steps to fulfill a community vision for a higher quality of life. In many ways, green growth is a variation on smart growth, although scaled up to a higher level.

A concept that has seen rising use in recent years, partly due to criticism of sustainability, is that of *resilience*: of resilient cities, regions, economies, societies, infrastructure, and so on. A term that it is firmly grounded in systems thinking, it describes the ability of systems or parts of them to maintain their essential structure and function in the face of disturbances or shocks, either from within the system itself or from outside forces (Gunderson 2000). The conventional wisdom is that a resilient economy is diverse and balanced enough to withstand such external shocks as a global financial crisis or catastrophic weather event. Similarly, a resilient city is one that is able to absorb disturbances or shocks (such as sea level rise, extreme weather events, or water shortages) from an external disturbance like climate change.

A recurring issue with green growth is its relationship to the core concept of modern economic and ecological discourse, that of *sustainable development*. Although used earlier, this concept emerged as a means of debating economy–ecology relationships in the 1987 report of the World Commission on Environment and Development (WCED 1987), *Our Common Future*. Known widely as the Brundtland report, the WCED constituted the first major, global effort to take on the conflicts among ecological and economic goals in modern societies (Langhelle 2017). The backdrop for the WCED was the tension between the developed economies (largely the OECD club of richer countries) and developing countries fighting to escape poverty. Developing countries worried that concerns in OECD countries about pollution, waste, land degradation, and so on would be used to limit growth. The task of the Brundtland Commission was to walk the fine line between aspirations for continued growth and concerns about its ecological effects. By merging economic and ecological goals, changing growth paths, conserving resources, and reorienting technology, it was argued, the world could meet human needs within planetary limits (*Our Common Future,* chapter 2).

Like green growth, sustainable development aims to reconcile economic growth with ecological protection (Fiorino 2010). Yet, for reasons explored in the next chapter, many sustainability advocates dislike the concept of green growth. They argue that it is ambiguous, at best, on constraining growth (although sustainable development is less than clear on this, as Langhelle 2017 points out); is too oriented toward rich countries and corporations; and places too little emphasis on the social issues of equity and empowerment. For now, it is worth noting that green growth and sustainable development are related; whether the first augments, replaces, or competes with the second is a matter for future debate.

Anyone looking for a hybrid concept might focus on *sustainable growth,* which for my purposes is essentially green growth. Others are *green jobs,* taken up in Chapter 3; the *green state,* a subject of Chapter 4; and such specific concepts as green infrastructure, green chemistry, green investment, and others that come up at many points. It is a rich and varied landscape.

## ECOLOGICAL LIMITS: WHAT CAN THE PLANET WITHSTAND?

The case for a greener economy rests on the many harmful effects that human activity has on the biophysical capacities of the planet. The notion of the concept of *the planet* is used loosely here; many ecosystem and resource limits are apparent regionally and locally as well as globally.

Documenting the case for the existence of ecological limits is not an aim of this book. That has been done and is being done in many places on a broad range of issues (e.g., IPCC 2014; Worldwatch Institute 2015; Kolbert 2014; Lubchenco 1998). My assumption is that ecological and resources limits do exist and at some point undermine the capacity of political, economic, and social systems at multiple levels to provide a reasonable quality of life. Just where those various limits lie and when they will be or have been breached is a topic of ongoing discussion, but it is not my main concern. Still, it helps briefly to consider evidence on ecological limits and what we know about where an *ecologically insensitive* or *growth-above-all* path could take us.

Finding signs of the long-term, damaging effects of growth is not difficult. Evidence on the effects of climate change alone will occupy any number of university classes, books, and careers. On climate change, of course, there are

the many reports of the Intergovernmental Panel on Climate Change (IPCC),
created by the United Nations to assess, monitor, and report on the state of
scientific knowledge. This could be augmented by assessments like the *Stern
Review on the Economics of Climate Change* (2006), which found that the costs
of ignoring climate change are far higher economically than those of dealing
with it (Wagner and Weitzman 2015). Effects on the United States are set out
in the National Climate Assessment (United States Global Change Research
Program 2014). Anyone wanting a call to arms could use Naomi Klein's *This
Changes Everything: Capitalism versus the Climate* (2014).

A range of highly respected organizations and individuals have tracked
national and global trends on many ecological and environmental health indicators (see Dryzek 2013, 27–51 and Boston 2011 for reviews). Their core message is that pressures on the earth's biophysical capacities are increasing due to
population growth, economic expansion, rising incomes, more mobility, use of
fossil fuels, land conversion, and other factors. All of these support a contention
that ecological limits exist, are being exceeded now or will be at some point if
current trends continue, and with consequences not only for the planet but our
economic and social well-being.

My goal in this section is to present a picture of the writing on planetary
limits to set the stage for the rest of the book. I begin with the foundation from
the *Limits to Growth*. As the title suggests, the thesis of this line of work is that
economic and population growth impose stresses on the biophysical capacities
of the planet and must be reined in at some point. I then turn to other ways of
thinking about planetary limits and review two brief cases of mainstream, fairly
recent assessments of the state of and trends in the stresses of economic growth
on ecosystems.

## The Limits to Growth

The work most often associated with limits in the earth's capacities is the 1972
study by a team from the Massachusetts Institute of Technology (Meadows et
al.), *Limits to Growth*, followed by two updates: *Beyond the Limits: Confronting
Global Collapse* (Meadows and Randers 1992) and *Limits to Growth: The Thirty
Year Update* (Meadows et al. 2004). Use of computers enabled a complex analysis for projecting trends in resource use and damage to the sinks (air and water)
where pollution and wastes accumulate. Although the specifics varied according to which of many scenarios was realized, the message was that "given pos-
tulated limits to resource availability, agricultural productivity, and the capacity
of the ecosphere to assimilate pollution, some limit was generally hit within a
hundred years, leading to the collapse of industrial society and its population"

(Dryzek 2013, 31). A major event in the emergence of modern environmental-ism, the *Limits* case challenged the postwar dominance of the economic growth mindset (Norgard, Peet, and Ragnarsdottir 2010). Although not always correct on many of the specifics, the essentials of the *Limits* thesis have largely been confirmed (Turner 2008).

Many assessments and critiques of the *Limits* argument exist. For my pur-poses, it is worth noting a few aspects of the argument and evidence. First is the argument that unabated, exponential growth at some point leads to a collapse of national and global economies; the issue is not just planetary but human well-being. Second, the process by which limits are breached is termed *over-shoot*, which occurs when there is rapid change, there is a resource and ecologi-cal limit to that change, and evidence or *signals* of those changes and effects are not available, are ignored, or appropriate responses are not taken. Third, the issue is that growth is exponential, not linear: "its increase is proportional to what is already here" (19). At a 4% annual growth rate, for example (lower than many emerging economies but elusive lately for developed ones), the global GDP would double in just 18 years. Fourth, the *Limits* are global: the effects will vary locally and regionally. Finally, although not a political analysis, the 2004 version offers this insight: "history does suggest that society has limited capac-ity for responding to these limits with wise, farsighted, and altruistic measures that disadvantage important players in the short term" (xvii).

A variation on the limits concept, noted earlier, is a 2009 exploration of a *safe operating space for humanity* in terms of planetary boundaries (Rockstrom et al. 2009). A team of scientists collaborated in defining and assessing the state of knowledge with respect to nine such planetary boundaries: atmospheric con-centrations of carbon dioxide; rates of biodiversity loss (measured by extinc-tion rates); stratospheric ozone depletion; ocean acidification; changes in land use (% of the global land cover converted to cropland); global freshwater use (human consumption); atmospheric aerosol loading (a measure of overall air particulate concentrations); chemical pollution (measures of the releases, con-centrations, and effects of harmful chemicals); and, as two separate indicators, the global status of the nitrogen and phosphorous cycles.

The conclusion was that three of the nine boundaries have already been exceeded: carbon dioxide, biodiversity loss, and the nitrogen cycle. For oth-ers, including ocean acidification, changes in phosphorous, freshwater use, and land use changes, the boundaries are being pressed, or the long-term trends for them should be a source of worry.

As Jonathan Boston notes, "there is no consensus on whether long-term exponential economic growth is technically feasible" (2011, 38). Indeed the explicitly growth-above-all argument either rejects the validity of planetary limits or asserts they may be overcome or managed. Still, Boston concludes, if continuing and exponential growth occurs through this century it "seems reasonable to conclude that such an outcome will be possible only if human activities are utterly consistent with the assimilative and regenerative capacities of the earth's biosphere" (39). If this were not the case, one could argue that green growth is unnecessary.

## Ways of Thinking about Ecological Limits

Some standard terms are useful in discussing ecological limits. One distinguishes among sources, sinks, and services. *Sources* are the water, energy, materials, food, fish, and other goods that make life possible, or at least life as people have come to expect it. *Sinks* are places where pollution and waste end up, the dumps of modern societies. *Services* are functions performed by ecosystems: water purification, waste sequestration, re-generation of soil nutrients, climate regulation, and maintenance of the gene pool, among others. All of these categories are crucial for sustaining human well-being: life without water, energy, clean air or water, and a functioning climate system would look very different, if livable at all.

Sources come in renewable and nonrenewable forms. Nonrenewable sources are a concern; running out of water or fossil fuels subtracts from a quality of life, to say the least. For decades, the notion of "peak oil" suggested this essential source of energy in modern economies would peak and eventually be gone. That this has not occurred so far is a theme of brown growth advocates. Still, renewable resources are preferable ecologically (discussed in Giddens 2011, chapter 2 and National Research Council 2010). We will not run out of sun or wind for energy. Some sources—fish or forests—are renewable but become scarce if overexploited. For ecological economist Herman Daly, the use of nonrenewable resources (e.g., fossil fuels or groundwater) should not exceed the rate at which renewable resources can be substituted; in turn, renewable sources (e.g., freshwater) should not be used faster than their rate of regeneration (also see Meadows 2004, 54).

Pollution and waste motivated the emergence of modem environmentalism. Air, water, land, and, more recently, the atmosphere are the sinks where pollution is deposited and absorbed. Most laws from the environmental decade of the 1970s were aimed at protecting sinks; the Clean Air Act, Clean Water Act, and Resource Conservation and Recovery Act are examples. A feature of these laws is that they focus on the sinks over sources, so that the Clean Air and Clean Water Acts were aimed at the pollution as it came out of smokestacks or discharge pipes rather than the sources and activities that caused the pollution in the first place. Daly's rule with respect to sinks is that the releases should not exceed the rate at which pollutants are absorbed or "rendered harmless" in their sinks. In the United States, sinks are protected largely through government-mandated technology controls on the sources of air, water, and land pollution.

The concept of ecosystem services has emerged as a major focus of ecological thinking in the last few decades and is central to the green growth concept. Chapters 2 and 3 consider this trend, including the United Nations TEEB project (The Economics of Ecosystems and Biodiversity 2010). One controversial practice is estimating the economic value of ecosystem services. These analyses, for example, assess the functions coastal estuaries perform in protecting coastlines from storm surge, filtering water pollutants, and providing spawning grounds for fish. Many critics of ecosystem valuation charge it turns nature into just another commodity (McCauley 2006), a criticism that is considered more in Chapter 2.

Several points are worth making at this stage. One is that US policy has focused more on sinks and less on sources and services. Until recently, energy and water efficiency were not prominent on policy agendas. The Clean Air and Clean Water Acts are designed to control pollution, not get at its source. Second, responding to one issue generates solutions for others. For example, conserving energy preserves a source, but it also protects ambient air and the atmosphere, two critical sinks. Similarly, moving away from fossil fuels and toward solar, wind, and geothermal energy for generating electricity replaces a nonrenewable source with a renewable one. It also reduces harm to sinks by controlling particulate, nitrogen dioxide, and carbon dioxide emissions. Preserving ecosystems protects vital services as well as air and water sinks. These *co-benefits* offer options for improving ecology and human health. Third, sources, sinks, and services are useful categories but often overlap. Soil is a source but performs critical ecosystem functions. Wetlands provide services but suffer as sinks when polluted or degraded.

## Two Cases on Limits

Before proceeding with this discussion on limits, I look briefly at two assessments pointing to an ecology–economy collision. These are not the work of ecological catastrophists, what John Dryzek terms *survivalists* (2013, 27–51), but of mainstream organizations concerned about prosperity: the OECD and the United Nations. My view is that if they worry about the collision of economic growth with ecological protection, then so should the rest of us. Both organizations have sponsored major reports on green growth that are examined in the next chapter.

The OECD includes 35 relatively affluent nations, at times referred to as "the rich man's club" of countries.[2] Its mission is "to promote policies that will improve the economic and social well-being of people around the world." Although prominently focused on growth, it also has shown a regard for ecological well-being, public health, and social equity. In 2012, the OECD *Environmental Outlook to 2050* examined likely demographic and economic trends in the next four decades and their ecological impacts in four areas: climate change, biodiversity, water, and the health impacts of pollution. Although far from what might be considered an environmental alarmist organization, the OECD concludes: "The reality is that, if we fail to transform our policies and behaviour, the picture is rather grim" (OECD 2012, 3). It adds that "prospects are more alarming than the situation described in the previous edition, and that urgent-and holistic-action is needed now . . ." (19).

Among the projections are that global population will increase from a current seven to more than nine billion, and the global GDP will nearly quadruple from current levels, a product of more people having higher incomes. That the increasing size of the global economy will impose even greater stress on the ecological capacities of the earth is a major and recurring theme. The global distribution of growth rates will vary. Already slower in developed (i.e., the OECD) nations, economic growth rates will slow down in China, India, and some other recent, rapid-growth countries. Although Africa will remain the poorest continent, many of its poor countries will exhibit the highest growth rates in the period 2030 to 2050. Demographic and behavioral changes linked to growth will lead to "evolving lifestyles, consumptions and dietary preferences" (20). In brief, this means larger populations consuming more, using more fossil fuels, converting more land to agriculture and other purposes, withdrawing more water, and eating more meat.

Among the projected outcomes from population and economic growth by 2050 are a 50% increase in greenhouse emissions; a doubling of deaths from exposures to air particulates, to 3.6 million annually; a 55% increase in global water demand, with up to 2.3 billion people living in "severely" water-stressed areas; and a 10% decline in global, terrestrial biodiversity. Despite the attention given to renewable energy in recent years, and the progress that is being made, the OECD projects that fossil fuels still will account for 85% of energy consumption in 2050. It projects "continued degradation and erosion of natural environmental capital to 2050 and beyond, risking irreversible changes that endanger two centuries of rising living standards" (20).

In the *Millennium Ecosystem Assessment*, the United Nations evaluated the state of and prospects for ecosystems around the world. Of the 24 major ecosystems assessed, fifteen (60%) were found to be degraded. Among the degraded ecosystems are capture fisheries, water supplies, waste treatment and detoxification, water purification, natural hazard protection, regulation of air quality, regulation of regional climate, erosion control, and aesthetic enjoyment (6). The biggest drivers of ecosystem change are habitat change due to such activities as land use, physical modification of rivers and water withdrawals; overexploitation of resources, such as fish stocks; the spread of invasive alien species; pollution of various kinds; and, of course, the effects of climate change (14). Ecosystem damages are seen as "a loss of a capital asset" (9).

The pace of change is accelerating: "The structure and functioning of the world's ecosystems changed more rapidly in the second half of the twentieth century than at any time in human history" (2). Indeed, humans changed the earth's ecosystems more in the last 50 years alone than any comparable time in history. A special concern, the *Assessment* observed, is the "established but incomplete evidence" of "nonlinear changes in ecosystems (including accelerating, abrupt, and potentially irreversible changes) that have important consequences for human well-being" (1). This non-linearity means that ecosystems may reach critical tipping points, beyond which they lose their essential qualities and fail to provide needed services.

Signs of the effects of human activity on ecosystems are everywhere: One-fifth of coral reefs are gone; another fifth are degraded. By 2012, three to six times more water was being held in reservoirs as was contained in natural rivers. An estimated 10%–30% of mammal, bird, and amphibian species around the world are threatened with extinction. More than half the synthetic nitrogen fertilizer used in the last century (it was first manufactured in 1913) was used in the last 25 years, which is part of the explanation for eutrophication and hypoxia occurring globally, where excessive nutrients (nitrogen and phosphorous) lead to abrupt changes in freshwater and coastal ecosystems, harmful algal blooms, and the emergence of oxygen-depleted dead zones in places like the Gulf of Mexico, Chesapeake Bay, and many other waterbodies around the world.

In its effects on human populations, ecosystem degradation on this scale is strikingly unfair. The *Assessment* concludes flatly that losses in ecosystem structure and functioning cause poverty and harm the poor, who often depend more on ecosystem services (such as water supply or climate regulation) and suffer from soil erosion, desertification, extreme weather, water stress, and changes in disease patterns. Evidence on climate change documents the vulnerability and lower adaptive capacity of the poor. The evidence on the status of ecosystems strengthens the green growth case.

## Limits and Ecological Policy

The premise of this book and environmentalism in general is that ecological limits matter. Indeed, the limits concept permeates ecological and health policy in the United States and many other nations. The Clean Air Act calls for National Ambient Air Quality Standards (NAAQS): health-based, scientifically informed, nationally uniform limits on concentrations of pollutants that protect public health and welfare with "an adequate margin of safety." The Clean Water Act makes states set water quality standards that recognize designated uses and science-based limits on pollution. Chemical laws like the Toxic Substances Control Act set limits on exposures to substances posing risks to human health or the environment (see Portney and Stavins 2000; Kraft 2015; Rosenbaum 2017; Davies and Mazurek 1998). The concept of *critical loads*, clearly stating an ecological limit, is the centerpiece of the European Convention on Long-Range Transboundary Air Pollution, adopted in 1979 and revised many times since (Bäckstrand 2017). A prominent global limit is the 2 degree Centigrade target that has been adopted by the Intergovernmental Panel on Climate Change, revised in Paris in 2015 to an "ambition" of 1.5 degrees, to avoid the worst effects of climate change (for an overview see Davenport et al. 2015).

In summary, my view of economic growth colliding with ecological limits assumes the following:

- Resource and ecological limits exist and are informed by scientific assessments. They are not bright lines but a series of shaded lines reflecting risks of critical or irreversible harm.
- Limits in sources matter, but the most serious challenges will be in sinks and services.
- Resources and ecological limits should be seen as playing out locally, regionally, and globally, and in the interactions among governance, economic, and ecological systems.
- Evidence on limits involves scientific uncertainty, although the direction of change and impacts is often reasonably clear, as climate change and ecosystem degradation illustrate.
- Resource and ecological limits inevitably will require a policy response; whether that is ending or reversing growth, rethinking and redefining it, changing its composition, or some combination of these is a matter of effective governance and smart policy design.

## IS THERE A PROBLEM WITH GROWTH?

In *Prosperity without Growth,* British economist Tim Jackson observes that "Questioning growth is deemed to be the act of lunatics, idealists, and revolutionaries" (14). It would be hard to dispute this. Few things are so universally agreed-upon, even in an era of contentious politics, than the desirability of and need for growth. Indeed, politicians compete in their ability to deliver more growth and higher incomes to constituents. Nearly everything in society is assessed on the basis of its relationships to economic growth. The quality of education turns on its effects on growth. Poor health and obesity matter because both may subtract from productivity and growth. Growth rates and their effects on employment, competitiveness, consumption, and investment are tracked by markets, financial institutions, policymakers, and voters.

The benefits of growth are obvious. It delivers a better quality of life, improves education and health care, allows for social safety nets and retirement systems, funds government services, enhances political stability, finances new medical technologies and treatments, and expands the prospects for flourishing in modern societies. Growth also makes it possible to satisfy human desires for novelty and acquisition, from luxury cars to the latest smart phone. Business leaders like growth because it opens up new markets, fuels consumption, and generates investment capital, among other things. Politicians like growth because it lets them create and distribute benefits, manage tax rates, reduce deficits, and keep various constituencies happy; an expanding pie is much easier to carve up than a shrinking one. Voters associate growth with more jobs, more promising futures, a greater array of options in life, and higher consumer satisfaction.

There is even evidence that economic performance, especially annual growth rates, influences presidential elections. The "time-for-change" model in political science suggests three factors that reliably predict presidential elections in the United States: the popularity of an incumbent president, measured by approval rating at mid-year; the length of time the incumbent's party has controlled the White House; and the state of the economy, measured by the real, annualized growth rate in the second quarter (April–June) of an election year. Although not the most significant of the three factors, growth rates matter: "the difference between running with a stagnant economy and running with a booming economy is substantial" (Abramowitz 2008, 695). Elected leaders are judged in part on their ability to deliver economic growth.

Yet there is a darker side to economic growth. Growth all too often degrades ecosystems; fuels status competition; increases (beyond a point) economic inequality; wastes energy, water, land, and other resources; undermines a sense of community; generates a range of social problems (if benefits of growth are distributed too unequally); and may lower the quality of life. The cases for and against growth are examined in Chapter 3. There is both an ecological and a social case against growth. My main interest is the ecological side, but the social case is relevant. Social aspects of growth affect its ecological impacts as well as the politics of responding to ecological issues. Indeed, a theme of this book is that ecological issues should be seen as part of a larger social and political agenda, not as separate and distinct. Similarly, as Chapters 7 and 8 argue, solutions to conflicts among economic growth and ecological protection may be found not just in the usual set of ecological strategies but in broader social and economic policies.

The dilemma is that growth is on a collision course with ecological limits. Since the emergence of modern environmentalism in the 1960s, there have been three answers to this dilemma. One is that *economic growth is ecologically and socially unacceptable* and must be stabilized or reversed, at least in wealthy countries. A second is that *economic growth should have priority over ecological concerns,* to the extent that pollution and ecological loss is the price we pay for prosperity. A corollary is that serious ecological issues will be resolved or managed through the normal operations of markets (so that prices of scarce materials will rise to allocate them efficiently), or that technology and human ingenuity will enable us to devise solutions, or that problems depicted by environmentalists are overstated and consequences overblown. This view is obvious in recent conservative politics in the United States (Layzer 2012), where growth and ecological protection are framed as zero-sums, as a set of dichotomous choices.

A third answer is that *growth and ecology can be reconciled in some way,* either by minimizing trade-offs, which has been the dominant theme in US environmental politics, or by seeking out positive relationships. The notion of minimizing trade-offs overlaps with the idea that growth and ecology pose zero-sum choices: that promoting one goal involves an almost inevitable sacrifice in the other. In this mindset, requiring technologies for controlling air emissions from steel plants delivers health benefits but raises the price of steel, puts US firms at a competitive disadvantage, and eliminates jobs. To take another example, protecting wetlands from being converted to farming saves a resource but reduces food production and its economic benefits. This view of nearly inevitable trade-offs characterized US ecological policy well into the 1980s. Chapter 3 considers the validity of assumptions about economy–ecology trade-offs.

The concept of green growth in this book accepts the existence of resource and ecological limits but seeks positive economy–ecology relationships. Green growth advocates recognize (in varying degrees) that ecological limits matter and have consequences, while accepting that some kind of growth is not only inevitable but desirable. From this perspective, stopping growth in its tracks is politically infeasible, economically risky, socially unfair, and ecologically harmful. At the same time, growth increases stresses on resources and ecosystems; unguided or ecologically insensitive growth ultimately undermines human and ecological well-being. Economy–ecology trade-offs are hard to avoid for near-term, specific choices, but in the longer-term context of the broader public interest, positive synergies exist and may be found.

So we have three sets of answers to the evidence of economic growth and ecological protection being on a collision course: one that accepts it and calls for an end to growth; a second that largely denies its significance and asserts the superiority of unguided growth; and a third that seeks a way to allow for economic growth in some form while also respecting ecological limits. Within the third are two sets of strategies: one accepting the inevitability of zero-sum choices, and another seeking positive-sum when possible—of *ecologically driven* or *green* growth.

Within the realm of politics and governance, which is where decisions about growth and ecology will play out in the coming decades, the concept of green growth may play useful roles. Two such roles are examined in this book. One is the use of green growth as an *issue framing* device. There is a great deal of evidence that words matter in policy debates and processes (Meadowcroft and Fiorino 2017, chapters 2 and 14). Skilled political operatives know that controlling the terms of debate and defining alternatives for responding to problems is a path to influencing outcomes. In a complex world, people rely on mental maps to organize and interpret information, competing political claims, risks and opportunities, and policy solutions. Issue framing aims to influence these mental maps, the ways of making sense of the world, by weaving "an intricate web of cause and effect that can be used to define problems, diagnose causes, attribute blame and responsibility, make moral judgments, and suggest remedies" (Guber and Bosso 2013, 439–440). Issue framing helps advocates or opponents of public policies tell a convincing story.

Advocates of green growth aim to reframe the old storyline of economic and ecological goals posing a set of almost inevitable trade-offs to one in which they may be, much of the time, compatible. The idea is to turn a presumed zero-sum into an actual positive-sum. Rather than arguing that "environmental regulation kills jobs," the case is that ecological protection creates investment opportunities, markets, and economic sectors that add family-supporting jobs. Instead of criticizing protection of coastal estuaries as restricting growth, recognize that they perform critical services.

A second role for the green growth concept is as a *policy agenda:* problem diagnoses, analytical methods, strategies, policy tools, and evaluative criteria. If green growth as issue framing is a means to shape debates and build a political coalition for change, its role as a policy agenda is to provide means of actually carrying out that change. One way of looking at it is that issue framing is more about politics and a policy agenda more about implementation, but it is more complicated than that. The roles of issue framing and policy agenda are interdependent: making a case for a green growth policy agenda supports its use in reframing relationships. Similarly, a valid reframing makes it politically possible to put a green growth agenda into place.

Green growth is contested politically. Critics from the right are suspicious of its emphasis on ecological issues and what it means for growth. In their minds, it involves too much collective action and government management of the economy. From the left, critics doubt the validity of the central proposition—that economies can grow and be green—and acceptance of economic growth. As is argued in the next chapter, green growth is a concept that builds from the center out, although the particular version set out in this book is more progressive than others, and it calls for a transition not only in economic and ecological policies but in social ones as well.

My focus is on the United States, especially in the final two chapters, but the need and opportunities for green growth are international. Indeed, most of the issues discussed in Chapters 2 through 6 app'v +o all developed countries and, to a large degree, emerging and poor ones             If there is any lesson to be drawn from the last few decades of ecological policy and politics, it is that these challenges are global, present similar challenges across all political and economic systems, and will require a higher degree of global, collective action than has occurred so far. This is a comparative analysis of the political economy of green growth with a focus on the United States.

## THE PLAN OF THE BOOK

The next chapter presents the concept of green growth—where it came from, what it means, what its critics say, and how to define it in socially acceptable and politically effective ways. It examines it as a *framing concept* and as a *policy agenda* for a green economic transition.

Chapters 3, 4, and 5 examine the economic, governance, and equity aspects. They go deeper into the concept, what it means from various perspectives, and conditions under which it may be achieved. Chapter 3 examines the ecology–economy relationship. This is at the very core of the concept, given its emphasis on reframing what historically was a zero-sum into a positive-sum. A careful look at the evidence suggests this relationship is far more complicated and interdependent than political debates reflect. This may be partly due to the mixed evidence; but it also is a reflection of the political incentives various economic interests have in confusing the debate and, in particular, continuing to push the old economy-versus-ecology dichotomy.

Chapters 4 and 5 turn to topics largely ignored in the field: governance and inequality. Why do some countries have better ecological and health policies than others? For that matter, why is California more of an ecological leader than Arkansas? Is there any such thing as a green state? Chapter 4 reviews what is known about the characteristics of governance systems that are well-suited to green growth. This sets the stage for a look at green growth politics in Chapter 7.

Inequality and its linkages with ecological policy, and green growth in particular, is the subject of Chapter 5. Part of the argument in this chapter is that too much is made of aggregate economic growth and not enough of the distribution of its benefits. It is true that equity is a core component of sustainable development and that ecological economists worry about equity. Yet economic inequality is expressed largely in normative terms, as something we should aim for. But is there a connection between inequality and prospects for green growth? And what effect could green growth have on economic inequality? This chapter sets out a case for how inequality reduces a society's capacity for strong ecological policies and a green growth path in particular.

Chapter 6 focuses on strategies for green growth. The range of ideas and proposals, what political scientist John Kingdon terms the *policy stream*, is rich and varied. The writing on green growth sets out an array of policies, investments, analytical approaches, and evaluative criteria, and these may be combined into an overall strategy. To be sure, many of the finer policy points need to be worked out: What are the advantages of a carbon tax compared to cap-and-trade? What mechanisms are effective for investing in habitat protection and climate mitigation? The chapter differentiates a green growth agenda from a conventional ecological policy agenda.

The last two chapters turn to the politics of green growth, focused on the United States. Of the developed countries, the United States is probably most locked into an economy-versus-ecology mindset. This is due in part to its institutional characteristics and political culture, typically described as competitive, adversarial, and fragmented (Fiorino 2006; Davies and Mazurek 1998). It also is a strategy used by advocates of brown growth to promote their own economy–ecology framing. Chapter 7 builds on the governance chapter and assesses US ecological performance, evaluates its capacities for green growth, and describes the role the concept plays in current US politics.

The last chapter takes up the really tough question: Is a green growth transition possible in the next three decades (my time frame for this analysis)? If so, under what conditions and with what political strategy could it happen? This chapter draws upon two leading theories of policy change to propose the outlines of a political strategy for a green transition. That such a transition *should* occur is a premise of this book. Whether it *will* occur and how is the focus of Chapter 8.

Three final points are worth making before moving into the origins and meaning of green growth. First, the concept is used as a kind of proxy for a variety of terms that aim to reframe the economy–ecology relationship in a more positive light. Concepts like sustainable growth, green economy, or smart growth are similar to green growth, so this book reflects on them as well. Second, green growth is not simply a middle ground, a compromise of economic and ecological goals. That is what ecological policy in the United States often has been—an effort to find a *balance* between the two. Green growth offers an alternative path and should be evaluated in that light. Third, like sustainable development, green growth is a theory in search of validation. Even assuming needed policies are adopted, investments made, behavior changed, and technologies deployed, questions remain about the feasibility and sufficiency of durable, green growth.

This book is being written in the first year of a new presidential administration and Congress. The United States moved from an administration that supported many elements of green growth (although not a Congress, which is why little happened legislatively) to one that embraces growth over ecological values. Whatever the near-term significance of this change, it is but the latest in a competition between two philosophies of economic and ecological governance. One is far more comfortable with collective action than the other, and it places value on public goods like clean air and water, a stable climate system, ecosystems, resource protection, and investment in green technology and infrastructure. The other is less favorable to public goods and collective action and prefers to rely almost entirely on markets and more growth-oriented technology. Periodic shifts in political power, like what occurred in 2016, not only detract from ecological progress but magnify the ecology–economy conflicts that dominate ecological politics. A green growth framing and policy agenda may allow us not only to moderate these shifts but also recognize and achieve positive relationships among political, economic, and social policy goals.

So this is the dilemma: Growth does many good things, but it has an ecological dark side. Still, few things are so universally desired or valued. Is green growth the answer? The next chapter turns to the concept and to why it matters.

# What Is Green Growth?

The previous chapter defined the issue as that of the colliding worlds of exponential economic growth confronting local, regional, and global ecological limits. This chapter presents a possible solution, although one that is by no means without its own problems and critics. In many ways, green growth illustrates what Anthony Giddens (1999) has termed a *third way* for ecological policy and politics. The notion of a third way originally was proposed as a means of bridging the political gaps between the right and left in the United Kingdom through a new politics of constructive, pragmatic policymaking. More broadly, the third way describes an effort to chart an alternative path between two strongly held, sharply defined, and apparently irreconcilable points of view. In 1990s British politics, it described the effort to navigate a coherent and politically feasible course between socialism and laissez-faire market liberalism. Prime Minister Tony Blair and President Bill Clinton were counted among its practitioners.

In the case of green growth, I see it as charting a conceptually similar alternative to the competing poles of unrestrained, unguided economic growth and de-growth, no-growth, or slow growth, each of which is associated to a degree with the right and left sides of the political spectrum. A negative or no-growth strategy is unlikely to gain political support and, as I argue in the next chapter, is not likely to be effective in dealing with the issue on its own. On the other hand, a growth-above-all scenario not only continues on a path toward ecological degradation—climate change, species and habitat loss, water insecurity, and the like—it undermines the foundations of our economic and social well-being. The concept of green growth is similar to Gidden's third way by presenting a pragmatic, politically defensible alternative to the other courses of action—not a compromise between the two, to be clear, but an alternative.

As with many concepts challenging old storylines and assumptions, green growth has its skeptics. There admittedly are grounds for skepticism. That we can maintain growth without stretching and, at some point, breaching ecological limits sounds, as economist Richard Schmalensee (2012, 56) puts it, like "having your cake and eating it too." His skeptical appraisal, he admits, "reflects an economist's strong negative reaction to claims that a large free banquet has been located under our noses" (2012, 56).

This chapter begins with the intellectual origins of the concept, which may be found in thinking from political science, economics, and business in the 1980s and 1990s. Even though these influences are not always explicit in green growth writing and practice, it is hard to imagine the concept taking the form that it does without them. I then turn to leading, mainstream expressions of the concept. Use of green growth and its sibling, the green economy, became widespread in the wake of the global financial crisis and recession of 2008–2009. My emphasis is on the international use by such organizations as the United Nations Environment Program (UNEP), Organization for Economic Cooperation and Development (OECD), and World Bank. The impact of green growth has been substantial, as even a brief review of the effects on national economic and ecological planning and policy reveal. The last two sections of the chapter look at criticisms of green growth, from both left and right, and set out my own approach to the concept.

## THE CONCEPT OF GREEN GROWTH

To one line of thinking, green growth is potentially, if not inevitably, an oxymoron (Brand 2012). That economies can expand in production and consumption and not suffer from ecological degradation is a proposition that defies common sense and a great deal of evidence. Economic expansion leads to production and consumption, energy use, urbanization, land and water use, habitat loss, and other pressures. Although economies become more eco-efficient as they mature, growth overwhelms this effect; for critics of green growth, a *decoupling* of growth from ecological harm is bound to fail (for a summary of this case, see Jackson 2011, 67–86).

Yet, as is argued in the next chapter, the relationships among economic growth and ecological protection are complex; ecological stresses do not necessarily increase linearly with higher incomes. First, empirical evidence suggests that some forms of health-related air and water pollution decline absolutely as economies and incomes grow (Fiorino 2011; Scruggs 2003). This is due in large part to demands for government action and improved governance. Second, economic growth is associated with slower rates of population increases and with social conditions, such as the improved status of women, which offset many sources of health and ecological damages. Third, policy choices and tools are available for decoupling, to a large degree, prosperity from ecological harm by guiding growth away from dirty and toward green economic sectors (Dellink, Bennis, and Verbruggen 1999; Jacobson and Delucchi 2009).

The concept of green growth recognizes these factors in its goal of reframing economy–ecology relationships. It goes further, however, in seeking out *complementary* and *synergistic* linkages through new patterns of investment; institutions that integrate across policy sectors; methods for valuing ecosystem services and incorporating them into decisions; policies that deliver ecological and social as well as economic benefits, like eco-taxes; technologies that improve well-being while using resources efficiently; incentives that shift consumption in ecologically benign directions, via tax or pricing policies; and regulatory standards that promote technology innovation and diffusion.

## Intellectual Antecedents of the Green Growth Concept

Concepts come from somewhere. They may begin with the writing of an economist or ecologist, the musings of a politician looking for a new policy pitch, or a chance encounter at a conference. If ideas matter, it is useful to ask where they come from and how they evolve. The intellectual origins of the concept of green growth may be found in innovative thinking among select groups of political scientists and economists in the 1980s and 1990s, as well as business scholars at about the same time. Over time, these ideas were incorporated into public debates, political advocacy, national and global discourse, and governmental planning. Three sources were influential: ecological modernization, ecological economics, and business eco-efficiency.

## Ecological Modernization

In political science, the concept's origins may be traced to *ecological modernization theory* in the 1980s. To that point, a central theme in writing on environmental politics was the need to fundamentally transform existing political and economic systems in developed countries. Liberal democracy was seen as inadequate for making difficult choices of lost growth, reduced consumption, and less material gratification. Capitalist systems, it was argued, are hardwired to go through inevitable cycles of investment, growth, and expansion. Only basic political and economic change, perhaps with authoritarian government and centralized economies, could avert long-term ecological catastrophe (Ophuls 1977 and Ophuls and Boyan 1998; summarized in Dryzek 2013, 27–51).

Ecological modernization presented an alternative vision by rejecting the idea that ecological protection and economic success inherently conflict. It is defined by such assertions as "economic development and ecological crisis can be reconciled to form a new model of development for capitalist economies" (Gibbs 2000, 10), or "environmental improvement can take place in tandem with economic growth" (Fisher and Freudenberg 2001, 704). It was further characterized by such statements as "the central institutions of modern society can be transformed in order to avoid ecological crisis" (Gibbs 2000, 11; also see Hajer 1995).

Competing versions of ecological modernization emerged over the years. For early proponents like Joseph Huber, it meant a private sector process of technology innovation, industrial transformation, and eco-efficiency. This version is still evident in industrial greening, decoupling, and eco-efficiency. It is expressed in Porter and van der Linde's work (1995) on the benefits to business of environmental innovation and by Amory Lovins and others in achieving eco-efficiency through their factor-four and factor-ten analysis (e.g., Hawken, Lovins, and Lovins 1999). Contrasting to this business-oriented thinking is writing by Martin Jänicke and others on the role of the state and public policy in green transitions. For them, ecological modernization is a more macro-level process of political development in which governance capacities are critical, and a focus on business is too narrow (Jänicke 1996, 2008, and 2012).

Mol and Sonnenfeld (2000, 6–2) define five aspects of eco-modernization: an emphasis on the changing role of science and technology as not only a cause but a solution to ecological problems; an appreciation of the role of private sector firms and markets in combination with public policy; a new role for the state, stressing decentralized, flexible, and consensual governance; different roles for social movements, which become partners and innovators as well as critics; and new discourses that reframe ecology–economy issues in ways that may generate more widespread political support. Other studies examine the political, social, and economic conditions under which a transition to a more ecologically advanced society develops. Among them are economic development; cognitive capacities in science and technology; effective, accountable governance with low corruption; an active civil society that both criticizes and collaborates; and participatory and policy-integrating capacities (Weidner 2002). On this point, research suggests that neo-corporatist, consensus-based systems are more suited for ecological progress than pluralist, adversarial ones (Liefferink et al. 2009; Scruggs 2003; Fiorino 2011), a finding that has implications for the ability of countries to implement a green economic transition.

Ecological modernization theory is lauded and criticized. Murphy (2000, 5) views it as a major contribution, "given that most work in environmental social science starts by assuming the inability of industry and the state to do anything other than create such problems" as ecological harm. Criticism of ecological modernization over the years reflects the same kinds of issues critics raise today with respect to the green economy. They see it as perpetuating the rich-country, corporate dominance that is the root of our ecological crises. Of course, the validity of such criticisms depends on which version of eco-modernization is on the table—the one focused on business eco-efficiency and innovation or the more systemic, institutional change version. Even advocates of the latter, however, recognize that "despite its impressive potential," ecological modernization theory is "not sufficient to ensure a long-term stabilization of the environment" (Jänicke 2008, 563). Many issues require lifestyle and perhaps basic social change; even dramatic gains in eco-efficiency are insufficient in the face of exponential growth.

Ecological modernization has been influential enough that John Dryzek includes it as one of nine alternatives in his book on environmental discourses. His description could serve as a cocktail-party version of green growth: "a restructuring of the capitalist political economy along more environmentally sound lines, but not in a way that requires an altogether different kind of political-economic system" (2013, 170). It captures the notion of an alternative to two existing, conflicting visions—one skeptical of growth and another reflecting a growth-above-all mindset.

## Ecological Economics

A larger influence on the concept is *ecological economics* as it developed in the 1980s and 1990s. Building on work of Herman Daly on limiting throughput in a steady-state economy, Nicholas Georgescu-Roegen on thermodynamics and entropy, and C.S. Holling on ecosystem stability and resilience, this school offered both a critique of the limitations in conventional welfare economics as well as a vision, concepts, and methods (van den Bergh 2001, 14). Its goals are "to provide an integrated and biophysical perspective on environment-economy interactions" (van den Bergh 2001, 13), to make economists aware of "ecological impacts and dependencies" and to urge ecologists to be "more sensitive to economic forces, incentives, and constraints" (Costanza 1989, 1).

Ecological economists seek to expand and reorient conventional economics in many ways. One is by placing natural capital—clean water, ecosystem services, forests, and the like—on not just an equal but a preferential footing relative to other forms of capital. Natural capital differs from financial or physical capital, first because it often has no substitutes, second due to the existence of ecological thresholds beyond which ecosystems may flip to an alternative state. That is, much natural capital is irreplaceable and many forms of damages to it are irreversible.

A second reorientation is that economies should be seen as sub-systems of the ecological system and subject to biophysical, planetary constraints. "Continuous exponential growth of any physical sub-system of a finite system is impossible" (Farley 2012, 43). The near-exclusive focus on growth (increasing real GDP) is a recipe for disaster due to the "overwhelming theoretical and empirical support for the existence of ecological and biological thresholds" (Farley 2012, 42). Ecological economics demonstrates a concern with the effects of growth, with development over growth, with distributions of income and wealth, and with alternative measures of progress.

Where ecological economists differ among themselves is with respect to growth. A core concept is Daly's (1973 and 1991) *steady-state economy*, in which the size of the economy does not expand beyond what is sustainable under ecological and biophysical constraints. Solutions to the growth issue vary, from a more managed, moderate growth (Victor 2008; Jackson 2009), to selective reductions in brown and expansions in green sectors (van den Bergh 2011), to de-growth through a deliberate contraction in economic scale (Alexander 2012; Kallis 2011).

A concern of ecological economics is valuing ecosystems and their services. They are undervalued because "they are not adequately quantified in terms comparable with economic services and manufactured capital" (Brat and de Root 2012, 6). In economic terms, ecosystems serve as a fund "capable of generating a flux of ecosystem services over time" (Farley 2012, 40). Among these are *provisioning* (food, freshwater, raw materials); *regulatory* (carbon storage, moderation of weather); *habitat* for species; and *cultural* services (recreation, sense of place).

Many of these ideas were captured in an early book explicitly using the term, *Blueprint for a Green Economy* (Pearce, Markandya, and Barbier 1989). It bridged conventional welfare and the newer ecological economics. It also made a case for recognizing the interdependence among ecology and economics and for viewing ecology as the foundation of economic success. This and a later volume (Pearce and Barbier 2000) argue that ecological valuation puts nature on the same level as the economy. This work differs from much ecological economics by accepting growth as necessary and allowing for some substitution of natural with other forms of capital.

Still, many core ideas of ecological economics are found in this work. The economy "is not separate from the environment in which we live" (1989, 4). A root cause of ecological harm is that ecosystems are not valued in markets, and "the elementary theory of supply and demand is that if something is provided at a zero price, more of it will be demanded than if there is a positive price" (5). They anticipate a criticism of green growth—that "the most resisted issue" in their approach "remains the idea of placing money values on environmental assets, the so-called monetization of the environment" (2000, xi). To the contrary, they argue "valuation is important because it places the environment in the same political dialogue as economic activity generally" (2000, 7). They attribute ecological degradation and resource inefficiency to the "failure of institutions, markets, and government policies to provide adequate incentives and investments for efficient and sustainable management of natural capital" (2000, 131).

## Business Greening and Eco-Efficiency

Another intellectual antecedent of green growth was a reconceptualization of business thinking on the relationship between ecological and business success. If green growth at a macro level reflects a rethinking of the old zero-sum as a potential win–win, it is in large part due to how many firms and business strategists changed their views in the 1980s and 1990s. In contrast to the view that firms should and would always seek to avoid ecological progress or innovation except when required by regulation, strategists and firms argued that investments in ecological performance, innovation, and reputation were critical to business success (as in Reinhardt 2000).

A watershed in the academic literature is the work of business professors Michael Porter and Claas van der Linde (1995). What is now known as the *Porter Hypothesis* is that "Properly designed environmental standards can trigger innovations that lower the total cost of a product or improve its value" (v). They argued that the old notion of stringent standards undermining efficiency and innovation relied on a false premise—that firms consistently act in economically rational ways. More specifically, conventional thinking assumed that firms discover all profitable innovations, all managers have perfect information about costs and options for reducing them, and incentives within firms are aligned with the goal of innovating. Business and environment strategists challenged these assumptions. In their view, pollution is not an externality that is not reflected in markets, it is "unproductive resource utilization" (105).

What is often overlooked in the Porter Hypothesis is the emphasis on *well-designed* regulation. In a critique of US regulation that I and others have found to be persuasive (Fiorino 2006, 93–94), they argue that the current system "often deters innovative solutions or renders them impossible" not because of the stringency of standards but how they are designed and administered. Specifically, *bad* regulation distracts from or does not fully realize the benefits of innovation when it stresses clean-up over prevention, mandates particular technologies, sets unrealistically short compliance deadlines, and subjects firms to high levels of uncertainty. In contrast, what they call *good* regulation relies on upstream solutions that prevent pollution rather than control or clean it up later, encourages a search for innovative compliance, and minimizes uncertainty by allowing the time and flexibility to come up with innovative, efficient solutions.

One of the best expressions of the eco-efficiency case is *Natural Capitalism: Creating the Next Industrial Revolution* (Hawken, Lovins, and Lovins 1999; also see Von Weizsacker et al. 2009). It offers a vision of a shift from an economy based on human productivity to one founded on "a radical increase in resource productivity" (ix). Capitalism will be seen as "a financially profitable nonsustainable aberration in human development" (5). They define four types of capital. Three—human, financial, and manufactured—play central roles in capitalist economies and are valued in markets. The fourth, natural capital, has not been valued in markets and is rapidly being depleted. Yet, without natural capital, the foundations of modern economic and social systems crumble. Natural capitalism is built on a four-fold strategy of radically increasing resource productivity; removing ecologically harmful market distortions, such as resource and extraction subsidies; reorienting economies to stress services over goods; and investing in natural capital: wetlands, forests, fisheries, water, and energy. Growth is tenable only with radical gains in resource productivity—by reducing ecological impacts by an order of magnitude.

The core ideas of each of these sources and their influence on green growth are presented in Table 2.1.

## Conceptual and Analytical Origins of Green Growth

We may trace the intellectual origins of the green growth concept to these influences: ecological modernization theory from European political scientists; the reorientation of a field through ecological economics; and insights from the business and eco-efficiency literature.

Ecological modernization provided a plausible political logic and prescription for reconciling the assumed polar opposites of economic growth and ecological protection. That it emerged from Europe—with its more consensus-based political cultures and less powerful fossil fuel industry—rather than the United States is not surprising. Although the United States was a leader in what Daniel Mazmanian and Michael Kraft (2009) term a *first epoch* of environmental protection, stressing technology-based, deterrence-based regulation, it fares less well in a third epoch, which involves a transition to environmental sustainability. The emergence of ecological economics is the most significant intellectual and analytical force in shaping the green growth concept because it

*Table 2.1* Intellectual Antecedents of the Green Growth Concept

| Source of Influence | Core Ideas Influencing the Green Growth Concept |
| --- | --- |
| **Ecological Modernization** (from political science) | • Positive ecology–economy linkages possible on macro scales<br>• Radical social and political change is not necessary<br>• Will demand more flexible, consensus-based governance<br>• Technology innovation plays a central role |
| **Ecological Economics** (from economics) | • Economic growth is subject to planetary limits<br>• Natural capital warrants special protection<br>• Economic equity is central to ecological goals<br>• Recognize the value of ecosystem services |
| **Business Greening and Eco-Efficiency** (from business writing and practice) | • Financial and ecological success not inherently incompatible<br>• Ecological innovation delivers business value<br>• Business may lead and/or play a central role in change<br>• Business success depends on preservation of natural capital |

reinvents economics to make it concerned with valuing, protecting, and restoring ecological resources. Finally, trends in business thinking and eco-efficiency were transformative. *If profit-maximizing firms link economic and ecological goals in positive ways, why not societies?*

Having interesting intellectual origins on its own does not make a concept relevant. Governments, policymakers, and institutions have to pick it up and bring it to the realm of practical discourse. Next are the major expressions of green growth and their policy impacts.

## THE CONCEPT IN PRACTICE: EXPRESSIONS OF GREEN GROWTH

Green growth broke through as a concept in global discourse, national planning, and local development in the first part of this century. It took center stage on the agendas of the World Bank, United Nations Environment Program (UNEP), Organization for Economic Cooperation and Development, (OECD), World Business Council for Sustainable Development, and others. This section considers three aspects of the concept in practice: Why did it break through when it did? How has it been expressed in practice? What political and policy impact has it had?

## Why Did the Green Growth Concept Take Hold When It Did?

The intellectual origins of green growth as a concept go back many years. It was only in the last decade ago or so that it became influential at a policy level. One explanation was the financial crisis of 2008–2009 and ensuing recession. Described as the greatest economic crisis since the 1930s, the recession was a challenge and an opportunity. The challenge was restoring confidence in financial markets and reinvigorating growth. The opportunity was channeling stimulus funds and other investments toward green economic sectors. Reflecting this view, a 2009 report from the OECD asserted not only that the "current economic crisis is not an excuse to weaken long-term efforts to achieve low-carbon growth" but the recession "can also open new opportunities—don't waste a crisis!" (OECD 2009, 7, 8).

A second factor was accumulating evidence on the effects of climate change. The fact of ecological limits, boundaries, or thresholds took on renewed significance (Meadows et al. 2004). The assessments on limits to growth now had real-world, global validation. Although threats to local and regional ecosystems had been evident for years—think of the Chesapeake Bay or Great Lakes or New England fisheries—the effects of climate change on sea levels, water resources, food production, health, habitat, and species brought the macro-level conflicts between growth and ecological well-being into sharp focus. Add to this the results of large-scale analyses of ecological threats, such as the Millennium Ecosystems Assessment (2005) and others (Boston 2011), and the time was ripe for thinking the world had to stop growing or grow in new ways.

A third factor in the rise of the green growth concept could well have been frustration with the progress of sustainable development (Brand 2012). Despite signs of incremental progress, the world had not changed dramatically since the report of the Brundtland Commission in 1987. Nationally, sustainable development has been nearly invisible in the United States, although used locally. Internationally, despite many initiatives, the concept has not delivered the transformational change many had hoped for. It may be that the concept of green growth offers a more politically accessible framing of ecology–economy relationships than sustainable development can.

John Dryzek argues that sustainable development and ecological modernization "bear a family resemblance," but the latter "has a much sharper focus than sustainable development on exactly what needs to be done with the capitalist political economy" (2013, 172). Similarly, I see green growth as more accessible in framing and overcoming economy–ecology trade-offs than the more elusive sustainable development. Global discourse may be reflecting that view as well.

## Mainstream Expressions of Green Growth

The expressions of green growth discussed here use *green* as their modifier, reflecting an emphasis on integrating ecological and economic goals, policies, and institutions. However, some use *growth* and others *economy* as the subject. In terms of policy framing, policy tools, and other aspects, the practical differences are small. In this book, I use *growth* over *economy* simply because it describes the challenge directly. There will be growth, so why not be clear about it?

The emergence of the green growth concept in recent years has been impressive. Its current relevance is due in part to the run-up to the Rio+20 Earth Summit in 2012. The "green economy in the context of sustainable development and poverty eradication" served as one of the themes. The emphasis was on synergies and win–win strategies, with green growth/economy as "a lens for focusing on and seizing opportunities to advance economic and environmental goals simultaneously" (UN 2010, 4). Green growth and economy proponents claim the concepts are not meant to replace sustainable development but to achieve the same long-term goals (UN 2010, 5). Nonetheless, tensions between the concepts and their advocates remain.

Reflecting this framing is UNEP's *Towards a Green Economy* (2011). For UNEP, a green economy is "one that results in improved well-being and social equity, while significantly reducing environmental risks and economic scarcities" (9). Such an economy "is not generally a drag on growth but a new engine of growth"; a "net generator of decent jobs"; and "a vital strategy for the elimination of persistent poverty" (10). Investing 2% of annual, global GDP, then about $1.3 trillion US, could create an economy that grows, but within ecological limits. This may be achieved by sustainably managing and restoring such natural capital sectors as water, forestry, agriculture, and fisheries, while increasing efficiency and reducing ecological impacts of transport, energy, manufacturing, and buildings. UNEP's macro-economic model projected that, after a brief period of slightly slower growth to replenish renewable resources, a green strategy delivers more economic growth, reduces poverty faster, and creates more jobs than does a business-as-usual scenario. UNEP clearly concluded we can have our cake *and* eat it.

UNEP models the economic and ecological effects of its 2% green investment scenario over the next several decades. *Towards a Green Economy* estimates that a green investment and policy scenario would still deliver a global increase in per capita income of 14% by 2050. At the same time, and contrary to the argument that growth inevitably degrades ecology, their model projects a 21% increase in forest land; a nearly 22% decrease in water demand; a 40% fall in primary energy demand; and a nearly 50% reduction in the global footprint to bio-capacity. Indeed, UNEP projects that its scenario will enable even *more* growth than would business as usual, after five to ten years of slower growth rates due to investments in natural resource sectors. The report concludes: the "the so-called 'trade-off' between economic progress and environmental sustainability is a myth, especially if one measures wealth inclusive of natural assets, and not just narrowly as produced output" (31).

Another prominent expression is the OECD's *Towards Green Growth* (2011). Green growth is "fostering economic growth and development while ensuring that natural assets continue to provide the resources and environmental services on which our well-being depends" (9). It is based on principles of sustainable natural resource use, energy efficiency, and fair valuation of ecosystem services. The reason for "putting green growth at the heart of development," as stressed in a follow-up report (OECD 2013), is that population increases require growth, and the form of that growth should be far greener than it has been in the past.

Like UNEP, the OECD offers an optimistic scenario of global, green economic prospects, if the right incentives and policies are adopted. Aside from investments in green sectors, these include eco-taxes, such as a carbon tax; well-designed regulation to promote innovation; energy, water, and materials efficiency; and cuts in subsidies for unsustainable activity related to fossil fuels, irrigation, and mining. The report also stresses the importance of economic valuation of natural capital and ecosystem services, as a way of recognizing their value in measurable terms.

A third example is the World Business Council for Sustainable Development's (WBCSD) *Vision 2050: The New Agenda for Business* (2012). The good news for business is "growth will deliver billions of new consumers who want homes and cars and television sets" (all quotes from the Executive Summary). In contrast, the bad news is that "shrinking resources and potentially changing climate will limit the ability of all 9 billion of us to attain or maintain the consumptive lifestyle that is commensurate with wealth in today's markets." The report sets out two goals: (1) "a standard of living where people have access to and the ability to afford education, healthcare, mobility, the basics of food, water, energy and shelter, and consumer goods"; and (2) "a standard of living [that] can be sustained with the available natural resources and without further harm to biodiversity, climate, and other ecosystems." The vision for 2050 is a world where "Economic growth has been decoupled from ecosystem destruction and material consumption and re-coupled with sustainable economic development and societal well-being."

The report does explicitly recognize the existence of planetary limits of some kind and sets out a strategy for fulfilling its two goals vision by 2050. Among the actions to be taken strategically are incorporating the costs of environmental externalities (e.g., pollution) into decision making; doubling agricultural output without increasing land or water use; halving carbon emissions; halting deforestation; achieving a four-fold to ten-fold increase in resource and material use; and achieving universal access to low-carbon mobility for the world's population. Not surprisingly, *Vision 2050* emphasizes ways to expand markets given growth and the need for product, technology, and market innovation. There also is a tendency to fault governance (i.e., public institutions and policies) rather than business for promoting ecological degradation.

For the World Bank, green growth is "efficient in its use of natural resources, clean in that it minimizes pollution and environmental impacts, and resilient in that it accounts for natural hazards and the role of environmental management and natural capital in preventing physical disasters" (2012, 2). A premise in *Inclusive Green Growth* (2012) is that "sustained growth is necessary to achieve the urgent development of the world's poor" and that "there is substantial scope for growing cleaner without growing slower" (xi). The report places a premium on *inclusive growth* sensitive to the needs of the poor; growth drives poverty reduction but must be equitable. Like UNEP and OECD, the Bank views environmental damages as "reaching a scale where they are beginning to threaten both growth prospects and the progress achieved in social indicators" (3). Such growth is affordable: "many green policies pay for themselves directly, and the others make economic sense once externalities are priced and eco-system services are valued" (4). Like its counterparts, the Bank bases its case on the costs of ecological degradation to economic and social well-being rather than the intrinsic worth of nature, a source of discomfort among critics. The Bank takes a standard green growth position: an expanding economy is needed to meet the needs of the poor; but it takes pains to emphasize the need for *inclusive* economic growth.

Among the strategies available for achieving green, inclusive growth are those that fix market failures, internalize externalities, assign property rights, improve governance, and influence behaviors. Table 2.2 lists several definitions of green growth and economy.

Several aspects of these reports are worth noting. First, they present both a *policy framing* (in this case, more of a *reframing*) and a *policy agenda*. All imply the existence of ecological limits, boundaries, or thresholds, but are vague on just where or when they matter. All accept a need for growth, seeing it as accelerating, continuing, or at worst declining marginally. All express a central tenet

*Table 2.2* Definitions of the Green Growth/Green Economy Concept

| | | |
|---|---|---|
| **United Nations Environment Programme (2011)** | Green Economy | "one that results in improved human well-being and social equity, while significantly reducing environmental risks and economic scarcities" (9). |
| **World Bank (2012)** | Green Growth | "growth that is efficient in its use of natural resources, clean in that it minimizes pollution and environmental impacts, and resilient in that it accounts for natural hazards and the role of environmental management and natural capital in preventing physical disasters" (2). |
| **World Business Council for Sustainable Development (2012)** | Neither explicitly; oriented to green growth | "a standard of living where people have access to and the ability to afford education, healthcare, mobility, the basics of food, water, energy, and shelter, and consumer goods . . . living in such a way that this standard of living can be sustained with the available natural resources and without further harm to biodiversity, climate, and other ecosystems" (Executive Summary). |
| **Organization for Economic Cooperation & Development (2011)** | Green Growth | "fostering economic growth and development while ensuring that natural assets continue to provide the resources and environmental services on which our well-being relies" (9). |
| **Green Economy Coalition (2012)** | Green Economy | "one that generates a better quality of life for all within the ecological limits of the planet" (undated). |
| **Institute for European Environmental Policy (Ten Brink et al. 2012)** | Green Economy | "a resource efficient, low-carbon, equitable economy that stays within a 'safe operating space'—or working within the planet's regenerative capacities and avoiding critical ecological thresholds" (34). |

of green growth thinking—that a business-as-usual growth trajectory at some point degrades the natural capital that makes well-being possible. Some suggest it may be necessary to rethink growth as a goal. Still, none calls for an end to or deliberate slowing of growth or incomes; that would undermine the validity of green growth as a framing concept.

As exercises in framing, or more specifically in *reframing* issues, these reports share such themes as integration, synergy, poverty elimination, minimizing trade-offs, efficiency, and the probability of ecology–economy win–wins. As policy agenda, they stress economic instruments, sector-based approaches, market valuation of critical ecosystems, and policy/investment linkage. The policy agenda for green growth is examined in detail in Chapter 6.

## THE IMPACT OF THE GREEN GROWTH CONCEPT

As a relatively new concept in ecological discourse, the long-term impact of green growth is yet to be established. It has been adopted in international policy debates and assessments, and there are signs of its influence at a national level, even in the United States. It is used to reframe ecology–economy relationships and may displace sustainable development as the framing concept of the day. As a policy agenda, its impact still is undetermined. Yet advocates have brought it into the mainstream.

With major organizations like the UNEP, OECD, and World Bank behind it, green growth does not lack international presence. These and other organizations created the Global Green Growth Institute (www.gggi.org), "founded on the belief that economic growth and environmental sustainability are not only compatible objectives; their integration is essential to the future of mankind." It develops resources and supports green economic planning in Indonesia, Brazil, Ethiopia, and elsewhere. Such organizations as the World Wildlife Fund, International Union for the Conservation of Nature, and New Economy Foundation formed a Green Economy Coalition (greeneconomycoalition.org) to promote the transition to a "resilient economy that provides a better quality of life for all within the ecological limits of the planet."

A brief country profile illustrates the influence that the UNEP formulation in particular is having at a national level. One country that embraced the concept is Ethiopia. Its *Climate-Resilient Green Economy Strategy* is framed as an effort to "unlock economic growth, create jobs for the growing population, and deliver wider socio-economic benefits" (FDRE 2011, 11). Its policy agenda is focused on energy, agriculture, forestry, buildings, and water. It developed as a strategy not only to avoid costs of ecological degradation but to leverage market options by, for example, generating renewable energy for export. It includes measures for leapfrogging to energy-efficient technologies in multiple sectors as well as for protecting and restoring forests. With its high growth rates, Ethiopia will test the efficacy and durability of a green growth agenda and serves as a laboratory for evaluating it, as will countries like South Korea (Matthews 2012).

What about the world's largest and historically most dynamic economy? The influence of and prospects for green growth in the United States are taken up in Chapters 7 and 8. For now, it is worth noting that, at a national level, the green growth concept has been visible as a reframing device. The Obama administration embraced the "clean energy highway" to create jobs, promote durable growth, and expand markets in energy efficiency and renewables. The opposition, in turn, has used the old ecology–economy zero-sum framing as a rhetorical strategy for protecting fossil fuel interests against such a transition. Green growth issue framing is apparent in other actions as well. For example, the Environmental Protection Agency (EPA 2013) states that "Water is vital to a productive and growing economy in the United States, and directly affects the production of many goods and services." Coalitions like the BlueGreen Alliance of unions and environmental groups stress the ecology–economy linkages of job creation and infrastructure spending. Green jobs are a theme used for linking economic strategies and ecological policies (Jones 2008).

The ideas of green growth, if not the term itself, are evident locally in the United States. Indeed, with terms like smart or sustainable growth, green growth is an organizing theme for innovative policies in cities across the country. Although many are framed in terms of sustainability, they stress economy–ecology synergies more than the social equity aspects (Saha and Paterson 2008).

## CRITICISMS OF GREEN GROWTH

Like many concepts that seek to reconcile real or perceived conflicts, green growth generates criticism as well as praise. For critics from the left, it is a cynical effort to justify continued, rapid, and ecologically and socially destructive economic growth. For critics from the right, it is an agenda to limit growth, expand government, undermine markets, and harm vital industries like energy and agriculture. At the same time, for its advocates, green growth offers a politically defensible and economically pragmatic path for reconciling the inevitability of and need for growth within ecological limits (Fiorino 2014a). Because it is contested politically, views on the concept are influenced by where one stands on economic growth and inequality, government's role in society, the legitimacy of business engagement, the intrinsic relative to instrumental value of nature, and even our definitions of human well-being and happiness.

I consider the more common criticisms of the green growth concept in two categories—those largely coming from the political left and those mostly from the political right. Criticisms from the left occupy most of my attention; they are more substantive and, from my point of view, more valid. Both critics find common ground in asserting that green growth cannot deliver as promised. From the left, the charge is that the policy agenda is not green enough to overcome the sheer weight of exponential growth. From the right, the claim is that greening sacrifices growth.

## Criticism Largely from the Political Left

One criticism of green growth—an obvious one given the concept—is that *it justifies continued, exponential, economic expansion.* For these critics, stopping or reversing growth is the only way out of our ecological dilemma. Herman Daly (1998) argues "it is impossible for the world economy to grow its way out of poverty and environmental degradation" (285). He adds: "To delude ourselves into believing that growth is still possible and desirable if only we label it 'sustainable' or color it 'green' will just delay the inevitable transition and make it more painful" (286). And yet this is precisely what green growth advocates propose.

The green growth case is that we can decouple ecological and resource impacts from the process of continued economic growth, defined as "an increase in the level of real GDP over time" (Pearce and Barbier 2000, 30). Indeed, the UNEP report claims not only that growth will not suffer, but we actually can *increase* GDP growth rates. Critics see this as misleading and unlikely, if not impossible. Although a relative decoupling is feasible, reducing ecological and impacts per unit of economic production and consumption only forestalls the inevitable reckoning. Eventually, the sheer weight of growth offsets even big eco-efficiency gains. Ecological economists cite the second law of thermodynamics and entropy in a closed biophysical system. Modern society transforms matter from "organized, structural, concentrated, low-entropy states (raw materials) into still more highly-structured commodities, and then through use into dispersed, randomized, high entropy states (waste)" (Daly 1991, 22). Physically, the effects of even very eco-efficient exponential growth are ecologically unsustainable.

Behavioral factors come into play as well, such as the *rebound effect,* where lower costs lead people to consume more goods or services. For example, energy-efficient cars lead to more driving that offsets the advantages of greater energy efficiency. "The existence of rebounds . . ." Blake Alcott (2010, 556, and 2008) argues, "means that policies to reduce population, affluence and energy intensity are not *sufficient* to reduce impact." He prefers to reduce the adverse impacts of population and economic growth by targeting harmful consumption directly.

Stopping growth is non-debatable in much ecology–economy writing. In a primer on the more radical version of a green economy, Mary Smith Cato writes that "If you only take away one idea from an introduction to green economics such as this it should be that green economics is opposed to continuing economic growth" (2009, 40). She adds: "one of the key demands of a green economist is an end to economic growth" (56).

Even writers sympathetic to the assumptions and goals of green growth recognize the need to address growth. A founder of ecological modernization, Martin Jänicke concludes that "high GDP growth cannot be 'green growth' because it cannot sufficiently be compensated by eco-efficient innovation" (2012, 20). Consider two growth rates over seventy years. A one percent growth rate leads to a doubling of GDP; a five percent rate translates into a thirty-fold increase. The latter, he concludes, is "the death sentence of any environmental strategy" (20).

Another concern among green growth critics is that *it commodifies nature— making it just another item on the market exchange table.* The authors of *Blueprint for a Sustainable Economy* argued, "the source of most environmental problems lies in the failure of the economic system to take account of the valuable services which natural environments provide for us" (2000, 1). The logic of their case was that only properly valued ecosystem services could play a role in decision making. Still, they realized that "the most resisted issue remains the idea of placing values on environmental assets, the so-called monetization of the environment" (xi).

Ecosystem valuation is, of course, a contribution of ecological economics. Ecological issues are more likely to gain attention if stated in economic terms. As Douglas McCauley (2006, 27) puts it, "if scientists can identify ecosystem services, quantify their economic value, and ultimately bring conservation more into synchrony with market ideologies, then the decision-makers will recognize the folly of environmental destruction and work to safeguard nature."

Having stated the case, McCauley then proceeds to challenge it. His objection is partly on principle. Rather than treating nature as a commodity, "we must strongly assert the primacy of ethics and aesthetics in conservation" (27). Mark Sagoff, another critic of viewing nature as a commodity subject to cost–benefit calculation, similarly asks (1998, 141): "Why is it so difficult for them [that is, advocates of attaching market value to ecological goods] to say that one may allocate resources not always as a perfect market would but on substantive, normative, and frankly ethical grounds?" It is far better to recognize that

"Nature has an intrinsic value that makes it priceless, and this is reason enough to protect it." (28).

There is a practical side to these challenges. What happens when ecosystem services cannot pass a market test? Is nature worth saving only when it is profitable? McCauley cites a Costa Rican coffee plantation where native bees provided some $60,000 a year in pollination benefits. When coffee prices fell, the plantation converted to pineapples, for which pollinator services were irrelevant. The value of pollinators fell to zero, and the case for protecting them disappeared. "If we oversell the message that ecosystems are important because they provide services," McCauley concludes, "we will have effectively sold out on nature" (28).

Many critics view green growth as *a ruse for preserving and even for increasing the economic and political dominance of multilateral corporations and financial institutions*. In this view, green growth advocates appear to respond to ecological limits while rigging the economy in their favor. One group critical of green growth and economy predicts their failure "due to the prevailing capitalist and imperialist conditions as well as the unquestioned faith in progress" inherent in globalized economies. "Instead of counteracting social disparities, racist, class- and gender-specific oppression," they charge, "strategies of the Green Economy amplify such tendencies." (Federal Coordination of Internationalismus 2012, 2; also see ETC Group 2011). Green growth replaces debate and change with an agenda of technology, efficiency, and management. Opportunities for actual political debate "could possibly close permanently with the sealant of the Green Economy" (4).

With a more nuanced view, Martin Khor warns that green economy and growth concepts could be used by rich nations to block economic development in poorer nations through trade policies, intellectual property rights, and aid programs. Developed countries, for example, could use economic greening "as a principle or concept to justify unilateral trade measures against the products of developing countries" (2011, 6). An illustration is a tax on imported products based on the carbon content. Similarly, subsidies to firms in richer nations may put poorer countries at a disadvantage in developing low-emission technologies. Environmental standards also could be used to condition "aid, loans, and debt rescheduling or debt relief" by the richer countries (13).

A fundamental criticism is that green growth and similar concepts are *inherently flawed because they seek solutions in the context of a capitalist system*. The problem—the root cause of our ecological dilemma—is capitalism itself, and solutions lie in radically changing or replacing market-based economies. James O'Connor argues sustainable capitalism is possible only "unless and until capital changes its face in ways that would make it unrecognizable to bankers, money managers, venture capitalists, and CEOs, looking at themselves in the mirror today" (1994, 158).

A *lack of attention to social issues of equity and empowerment* also draws criticism. The standard "three-legged stool" of sustainable development includes ecological, economic, and social components. Green growth and green economy focus on the ecological and economic, as the names suggest. In the context of sustainable development, the social dimension has referred to substantive issues of economic equity, health care and education, and access to such basics as housing, energy, water, and food, along with procedural issues of citizen engagement, empowerment, and political transparency. Expressions of green growth do give attention to these issues, largely in stressing economic growth as a path out of poverty and in acknowledging the need for some kind of equitable distribution of the benefits of that growth. The World Bank's interest in *inclusive* growth is an illustration. Still, the overriding emphasis is on the ecology–economy relationships, with the "softer" social issues typically relegated to the second tier of concerns and solutions.

Finally the pragmatic question: *Is green growth even possible* without at least a leveling off of growth and a scaling back of economies? The de-growth school argues that rich countries have to do serious economic down-sizing while poor ones grow to a modest per capita income of, say, $15,000–$30,000 or so annually and level off. A 2013 essay by Ivan Turok and Jacqueline Borel-Saladin poses the right question in asking "whether greening the economy will achieve enough to alter the current unsustainable trajectory of the global economy and enable it to stay within the 'safe operating boundaries' of the planet" (2013, 291). Specifically, they ask:

[W]ill the scale of change from 'business as usual' be sufficient to prevent excessive global warming and other environmental catastrophes, bearing in mind continuing population growth and pressures to increase consumption?

Can a new sustainable development path be engineered by manipulating resource prices and stimulating new technologies?

Or does the underlying market-based, short-term, growth-oriented paradigm of the global economy need to be replaced?

What do we make of such criticisms? We may begin with the asserted deficiencies of capitalism, defined as "an economic system characterized by private or corporate ownership of capital goods, by investments that are determined by private decision, and by prices, production, and the distribution of goods that are determined mainly by competition in a free market" (Merriam-Webster. com). The alternative is state or collective ownership and decision making. It is hard to disagree with the assertion that capitalism as it was practiced historically has not been especially sensitive to ecological degradation, although in recent decades we have seen attempts to change this pattern in the programs, laws, and ministries created in most parts of the world.

One problem with the capitalist critique is that state ownership and decision making have been no better and generally have been worse. The Soviet Union and Eastern Bloc are hardly poster children for ecological sensitivity. Since the 1960s, the progress has come in capitalist, democratic nations of Western Europe, North America, and Japan, not state-driven economies. China, a state-driven economic system, has so far not been a model of ecological sensitivity.

Another problem with the capitalist critique is that the alternatives are unclear. To be sure, the models offered by communal decision making and the "shared economy" at local levels offer interesting and useful models of economic organization, but they are hardly effective at a large scale. They may have an effect in the context of a more enlightened capitalism but in limited applications; they are an unlikely path for respecting ecological limits at macro-levels.

Then there is the criticism that green growth neglects the social agenda, specifically economic and political equality. Here, green growth presents a clear contrast with sustainable development, where social issues are central. I have two responses. First, the social aspects of sustainable development have been problematic in the United States and undermine its value as a framing device. Second, however, inequality is critical for green growth and should be incorporated more explicitly. Ecological economists are on target regarding economic inequality. Indeed, Chapter 5 argues they are even more correct than often is assumed, for reasons not fully appreciated.

That green growth in some of its expressions justifies continued growth and commodifies nature are valid criticisms. Indeed, its very definition is designed to justify economic growth. This makes it unacceptable to critics, to whom the only options are de-growth or no-growth. I agree that rethinking growth and what it means to quality of life is essential. However, focusing only on economic growth is bad politics and poor strategy, for reasons set out in the next chapter.

The concern about commodifying nature raises ethical and practical issues. That nature should be valued for its intrinsic qualities and not just its economic value to humans is entirely valid. It may well be, as Douglas McCauley puts it, that "We will make more progress in the long run by appealing to people's hearts rather than to their wallets" (2006, 28). Still, that approach has not been sufficient in the past, and the pressures for near-term growth and economic security raise doubts about it being enough in the future. Taking a practical step toward appreciating the economic value of ecosystems and natural resources does not have to diminish their intrinsic value; the utilitarian does not necessarily drive out the intrinsic.

As for the concern that ecosystem valuation makes wetlands, forests, and so on vulnerable to exploitation, the economics are only one factor among many that should be considered. In a response to McCauley, Walter Reid (2006, 749) writes, "useful roles played by a watershed in water purification, a woodland for recreation or a forest for carbon sequestration are just some of the many factors used to help convince a government of the merits of protecting certain areas from development." Likewise, Robert Costanza writes, "Ecosystems are critical to our survival and well-being for many reasons—hearts, minds and wallets included" (2006, 749). "If nature contributes significantly to human well-being," he adds, "then it is a major contributor to the real economy" (2006, 749). Market valuation is useful in recognizing ecological services and assets, is one of many factors to consider, and does not necessarily diminish their intrinsic value.

That a green growth framing and policy framework may not be enough, in the long haul, to allow us to remain within ecological and resource limits is a reasonable assertion. What is clear, at least to many of us, is that green growth offers both a plausible political rationale and workable policy framework for realizing a *far greener economy* than will occur under business as usual. Whether it leads to long-term, perpetual green growth is a theory in need of validation.

## Criticisms from the Political Right

What about the objections from the right side of the political spectrum? Why would economic and political conservatives not embrace a concept that accepts the inevitability of economic growth, even if more broadly conceived than in the past? The reality is that, at least in the United States, ideas of green growth and economy are disliked and often derided by conservatives. Their objections come in two forms. One is that *green* and *growth* are irreconcilable: Restricting fossil fuels, protecting land from development, changing agricultural practices, and so on, elevate nature over humans by constraining growth, killing jobs, and making firms uncompetitive.

Another objection is that green growth, sustainable development, and the like are just vehicles for realizing liberal goals. Washington *Post* columnist Charles Krauthammer wrote in 2009 that "environmentalism is becoming the new socialism, i.e. the totemic ideal in the name of which government seizes the commanding heights of the economy and society." More recently, criticizing sustainability on college campuses, his colleague George Will observed that "the term 'sustainable' postulates frugality and scarcity that entail government planners and rationers to fend off planetary calamity while administering equity" (2015). He adds, "The unvarying progressive agenda is for government to supplant markets in allocating wealth and opportunity."

In sum, criticism from the right concentrates not only on the *green* side of the equation but on the balance of government and the private sector, regulation and markets, collective and individual action. Underlying this view is the belief that markets and technology will solve any ecological problems, in what John Dryzek terms a *Promethean* environmental discourse (2013).

Politically, I see two explanations for such criticisms from the right. To begin, concepts like green growth attempt to refute the long-standing argument that ecological policies are bad for the economy. Framing concepts like green growth, green economy, and clean energy remove a powerful weapon in the conservative arsenal—that a path exists to reconcile economic vitality with ecological quality. Green growth removes a major rallying point from the pro-market, pro-growth, pro–fossil fuel political playbook and can help to legitimate environmentalism.

A second tactical, political explanation is a simple matter of political coalitions. Most opponents of economic greening are tied to fossil fuel interests. Members of Congress most visible in opposing climate action come from coal, oil, and gas states like Oklahoma, Texas, West Virginia, and Louisiana. In contrast, advocates come from states that lack such resources on any scale, such as California, Hawaii, Massachusetts, Maryland, and Vermont. Both in terms of financial support and political needs of constituencies, conservatives are tied to fossil fuels.

Both criticisms—that anything green beyond a point harms economic growth and so green growth is impossible and that green agendas are founded on intrusive government—carry weight in conservative circles and have influenced public perceptions of green policies, whether linked to growth or not (Layzer 2012; Klein 2014). In fact, however, the evidence reviewed in Chapter 3 suggests that ecological protection has had little growth-constraining effect. As for the big government argument, green growth does involve more collective action than advocates of limited government would care to see, without a doubt. That it is a vehicle for radical social transformation, destruction of markets, and socialism goes well beyond its scope and intent.

## BUILDING A BETTER GREEN GROWTH CONCEPT

Although these treatments of green growth share characteristics, there also is room for interpretation. Like other environmental concepts that influence our thinking, green growth is a theme with variations. This conclusion presents some modifications to the concept in response to many of the criticisms as well as sets out a view of green growth for the rest of the book.

*Greener* growth is entirely possible under the reframing and policy agenda embodied in the concept. Renewable energy, resource efficiency, smart urban growth, new models for agriculture or transportation—the list goes on. The question is whether or not this is enough given the increases in economic scale anticipated in the coming decades and beyond. If it is to be effective as a framing concept and policy agenda, some modifications will help. These come out in the rest of the book, but it is worth highlighting them now to give an overview. They include:

Be realistic in accepting, as most green economy proponents do, that growth of some kind will continue, but rethinking and redefining it is essential. This involves recognizing that richer is not always happier; status competition is socially and ecologically harmful; and GDP and income are narrow measures of well-being (Kubiszewski et al. 2013).

Recognize economic and political inequality. Equitable growth is less damaging and more ecologically responsible. Inequality leads to more consumption; insecurity; and a harmful erosion of social trust, capital, and the capacity for collective action.

Beyond rethinking what growth means, be "indifferent or neutral about it" in evaluating goals and developing strategies (van den Bergh 2011, 882). Rather than call for overall de-growth, van den Bergh argues, we should focus on economic activities and sectors such as fossil fuels, sprawl, large-scale agriculture, and others with *selective de-growth*.

Build the concept on the irreplaceability of ecological assets and services, for their own sake as well as their economic value. Ecological economics provides a basis for doing this, but it would help allay the concerns of critics if there were a greater appreciation of ecological goods on their own and not just for their instrumental value.

Recognize directly that business greening through eco-efficiency and innovation is necessary but insufficient. Government plays a role by putting a price on carbon, reforming subsidies, linking policy across sectors, reorienting investments, promoting new technologies, pricing resources effectively, and other measures (Fiorino 2014a).

Like any macro-level concept that aims to reconstruct how we think about issues and solutions, green growth offers ample grounds for criticism. It could be used to justify marginal adjustments from business as usual as a way of sustaining a growth-at-all-costs mindset. It also could be the basis for a politically effective reframing of ecological and economic issues and a pragmatic blueprint for change. It sets out a third way between the politically unrealistic, risky view that economies need to stop growing or actually contract, and the ecologically irresponsible view that ecological limits do not exist or will be overcome through technology, innovation, and the benefits of greater wealth. At the same time, if it is to prove durable and effective as a long-term framing device and a policy agenda, it should be revised to be an equitable, defensible, and systemic strategy for change. Then its value as a long-term innovation ultimately may be realized.

The next three chapters take apart the concept of green growth by exploring the three issues of economics, governance and politics, and social equity. My objective is to bring together evidence on each to further evaluate the validity of the green growth concept. I return to the usefulness of green growth as a framing concept and policy agenda in the final three chapters.

# Ecology and Economy: Partners or Antagonists?

For nearly half a century, the heart of the struggle over environmental policy in the United States and most other nations has turned on the relationship between ecology and the economy. Critics of ecological protection charge that controlling pollution, preserving wetlands, and limiting land use undermines growth, impairs competitiveness, increases consumer cost, and destroys jobs. Advocates of ecological protection assert, in turn, that unguided growth in pursuit of ever-more material gratification threatens health and degrades vital ecosystems and resources.

Given these competing assertions, the policy strategy for the last five decades in the United States has been to seek an acceptable ecology–economy balance. Expand the economy, create jobs, and make people richer, but protect them from serious effects of pollution and ecological harm. Or, from the other side, strive for clean water and maintain ecosystems, but grow and prosper. It has been a strategy of *minimizing the adverse trade-offs* among ecological and economic goals.

That this strategy of minimizing trade-offs has delivered value is clear to most of us. Take air quality as an example: levels of harmful pollutants have fallen considerably. Despite well over a doubling of GDP, a doubling of vehicle miles traveled, population growth of over forty percent, and a 25% increase in energy consumption between 1980 and 2015, the aggregate emissions of six major pollutants regulated under the Clean Air Act fell by 63% (summarized in Kraft 2015, 32–34; also see EPA 2016). Since 1990 alone, according to the EPA, ambient concentrations of nitrogen dioxide have declined by 54%; lead by 99%; ozone by 22%; particulates by 39 and 37% (depending on particle size); and sulfur dioxide by 81%. The Clean Air Act is a major success of US domestic policy

The record for other problems is less impressive, or at least less clear. Despite major reductions in water discharges from point sources like sewage treatment plants and industrial facilities, pollution from nonpoint sources (such as runoff from farms and urban storm water) is still a problem. Hazardous wastes are handled more responsibly now than decades ago, and some harmful chemicals (asbestos and lead, for example) are no longer in active use, although serious legacy issues remain, as the 2016 Flint water crisis illustrates (Bellinger 2016). Wetlands are better protected than in the past, but more than half are gone. In sum, minimizing trade-offs was effective at times, less so at others (for a summary, see EPA's *Report on the Environment*).

Green growth aims to move from a strategy of mostly minimizing negatives to one of maximizing positive relationships among economic and ecological issues. The elements of a green growth agenda are presented in Chapter 6. For now, two brief examples make the point.

One is energy efficiency, a classic no-brainer among economy–ecology synergies (Keane 2012). Using less energy saves money; reduces greenhouse gas emissions; cuts air pollution that damages health, such as particulates and nitrogen dioxide; reduces demand for water, which is affected by energy production and use; and helps protect habitat. Green infrastructure is another example; it uses natural forces to protect water quality and resources in place of standard "gray" construction. Roof gardens, swales, or cover crops protect water quality at a fraction of the cost.

The arguments underlying green growth in no way should be interpreted as denying the existence of trade-offs, because they do exist. Preserving a wetland makes land unavailable for cultivation or other commercial purposes. Granting a permit to a new plant increases emissions, even with strict controls. Shifting water from irrigation to municipal use affects farm production. Still, such trade-offs are mostly short-term and put specific interests ahead of overall well-being.

This and the following two chapters take on three issues critical to assessing the green growth concept: the interactions among the economy and ecology, especially that of economic growth in the face of ecological limits; governance for green growth; and economic inequality.

The assumption underlying the concept of green growth is that the economy and ecology *should* and *may* be conceived of or managed more as partners than antagonists. This contradicts many decades of political struggle over the *balance* that should be maintained among economic and ecological goals. If advocates of the zero-sum relationship are correct, and economy–ecology interactions are nearly always antagonistic, the concept of green growth is, as many critics claim, little more than a ruse, a fantasy of having your cake and eating it too. If, on the other hand, such interactions are or can be positive—if economic and ecological goals may be framed as being at times positive rather than antagonistic—green growth may have validity and be worth pursuing.

This chapter explores the complexity of economy–ecology relationships as a way to appreciate the strengths and limits of the concept of green growth. It presents several arguments:

- The net effect of economic growth (increases in real GDP and incomes) is to increase ecological pressure, *as growth has been pursued to this point.*
- The negative economic impacts of progressive ecological policies are overstated, as is reflected in the evidence on the prospects for coming decades.
- The ecological impacts of growth are not always uniformly negative; growth may support and enable health, ecological, and resource protection.
- Debates about growth versus ecology are oversimplified, for many reasons, and they distract us from effectively managing economy–ecology issues.

## THE ECONOMIC EFFECTS OF ECOLOGICAL PROTECTION

The analytical basis for ecological policy in the United States has always contained large doses of economic analysis (Stavins 2005). This comes in three forms (EPA 2010). One is economic impact analysis, which looks at the cause-and-effect relationships of ecological and health protection policies on costs of producing goods and services, consumer prices, employment, and so on. The idea is to assess the economic impacts of a policy and make adjustments if they are too negative. Second is cost-effectiveness analysis, which evaluates policies by the costs per unit of a desired outcome, like tons of air pollution reduced or premature deaths avoided. Third and most controversial is cost–benefit analysis; it "monetizes' (puts in dollar terms) the expected negative (costs) and positive (benefits) outcomes related to policies, with a goal of minimizing the first and maximizing the second; it aims to generate net social benefits (Morgenstern 1997).

What each of these methods shares is an assumption that ecological policymaking is all about managing or balancing a series of trade-offs. Economic impact analysis tells us how to minimize the adverse effects of a decision to, for example, reduce water pollution through new technologies. Cost-effectiveness analysis takes a set of policy options and tells us which are least costly, given the goals. It aims to generate the most bang for the buck. Cost–benefit directs us to produce more societal benefits than costs, based on a series of calculations that attach a market value to the likely outcomes. All are useful tools, but they are designed to balance trade-offs.

All three share biases. Most important, and already mentioned, is a focus on minimizing negatives rather than maximizing positives. There is an assumption of trade-offs that have to be managed. A second bias is that these methods focus on the short term and are narrowly framed. Evaluating the costs and benefits of stricter standards for coal-fired power plants, for example, ignores the option of generating power in other ways, such as through wind or solar sources. Put simply, most economic analysis kicks in at a retail rather than wholesale stage of decision. For cost–benefit, a third bias is that the benefits typically are based on the sum of the willingness of individuals in a society to pay for benefits like a coastal estuary or wetland; this may not reflect their long-term value, their irreplaceability, or the irreversibility of actions that damage them.

Green growth is based on the notion that positive ecology–economy outcomes are possible. If green growth is a valid concept, it helps to assess the economic effects of ecological policies so far in the United States as well as to consider the economic future effects of a green growth path.

## Have Ecological Policies Harmed the Economy?

Critics of ecological protection, such as those opposed to mitigating greenhouse gas emissions or managing releases of nutrients in water, argue that such policies damage the economy. Typical is a 2014 statement from Thomas Donohue, President and CEO of the US Chamber of Commerce, who asserted on regulation generally (but emphasizing environmental regulation): "Projects are being sidelined, jobs are being lost, and freedoms seriously undermined by an out-of-control regulatory bureaucracy. Too much regulation creates uncertainty, drives up costs, suppresses hiring and investment, and threatens our competitive edge in a global economy." Washington *Post* columnist Ruth Marcus (2012) wrote a few years earlier, with respect to critics of regulation: "It is a seemingly immutable law of modern Republican rhetoric that the word 'regulation' can never appear unadorned by the essential adjective 'job-killing.'"

Are ecological and health policies necessarily bad for the economy? Evidence suggests that claims of lost growth, massive job loss, and diminished competitiveness are overstated. In a review of economy-wide studies of regulation, Isaac Shapiro and John Irons observe, "The most common general studies are of environmental regulations, and these have consistently failed to find significant negative employment effects" (2011, 3). Although dated, a 1994 review found that, of nine economy-wide studies, seven determined that environmental expenditures increased aggregate employment, one found lost jobs, and the other had mixed results (Goodstein 1994, 5). A more recent study found environmental regulation created jobs in some areas and displaced them others, but "the net effect on employment is positive" (Bezdek, Wendling, and DiPerna 2008, 63). An oft-cited study by Resources for the Future studied four highly polluting industries (petroleum, plastics, pulp and paper, and steel), where employment effects are most likely to be negative, and found slightly positive job outcomes in two—plastics and petroleum—with no statistically significant impact in the others (Morgenstern, Pizer, and Shih 2002). Similarly, a study of southern California, with its stringent air quality rules, found "no evidence that local air quality regulation substantially reduced employment" and may have "increased labor demand slightly" (Berman and Bui 2001, 265, 293; also Thomas 2009). A few studies find evidence of some job loss, but Shapiro and Irons conclude that research "tends to show that the broad fear of substantial regulation-induced job loss at the industry level is unfounded" (17).

Other claims are that regulation reduces growth and encourages the outsourcing of employment, of job losses due to "pollution havens" in developing countries with low labor costs. One study on overall growth effects is from 1990; it found environmental regulation reduced the gross national product by 2.6% over the study period (1972–1985), which translates into a 0.19% lower annual growth rate (Shapiro and Irons 2011, 15, citing Jorgenson and Wilcoxen 1990). Assume for a moment that health and ecological protection subtract a fraction of a point from annual growth rates (also see Jaffe, et al 1995). Given what we know about the ecological and health costs of conventionally brown growth, is this too high a price?

Other analyses find little support for the claim that environmental rules lead industry to move to countries with lax pollution controls to save money. Firms move offshore for many reasons, such as labor costs and quality and access to markets, and environmental costs are a minor factor in such decisions. A review of research on the role of regulatory costs found no pattern in the results; some studies showed negative effects, and others did not (Pasurka 2008). Some studies using different methods find evidence of a pollution haven effect, especially in manufacturing, but this will be less significant as other countries' standards become more stringent (Shapiro and Irons 2011, 19). Yet another study (Eskeland and Harrison 2003) found little support for the pollution haven hypothesis; many more complex factors were in play. Still, even though job losses due to pollution havens are minimal, they do occur in specific sectors; this reinforces the need for global, collective green growth strategies, as discussed in Chapter 8.

Of course, another way of looking at the economic effects of environmental regulation is in terms of its benefits: fewer premature deaths, better health, cleaner air and water, functioning wetlands, fewer contaminated aquifers, more ecosystem services, less lead poisoning, and so on. Benefits may be seen simply as costs avoided, and rapidly growing countries like China and India experience the high costs of growth in the form of dangerous air and water pollution and degraded ecosystems. Indeed, advocates of a growth-above-all mindset should recognize that "conservative estimates of illness and premature death associated with air pollution in China cost 6.5% of China's GDP per year" (Gallagher and Lewis 2016, 338).

Although a detailed accounting of benefits is not my goal, a few cases are worth noting. The Clean Air Act offers striking examples of health benefits that may be expressed in economic terms. Between 1970 and 1990 the Clean Air Act yielded benefits of some $22 trillion and costs of about $0.5 trillion (central estimates from a range of benefits) in premature deaths and health effects avoided (EPA 1997). Between 1990 and (projected) 2020, a later analysis found that the benefits of the Clean Air Act exceeded costs by a central estimate 30–1 ratio, avoiding 230,000 premature deaths, 75,000 bronchitis cases, 120,000 emergency room visits, and 17 million lost work days annually in 2020 (EPA 2011). To summarize: "cleaner air leads to better health and productivity for American workers as well as savings on medical expenses" (EPA 2010, 3).

The EPA's Clean Power Plan for reducing $CO_2$ emissions from coal-fired power plants, issued in final form in 2015, was estimated then to deliver some $34–54 billion in annual benefits for costs of $8–9 billion. These annual benefits included 1,500 to 3,000 fewer deaths, 90,000 fewer asthma cases in children, and some 300,000 avoided lost work and school days by 2030 (EPA 2015). Although, as critics are quick to point out, the program was expected to increase the unit costs of energy to consumers by 2030, the expected energy efficiency gains would offset this; these would deliver average annual savings of over $80 per household by 2030. Despite claims by Republican leaders of the House Energy and Commerce Committee that "it's lights out for jobs and the economy" as a result of the plan, the effects overall were positive. Taking into account all the effects, one study estimated that the Plan would yield a net gain of 74,000 jobs in 2020 and 263,000 in 2030. These are small given the US labor market, accounting for 0.1 and 0.2% of all jobs, but belie claims that major job losses will occur (Industrial Economics 2015).

On the other hand, there would also be a loss of some 20% of coal mining jobs (10,000 jobs) and 12% in electric utilities (40,000 jobs) by 2030 (Industrial Economics 2015; Cushman 2015). These sector- and geographic-specific losses drive the climate debate, as do ideological conflicts over the role of government.

Still, this underscores the need for economic support and assistance for hard-hit sectors in any policy-driven economic transition, including green growth.

## Do Positive Economy–Ecology Relationships Exist?

The theory of green growth is that positive economic–ecological relationships exist. Again, this does not mean trade-offs are not out there; they are, on specific issues and with respect to particular interests. Often they are unavoidable. A green growth framing asserts that as we look at choices broadly, from a societal perspective, the opportunities for positive-sums expand. The discussion of the economic effects of ecological policies established that negative trade-offs to this point often have been overstated. Perhaps some growth was lost at the margins; employment fell in some sectors but was offset by gains in others; movement of jobs offshore was caused by labor and other costs more than ecological policy. Negative effects were modest, especially given the many health and ecological benefits.

The weakness of the negative economic case establishes part of the validity of green growth as a concept. Ecological policies based on a goal of minimizing trade-offs did not fulfill widespread predictions of economic dislocation and harm. What if, looking ahead, we turn the question around: Could the right investments and policies deliver economic and ecological win–wins: more jobs, more competitive firms, and a stronger, fairer economy? One such view comes from Van Jones' *The Green Collar Economy*, which argues "we can fight pollution and poverty at the same time" (2008, 14). The key is green collar jobs, which he terms a "family-supporting, career-track job that directly contributes to preserving or enhancing environmental quality" (12).

Evidence exists to support Jones' claims: clean energy investments generate more jobs per dollar than do traditional fossil fuel ones. A 2009 analysis found that investment in six clean energy categories (building retrofits, mass transit, smart grid, wind, solar, and biomass) yielded from two to three times as much employment as an equivalent amount in oil, gas, or coal (Pollin, Heintz, and Garrett-Peltier 2009). This is because clean energy sectors are more labor-intensive than fossil fuels, generate more jobs per unit of investment, and rely more on activity occurring within the United States (including manufacturing and construction) and less on imports (in the case of oil). A 2014 update of this analysis calling for $150 billion in clean energy investment reached similar conclusions, although the specific ratios were different (Pollin, Garrett-Peltier, and Heintz 2014). Other analyses stress the job-creating potential of clean energy (e.g., OECD 2011, 89–93). These differences matter; much of the rationale for growth is to maintain employment.

The goal of this part of this chapter was to document an *absence of the negative*; to show that claims about inevitable societal trade-offs are overblown and that positive economy–ecology synergies are possible. There is a fair degree of evidence that ecological protection does not inevitably undermine prosperity. What about the other half of the picture: the effect of economic growth on ecological well-being? My assumption is that the net effect of growth over time is increased stress on ecosystems and resources, especially if action to mitigate growth impacts is not taken. Yet the ecological and health effects of growth are not uniformly negative. The next section considers the complexity of the relationships among economic and ecological outcomes.

## FURTHER EVIDENCE ON THE ECONOMY–ECOLOGY RELATIONSHIP

The difficulty with a simple "growth harms the environment" argument is that it is mostly but not entirely true. If growth is uniformly and linearly bad for health and ecology, why do wealthy countries rank higher than poor ones in indices like the Environmental Performance Index? If wealth and ecology are incompatible, why are states with strong ecological policies (California, Connecticut, or Minnesota) better off economically than those with weaker policies (West Virginia or Mississippi)? Why would cities viewed as sustainability leaders (Portland, OR, Seattle, and San Francisco) also be among the most prosperous? These examples do not prove that economic and ecological goals are related causally; that is much harder. They do, however, suggest that economy and ecology goals are not inherently and necessarily incompatible.

In fact, understanding the relationships among growth and ecology has been the subject of social science research at the national level, although less so at state and local levels. Among the conclusions from this research are that growth has both negative and positive effects, that it may have beneficial consequences for society and governance that offset to some degree its more harmful effects, and that economic growth is one of many factors affecting ecological quality.

Much of the evidence for these conclusions comes from research on the Environmental Kuznets Curve (EKC). This is part of broader research for explaining variations in ecological and health protection on the basis of factors like per capita income (Barrett and Graddy 2000; Dasgupta et al. 2006; Scruggs 1998; Gallego-Alvarez and Fernandez-Gomez 2016; Lorente and Alvarez-Herranz 2016); institutions and regimes (Crepaz 1995; Farzin and Bond 2005; Jahn 1998; Bernauer and Koubi 2009); geographic or demographic features, such as urbanization or population density; and even such regional affiliations as membership in the European Union (Liefferink at al. 2009; Holzinger et al. 2011).

My focus here is on income–ecology relationships, although these are linked to the social and political factors examined in Chapter 4.

The EKC is based on Simon Kuznet's analysis (1955) of the connections between economic growth and inequality. This original Kuznets Curve found that inequality grew early in the growth process but declined later. Likewise, the EKC asserts that pollution increases early in growth and then begins to decline past some level of income (see Grossman and Krueger 1995; Cole, Rayner, and Bates 1997; Dasgupta, et al. 2001). Where this "turning point" occurs varies, based on the adverse health or ecological outcomes being studied. With visible, highly relevant air and water pollutants like sulfur dioxide in air or metals in water, this turning point may come relatively early, in the $8,000–$16,000 range (Perrings and Ansuategi 2000; Levinson 2002; Dinda 2004; Munasinghe 1999). For other issues—wilderness protection, greenhouse gases, or waste generation—it comes later, if at all (Cole, at al 1997).

This research should be interpreted carefully (Stern 2004; Stern, Common, and Barbier 1996; Tan 2006). Advocates of unrestrained growth often use it to argue that growth magically solves problems—that we can grow our way out of ecological trouble. There is no basis for this. Pollution *may* decline as societies become more prosperous for many reasons, only a few of which are a direct result of growth (Dasgupta et al. 2006; Esty and Porter 2005; Tan 2006). As growth proceeds and a middle class emerges, post-material concerns about quality of life loom larger. Citizens call on governments to act. Governance, technical, and scientific capacities expand, information is more available; as ecological policies take hold, pollution falls. In sum, growth creates the conditions for responding to problems. If growth improves ecological well-being, it is mostly through better technology, eco-efficiency, and governance (Weidner 2002).

Two aspects of growth appear to reduce pollution independently of political and social change: using resources more efficiently per unit of production (eco-efficiency or relative decoupling) and shifting from a manufacturing to a service economy. In the first, it is clear that as economies mature, technologies emerge, competitive pressures increase, analytical tools improve, and resource costs grow, firms do more with less (Hawken, Lovins, and Lovins 1999). Dramatic gains in eco-efficiency were made in recent years. Some were due to regulation, but many were due to technology and management. In the second, moving from a manufacturing to service economy supports declines in pollution and the use of resources like water and energy.

Figure 3.1 is a summary of trends from 1980 to 2015 in the relationships among drivers of pollution increases (GDP and population growth; vehicle miles traveled) and emissions. The United States has achieved a *relative* decoupling in energy consumption and carbon dioxide emissions and an *absolute* decoupling in aggregate emissions of the six major pollutants regulated under

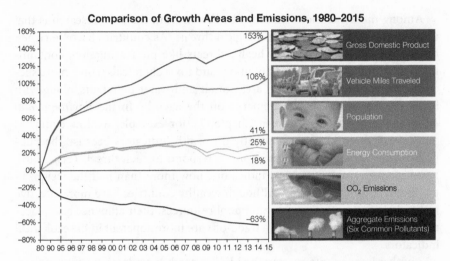

**Figure 3.1** Relationship of Pollution Drivers, Energy Consumption, and Emissions
SOURCE: US EPA: https://www.epa.gov/air-trends/air-quality-national-summary.

the Clean Air Act (ozone, nitrogen dioxide, sulfur oxides, carbon monoxide, particulate matter, and lead). Energy consumption and carbon dioxide emissions historically were not regulated; the major air pollutants were. This demonstrates that gains in technology, better management, and efficiency led to some relative decoupling, but that government regulation applied through the Clean Air Act led to an absolute decoupling of major air pollutants from economic growth.

Other qualifications apply to the EKC (Stern 2004; Levinson 2002). Harms that are less politically salient or visible—greenhouse gases leading to climate change are a prime example—are unlikely to exhibit the same kinds of turning points occurring with growth (Duwel 2010). The classic, inverted U-shaped curve may not always apply; pollution levels may decline, then level off or increase in later stages of growth. Moreover, because most of this research is on developed countries, the pattern may differ for emerging economies. Indeed, there are opportunities to help developing countries "leap-frog" over the historical curve of the EKC and move more directly to ecological protection, especially with technology and other forms of assistance from developed countries. Most important, the EKC applies more to some kinds of harm than others. The more salient the harm, the more people will demand action and a coalition supporting strong ecological policies will emerge (Duwel 2010). The contrasts between health-related pollutants like particulates or metals and greenhouse gases, the effects of which mostly are shifted to future generations or the global commons, are illustrative.

Among the conclusions that may be drawn from the EKC research is that it applies to health more than ecological threats. As countries become richer, they begin to address obvious health threats like poor sanitation, contaminated drinking water, local air pollution, and toxic chemicals (some more successfully than others). Later an array of air and water pollutants, along with losses of species and habitat, emerge on the agenda. In the *Environmental Performance Index* (discussed in Chapter 7), for example, wealthy countries outperform poorer ones consistently on health indicators because the public demands it, and society can afford to respond to such threats (Hsu 2016). Performance on the ecological indicators, now more than half the weight in the index, is far more mixed. Although wealthy countries have more effective institutions for protecting common pool resources, their affluence also places more stress on them. The growth trade-offs are more apparent in the ecological indicators.

Another issue in interpreting the EKC research is explaining why countries at a similar level of economic development, as measured by per capita income, perform differently. In nearly all assessments, for example, Sweden, Denmark, Norway, and Finland adopt stronger policies or exhibit better ecological results than others with roughly similar incomes, including the United States (discussed in Chapters 4 and 7). Two explanations for such differences—political institutions and economic inequality—are explored in later chapters. What matters for now is that incomes alone do not explain performance; other factors also determine national capacities for greener growth.

What lessons may be drawn from EKC research regarding the potential for green growth?

- Economic growth and rising incomes do help with some problems, although more on the health than ecological side of the ledger. Examples are the capacity to adopt sewage treatment, treat drinking water, or shift home heating from wood or coal to natural gas or renewables.
- There is a demand side to the picture also. As incomes rise, material needs are met, and a middle class emerges, issues like pollution or ecological loss become more of a priority.
- There is nothing magical about the EKC, when it applies. The bottom line is that politically, government has to do something, and economic growth creates conditions that may enable some degree of progress on environmental health and ecological protection.
- It is not just higher incomes but capacities flowing from them, in more democracy and better governance (see Chapter 4), that make a difference in policy and performance.

- The EKC relationship applies best to problems that matter to voters (like unsafe water or urban air pollution) and those for which financial or technology solutions are available.

In the United States, the case for inevitable trade-offs between economic well-being and ecological quality finds little support in city-level studies. In one of the more comprehensive analyses, Kent Portney observes: "if the expectation is that cities investing in sustainability do so at the risk of sacrificing economic growth, this does not seem to be true" (Portney 2013, 146). In a simple bivariate analysis of the correlation between a city's ranking in his *Index of Taking Sustainability Seriously* and changes in per capita income from 1990 to 2009, he found that those with the most income growth also had the best sustainability programs, and "other cities that have struggled economically are those that have made the weakest efforts on sustainability—Wichita, Santa Ana, and Detroit among them" (145). Whether affluence causes or results from sustainability is hard to say. Clearly, however, a sustainability commitment is not inconsistent with high incomes.

There is evidence that local ordinances restricting land uses do not impair and may facilitate growth. One study found: "communities that began growth management one or two decades ago have performed better in economic terms than other communities" (Nelson and Peterson 2000, 277). Local entities defined a vision and fulfilled it: a form of *guided growth* (Jeong and Feiock 2006).

Policy designs also influence ecology–economy interactions. A study of state ecological policy found when regulations are "unclear, complex, or subject to frequent and unpredictable changes or revision, it creates regulatory uncertainty" (Feiock and Stream 2001, 315). Poorly-designed rules increase costs and magnify economy–ecology trade-offs, a finding consistent with Porter and van der Linde's distinctions among *good* and *bad* regulation and my own case for a new environmental regulation (Fiorino 2006). The study concludes: "states with stringent regulation but stable and certain patterns and processes of regulation may have some hope of enjoying a growing economy as well as the social and environmental benefits resulting from regulation" (315).

That ecological and health protections undermine prosperity is the traditional case against government intervention. Imposing controls on a source of air toxins, blocking construction to protect an endangered species, banning oil drilling in a sensitive offshore area—all may impede growth in specific cases and the near term. Framing the decisions in a wider context presents a different picture. The costs would be near-term and narrow, and the benefits to society of protecting ecological protection large.

In sum, the economic case against well-designed ecological policies is overblown. Ecological policy has not harmed the economy noticeably; nor has it caused wide-scale job loss, forced firms to locate overseas, or made them close in large numbers due to foreign competition. Any employment effects that have occurred are insignificant in an $18 trillion economy with some 150 million jobs. Losses occur in some economic sectors but are offset by gains in others.

Of course, political debates are rarely engaged on the basis of overall societal interests, especially in a pluralist, fragmented system like the United States. This is what distinguishes the *economic* from the *political economy* aspects of green growth, a subject taken up in Chapters 4 and 7. For many, however, claiming that ecological protection is consistent with growth ignores the source of the problem. From this point of view, the problem *is* growth. The shock effect of the growth projections for later in this century, in which the 2050 GDP of China (in 2006 US dollars) will exceed $60 trillion, followed by the United States and India (each over $40 trillion), Brazil and Mexico ($8–10 trillion, and so on is huge (PWC 2015, 3).[1] That the global middle class may triple by 2030 is good news, but it could break the bank of global ecological limits. With these numbers, the goal may be less about maintaining than *stopping* or *reversing* growth.

## THE MIXED EFFECTS OF ECONOMIC GROWTH

The near-universal preoccupation with economic growth raises many questions: Are the effects of growth always positive? Is more growth the answer to a better life? Does growth beyond a point harm more than enhance human well-being? Despite wide acceptance of the goal of maximizing wealth and incomes, we have evidence documenting a darker side of growth.

There are social and ecological critiques of growth. Although I focus on the latter, the former also is relevant. The social critique starts in the early 20th century in Thorstein Veblen's notion of conspicuous consumption: "ostentatiously displaying wealth while ignoring the rest of the population" (Vergragt 2017, 314). More recently, Fred Hirsch offered an insightful analysis in his 1976 volume, *The Social Limits to Growth*. Like all growth critics, he recognized that societies should meet basic material needs for food, shelter, education, health, and so on. Once such needs are met, however, the social limits to growth come into play, when satisfaction begins to depend more on one's income *as it compares to others* than on meeting material needs: "What individuals actually get, in important aspects of their consumption and job satisfaction, has been seen to depend on their relative income position rather than on their absolute income" (113). High incomes are seen as necessary to maintain one's status in society, which in turn leads to cycles of ever-rising aspirations. As Hirsch puts it: "If everyone stands on tiptoe, no one sees better" (5).

A leading happiness scholar is Carol Graham of the Brooking Institution, who surveyed the field in a 2011 book, *The Pursuit of Happiness: An Economy of Well-Being*. Consistent with work by Easterlin and others, she also finds that relative income may matter more than absolute income, once basic needs are met. On average, poor people around the world are less happy than the wealthy, but very poor people still may be happy, at least in short-term life satisfaction. Low-income people in low-income countries are happier than their low-income peers in wealthy ones. The relationship of income to well-being is more complicated, however, if we consider other measures. Life satisfaction and contentment level off at some income threshold, but income is more closely correlated with measures reflecting "the capacity to lead a fulfilling life" (2011, 31). On the growth issue, Graham reports that people in rapidly growing countries are less happy than those in more moderate-growth ones (controlling for income), suggesting that economic uncertainty is a factor to consider, even when the trend is toward growth and higher incomes.

Graham reports one finding relevant to growth–ecology relationships: People with prospects of upward mobility "are much more likely to invest in their own and their children's future"; those with lower future prospects are less willing to make such investments (2011, 43). In economic terms, people with lower prospects of upward mobility have higher discount rates, meaning they are less willing to invest in the future. This suggests that, in declining economies with perceptions of a lack of future prospects, it may be harder to sustain political support for action on climate change and other, future-oriented public goods (also see Boston 2017 on this).

This research matters for both the ecological and social critiques. Growth is not always a reliable indicator of well-being, at least past some income level. There is empirical support for arguing that relative incomes matter, and that continued growth creates a perceived need for ever-higher incomes as people seek satisfaction in status composition and positional goods. Many forms of consumption—larger houses, luxury cars, elite schools, the latest phone—show that one has reached a station in life, a sign of status and having arrived. As Jackson puts it: "Material things offer the ability to facilitate our participation in the life of society" (2011, 98).

This all matters in thinking about how to "live a good life on a finite earth." Like the overall economy–ecology relationship, connections between growth and happiness are complex. Some measures (near-term satisfaction or happiness) *decouple* from income at some point, while others (self-fulfillment) may not until later, if at all. It does seem that affluence breeds a search for yet more affluence in the sense of "keeping up with the Joneses," as the vernacular puts it, and encouraging socially constructed and ecologically damaging growth and consumption (on the possible political consequences, see Edsall 2015). This reinforces the need to rethink the role of growth in well-being as a cultural matter; it also commends the use of measures like the Genuine Progress Indicator, an alternative to GDP discussed just below. It should encourage more thought on the social and ecological effects of inequality, as I do in Chapter 5, as well as consequences for the capacity to undertake collective action in pursuit of green growth.

The declining benefits of growth are documented at a country level in the *contracting threshold hypothesis*. This concept requires a discussion of the Gross Domestic Product (GDP) as an indicator of economic and social well-being and of its ecological economics alternative, the Genuine Progress Indicator (GPI). For our purposes, GDP is the sum of the value of goods and services produced in an economy in a year, adjusted for inflation (see Jackson 2011, 123–126). It was developed in the late 1930s under the guidance of economist Simon Kuznets to account for the economic production of a country in one standard measure. GDP was institutionalized after World War II as "the standard tool for sizing up a country's economy" (Dickinson 2011) and eventually much more. As one writer puts it, GDP is "the ultimate measure of a country's overall welfare, a window into the economy's soul, the statistic to end all statistics" (Dickinson 2011).

For its critics, GDP falls short as a measure of well-being (Nijaki 2012). For a start, it counts as additions to GDP activities that detract from long-term well-being, like destruction of a critical natural asset (e.g., a tropical forest). Although the income from the sale of timber is added to GDP, this is a lost asset. Expenditures on controlling pollution or cleaning up disasters like the 2010 Deepwater-Horizon oil spill count as positives. Nor does GDP account for the costs of inequality, crime, or other social ills. Much work, like caregiving for children and the elderly or unpaid household labor are omitted (Kubiszewski et al. 2013). Ecologically, failing to account for lost resources and depleted natural capital is a major deficiency of GDP to measure societal well-being (for other critiques, see Lawn and Clarke 2010, 2214–2215; Daly and McElwee 2014).

Ecological economists have developed an alternative yardstick that changes the focus from one of "maximizing production and consumption" to "improving genuine human well-being" (Kubiszewski et al. 2013, 67). Called the "Genuine Progress Indicator" (GPI), it aims to provide a fuller assessment of positives and negatives in national income accounts by including such factors as ecological and health protection, full employment, economic inequality, product durability and reliability, and resource efficiency as positives. Comparisons of GDP and GPI demonstrate that they move roughly in parallel to a moderate level of per capita income and then begin to diverge—at about $30,000–$50,000 in wealthy countries (Graham 2011, 17). This divergence or decoupling of the two indicators occurs, however, at lower income levels in developing countries—at which point the GPI starts to decline while the overall GDP continues to increase.

Why the divergence in the GDP–GPI relationship between the wealthy and developing countries? This is where the contracting threshold comes into play: it is *the point where the costs of further growth begin to exceed the benefits* (as measured by GPI); to be more precise, it is where the marginal costs of growth begin to exceed the benefits. One study comparing GDP and GPI at a country level finds that rich countries (those that developed early, like the OECD club) crossed the threshold at higher income levels than poorer ones growing later (Lawn and Clarke 2010). As a result, "the marginal costs of an increment of GDP growth in a full world are likely to be substantially higher than in an empty world" (Lawn and Clarke 2010, 2218). While countries like Australia, Japan, and New Zealand continued to enjoy quality of life benefits (as measured by the GPI) up to per capita incomes in the $15,000–$28,000 range (in 2004 dollars), ones like China, Vietnam, and Thailand crossed the threshold at much lower incomes. This is due to pollution and ecological degradation (e.g., climate change) and because rich countries export polluting sectors to developing ones. In response, Lawn and Clarke want to improve eco-efficiency, invest in natural capital, preserve critical ecosystems, and use systems of tradeable permits. They argue that rich nations should "halt the increase in their own GDP and immediately begin the transition to a steady-state economy" (2222) as a matter of global equity and fairness.

## Is No-Growth or De-Growth the Answer?

Stopping or reversing growth is one possible response to a collision of economic growth with ecological limits. If ecology cannot adjust to the economy, as Douglas Booth (2004) puts it, then maybe we adjust the economy to ecology, by keeping GDP and incomes within local, regional, and global ecological limits. In effect, we scale the size of the economy to the planet.

Herman Daly, a founder of ecological economics, is a leading exponent of a *steady-state economy*. I should point out that Daly would not accept the green growth case today, viewing growth by definition as unsustainable (1998). Still, consistent with the green growth concept, he argued the economy should be seen as existing within the ecological system, which means it has to be adjusted to finite ecological limits. Writing in 1991, he stated that a "U.S.-style high-mass consumption, growth-dominated economy for a world of 4 billion people is impossible" (1991, 6).[2] A steady-state economy is one "with constant stocks of people and artifacts, maintained at some desired, sufficient levels by low rates of maintenance 'throughput', that is, by the lowest feasible flows of matter and energy from the first stage of production . . . to the last stage of consumption" (1991, 17). Although economies might grow and still maintain a steady state with dramatic eco-efficiency gains (that is, relative decoupling), say with gains from technology innovation, Daly doubts that alone can work. Sustainable growth "when applied to the economy is a bad oxymoron—self-contradictory as prose, and unevocative as poetry" (1998, 285).

The pace of economic growth and its ecological impacts, as well as the social critique of growth, have inspired proposals for outright *de-growth*, "an equitable downscaling of production and consumption that increases well-being and enhances ecological conditions" (Alexander 2012, 351). The premise of this concept is that "growth in the highly developed nations has become socially counter-productive, economically unsustainable, and uneconomic" (Alexander 2012, 349). In rich countries, economic growth has not delivered full employment, eliminated poverty, nor protected the environment (Victor 2008). The thesis of de-growth advocates is that both the happiness research and various ecological assessments establish that the costs of growth now exceed benefits, and it is time to rethink the near-obsession with economic growth.

Of course, developing and poor countries should not be expected to "de-grow." As a matter of equity, countries early in their growth process should be allowed to reach a moderate income level sufficient to meet basic needs and capabilities for a good life (perhaps in the range of $20,000–$30,000 or so in annual per capita in ). Reflecting what the contracting threshold hypothesis documents empirically, economic downscaling in rich countries and modest growth in poor ones, so the case goes, maximizes happiness and well-being but within ecological limits.

How does a de-growth agenda look? It would maintain employment while shrinking the economic pie—GDP and average incomes. Work sharing (two or more people sharing a job) and reduced work weeks are prominent. Other measures include scrapping GDP for GPI; adopting aggressively progressive tax rates, perhaps a 100% marginal rate above some level; restraining profligate consumption with tax policy and limits on advertising; promoting work cooperatives and a barter economy; confiscating inheritances so wealth does not transfer to a next generation; and instituting a guaranteed annual income (for an in-depth discussion, see Alexander 2009).

It is hard to determine how much of this agenda is driven by ideological antipathy toward modern consumer society and how much by concern over ecological limits. Some ideas do make sense ecologically: alternatives to GDP, more progressive taxation, and guaranteed incomes. All aim to reduce inequality, proposed in Chapter 5 as a condition for greener growth. All fall in the realm of the possible, under the right conditions and leadership. Still, some show an impressive disregard for the plight of low-income groups in rich countries. Many low-income earners in the United States, for example, struggle with two jobs just to stay above water. Without more basic reforms, work sharing and reduced work weeks are not fair or realistic options. Despite its potential social and ecological value, it is hard to see de-growth on its own enable us to stay within ecological limits without big changes in energy, transport, agricultural, manufacturing, and other systems.

Offering more nuanced ideas on managing or moderating growth are Tim Jackson and Peter Victor. Jackson does not take on GDP directly and call for quantitative de-growth; he prefers cultural, structural, and policy changes to delink prosperity from growth and take advanced economies off the treadmill. His solutions may be summed in three ideas: establish ecological limits; fix the economic model under which most countries operate; and change the social logic underpinning growth (2011, 173–200). The first focuses on policy, with many standard tools in the green growth repertoire, like emission caps and subsidy reform. Fixing the economic model means changing growth-oriented macro-economic policies, valuing natural capital, investing in ecology, and revising income accounts like GDP. He wants new investment for job creation. His more ambitious ideas aim to change the *social logic*: dismantle the culture of consumerism, reduce inequality, strengthen social capital, and reform work-time practices (173–184).

Another thoughtful analysis is Peter Victor's *Managing without Growth* (2008). He argues that larger economies and higher incomes have failed in three areas: maintaining full employment, eliminating poverty, and avoiding ecological degradation. Using Canada as a case, Victor examines how a slower-growth scenario might unfold and actually enhance quality of life. Still, Victor criticizes actual de-growth, finding risks in "deliberately and dramatically slowing the rate of growth" (178). De-growth or no-growth "can be disastrous if implemented carelessly" (183). As an alternative, he favors planned, well-managed, moderate economic growth founded on a more diverse set of social goals than those used in current policy.

This review of thinking on economic growth and its ecological impacts highlights several issues underlying the green growth concept. One view not considered in depth here is that of maximizing growth whatever the ecological costs, relying on human ingenuity, efficient markets, and technology to enable us to stay within or overcome planetary limits. John Dryzek labels this a *Promethean* worldview, in which "natural resources, ecosystems, and indeed nature itself, do not exist" (59). Embraced by many in US politics, it is inconsistent with a green growth path.

Also relevant is rethinking quality of life, built on recognition of the social and ecological costs of current growth models. With governments unlikely to lead such a rethinking, many scholars and activists see prospects in a "bottom-up cultural shift toward different lifestyles and conceptions of well-being" (Brown and Vergragt 2015, 2). Generational shifts are one source of hope for many: "the changing aspirations, lifestyle choices, and broader circumstances of the large millennial generation may make them the most likely place for a cultural shift" (2). Interest in urban collaborative living, the shared economy, peer-to-peer economy, or collaborative consumption is not at all incompatible with my conception of green growth. Yet, in my view, they will not be sufficient, and more basic political and policy shifts also will be necessary.

## Should We Just Be Neutral about Growth?

Why is growth so important? Why is it a nearly-universal goal of governments around the world, including (and especially, it seems) the United States? Are people really all that greedy?

For poor countries struggling for minimal well-being, the answers are obvious. For wealthy ones at high levels of prosperity, the answer is more complicated. That perceived well-being tends to level off at medium income levels, as revealed in the happiness research, has not influenced growth aspirations, public policy, or political debates. The idea that governments can save the environment by cutting back on socially driven consumption has little traction. Indeed, a US president deliberately working to shrink the economy and reduce incomes would probably be impeached.

Typical explanations for the emphasis on economic growth as a priority are that it

- Is necessary for creating jobs and keeping unemployment rates low
- Expands the economic pie as needed to maintain social harmony and political legitimacy
- Generates revenues needed to fund retirement and social safety net programs
- Provides resources for governments to provide desired services to their citizens
- Enhances national prestige, security, and defense capabilities
- Creates wealth that nations may translate into global influence, including military power
- Enables people to enjoy a higher standard of living and exert more control over their lives
- Allows people to be optimistic about their futures and that of their children

These are so compelling that it is hard to imagine an ecological strategy built explicitly on a no-growth or de-growth platform. This feeds into zero-sum arguments pitting one goal against the other. History shows that, when in conflict, ecological goals usually give way to economic ones.

My approach builds on work of Jeroen van den Bergh, a Dutch economist who thinks we should be "indifferent or neutral about economic growth" (2011, 882; also see 2010). He calls for a mindset based on *A-growth*: that we should be agnostic about aggregate growth (i.e., GDP). He distinguishes five types of de-growth; each may stand alone or be combined with the others:

1. *GDP De-Growth*: This is a prescription of growth critics; reduce economic scale (GDP and incomes) to lessen ecological and resource pressures. Eliminate growth as a cause of harm.
2. *Consumption De-Growth*: Through aggressive use of eco-taxes, limits on advertising, and so on, reduce consumers' ability to satisfy desires for consumption. The idea is that excess consumption is driving ecological degradation and should be greatly reduced.
3. *Work-Time De-Growth*: Require shorter work weeks, more vacations and holidays, and earlier retirement. This reduces incomes and the ability to consume goods and services.
4. *Radical De-Growth*: This calls for a complete escape from capitalist economies and their emphasis on continual expansion, investment, and ecologically damaging consumption.
5. *Physical De-Growth*: Reduce the size/scale of ecologically damaging components of the economy in a strategy of selective de-growth, targeting sectors imposing the most stress.

Each has limitations as an ecological strategy. Simply scaling back GDP has effects in the short term, but it is a blunt instrument that may not yield ecological benefit. It will certainly fail politically. Giving up the positive effects of growth (like having investment capital) is risky economically—a de-growth strategy could easily spin out of control. De-growth focused broadly on consumption also is a blunt instrument that is difficult to apply and has uncertain ecological benefits. Would it rely on rationing? Limits on advertising are hard to implement and raise free speech issues in the United States. Still, targeting specific forms of harmful consumption through social pricing (e.g., a carbon tax or better pricing of water) may be an element in a selective de-growth strategy. Work-time de-growth may improve the quality of life and warrants discussion, but will affect little ecologically; it also raises issues of income sufficiency, affordability, and fairness.

That capitalism is the root source of ecological problems—by generating constant growth with little regard for ecosystems—is a staple of critical thinking (an example is O'Connor 1994). If we dispense with the excesses and failures of capitalism, as the argument goes, we can give ecological and social problems the needed priority. Is this at all realistic? What is the alternative? Have centrally planned economies demonstrated ecological sensitivity? Many writers blame our ecological dilemma on capitalism generically; a closer look reveals that they often are blaming specific *forms* of capitalism. In her book on climate change, for example, Naomi Klein (2014) poses the issue in her subtitle as *capitalism versus the climate*. But her concern actually is with the problems of *neoliberal capitalism*, which is a more specific and a far more valid critique.

My conception of green growth fits best with a strategy of physical, selective de-growth. To a degree, that is what a conventional pollution control strategy is built upon: identify harmful impacts of growth, like air or water pollution or species loss, and mitigate them. Yet a green growth strategy differs from a conventional one. It focuses less on the actual, visible by-products of growth and more on the underlying activities causing them. In this sense, it reflects a strategy of *pollution prevention*, which has been difficult to implement with current laws and policies (Geiser 2004). In pollution prevention, for example, the focus shifts from controlling air pollution at point of release to designing energy and transportation systems that are not polluting. More importantly, green growth seeks positive linkages of economic and ecological goals. That such linkages exist and are achievable, given a right mix of investments, technologies, policies, and behavior, is the core premise of green growth. These are examined further in Chapter 6.

As discussed in Chapter 6, a targeting of ecologically damaging economic sectors (coal-fired power plants, chemicals) figures prominently in the green growth policy agenda. A 2011 analysis comparing damages to economic value added from several industry sectors identified the major sources of air pollution as utilities (from coal plants), agriculture (crop and livestock production), and transportation (especially truck transport). Physical de-growth or changes in factors that are driving pollution impacts from these sectors would significantly lower US air emissions (Muller, Mendelsohn, and Nordhaus 2011). The Sierra Club recognized this in its *Beyond Coal* campaign, which claims to have caused the shutdown of 200 coal-fired power plants as of June 2016 (http://content.sierraclub.org/coal/).

An ecological strategy built explicitly on de-growth, no-growth, or slow growth is not only politically unrealistic, it could undermine prospects for a green transition. First, as a matter of politics, an anti-growth focus reinforces old assumptions about zero-sum trade-offs that empower opponents of ecological policy. It is no accident that critics of climate action build their case on claims of lost jobs, slow growth, and less competitiveness. Second, as Victor (2008) suggests, there are risks to "deliberately and dramatically" slowing growth rates. Signs of such deliberate de-growth could initiate a vicious cycle of crashing markets, deleveraging, and deflation, making "degrowth as an explicit strategy option . . . economically unsustainable and infeasible" (Tokic 2012, 49; see Kallis 2011 for a counterpoint). And, it is important to remember, those most at risk in global de-growth are people the anti-growth critics most want to protect: the low-income and vulnerable.

There are other reasons to be skeptical of a deliberate anti-growth agenda. One is political legitimacy. Economic well-being is critical for stability and legitimacy. An anti-growth platform, particularly if it spins out of control, may undermine that stability. As the next chapter discusses, political stability is a prerequisite for effective ecological governance. Other issues to consider include the effects of a shrinking economy on social trust, and thus the means to act collectively for addressing problems; the reduced capacities for investing in technologies; and the pattern in which support for ecology declines in times of economic uncertainty (Daniels et al. 2013, 470). On the last point, opinion surveys in Europe after the financial crisis found that more unemployment reduced perceptions of climate threats, while a growing GDP increased them. Indeed, a 5%–9% rise in unemployment lowered perceived climate threats by 10% in surveys (Chong 2015, 127).

So what is being neutral about growth? It means not focusing on growth as the primary goal. It means an anti-growth or even a trade-offs message is as unwise economically and politically as one of growth-above-all. It encourages use of alternatives to GDP, like the GPI, that measure quality of life more broadly, including ecological protection. Being neutral about growth allows us to aim for economic and ecological strategies that can expand the availability of durable, family-supporting, socially beneficial employment, not just aggregate growth. Most important, being neutral about growth helps neutralize the zero-sum arguments that political opponents have used to block action on global climate change and other ecological policies.

## THE ECONOMY–ECOLOGY RELATIONSHIP: WHAT DOES IT MEAN FOR GREEN GROWTH?

This chapter offers lessons for green growth. Yes, growth drives ecological pressure and brings us closer to local, regional, and global limits. Yet this is a more complex relationship than is often assumed. One lesson is that ecological policies have not had the adverse economic effects claimed by critics. The evidence shows that the standard complaints of stunted growth, lost jobs, and diminished competitiveness are overblown. This is not to say there have not been adverse effects in particular sectors or that development has not been blocked due to ecological policies. Overall, however, the economic effects have been modest, and in some cases positive.

Second, although growth over time adds to ecological stress, it has positive effects. An obvious one: rising incomes improve the status of women, and population growth rates fall. Another is that economies become more eco-efficient and reduce pollution and resource use per unit of economic activity (although less so for ecosystem degradation). Economic growth also creates conditions under which governments respond to pollution; this is not a magical outcome of growth but a matter of demand for ecological and health protection and having technological, financial, and administrative capacities for managing, if not necessarily resolving, problems. This research on the growth–ecology relationship should be interpreted carefully: it applies to some but not all problems; it may take different forms (for the EKC, maybe an S-curve rather than an inverted U, for example); and it has been observed largely in the advanced economies.

Third, deliberate slow-growth, no-growth, or de-growth is unlikely to succeed—smaller brown sectors do not on their own deliver a better environment—and could very well undermine greening. Although the Great Recession delivered short-term ecological benefits, including a fall in US greenhouse gas emissions, it reduced political support for climate action by fueling public concern on the economy and reinforcing the appeal of the zero-sum arguments. Being neutral about growth—perhaps Victor's *managed growth* or Jackson's *prosperity without growth*—is a more realistic platform. Economies will grow. They need to grow in ecologically sound ways.

Accepting the inevitability of growth does not mean that economic strategies do not play a role in green growth; indeed, integrating economic with ecological policies is a hallmark. Some macro-economic and social policies make sense: aiming for a more labor-intensive economy; raising marginal tax rates for high-earners; taxing damaging consumption, such as in a carbon tax; and reducing income inequality to spread the benefits of perhaps modest growth rates more equitably and, as Chapter 5 argues, enhance the value given to public goods within a society.

Finally, the happiness research is relevant. It suggests, at a minimum, that well-being does not always rise in lockstep with growth and incomes. A sense of community, strong family and social relationships, good health, control over one's life, *opportunities for flourishing*—all of these depend partly on growth and incomes; but they also reflect other factors that should be reflected better in measures of well-being. GDP is something, but it is not everything.

## NEXT: THE ROLE OF GOVERNANCE

A weakness in green growth writing is neglect of governance and politics. The reports from Chapter 2 are meticulous in describing the need for new growth models; the conflicts and synergies among economic and ecological factors; the policies and investments needed for a green economic transition; and for new, integrated ways of measuring progress. Yet they do not shed much light on the qualities of governance that should be associated with green growth or the political conditions under which a durable transition to a green growth path may occur. They usually end up stating something like "it all depends on the politics" and leave it at that.

In the end, however, politics is the make or break. If political coalitions cannot be built to support policies on issues like climate change, water security, ecosystem protection, and so on, all the strategies and analyses in the world will not matter. If political leaders cannot navigate the institutional and cultural features of governance systems, green growth is an empty vision. Why do some countries do better ecologically than others? What is good ecological governance? Under what conditions do political systems give priority to ecological problems and integrate them with economic and social issues? The next chapter examines these issues.

# Ecological Governance

Many proposals on green growth and ecological policy run aground on the shoals of governance and politics. Evidence of human activity stretching or exceeding ecological and resource limits is all around us. Many of the policy solutions make irrefutable sense as a matter of overall well-being. Is it really wise to continue pumping greenhouse gases into the atmosphere and set off eventually catastrophic changes in the global climate system? Does California want to run out of water because it cannot allocate it effectively or use it efficiently? Is irreversible loss of the ecological benefits of the Chesapeake Bay or the Great Lakes something we even want to contemplate? Is a long-term saturation of ecosystems by persistent organic toxics a good thing?

After making the case for responding to these issues, green growth assessments typically end with frustrating conclusions along lines of "however, the political barriers are formidable." The problems are real; despite the scientific uncertainty about particulars, the worlds of economic growth and ecological integrity are on a collision course. Policy solutions like a carbon tax, measures to protect critical ecosystems, more sensible and sustainable water allocations, and low-input agriculture are applied unevenly, if at all. In the end, a messy thing called *politics*, and its handmaiden *governance*, get in the way of actions that enhance collective well-being.

Given that most experts working on issues like green growth are trained in economics, ecology, health, law, or engineering, this frustration with politics and governance is unsurprising. It is, however, one of the missing pieces of work on green growth and sustainable development.

The heart of the political problem is that *the short term tends to crowd out considerations of the long term, and narrow interests often take precedence over collective ones.* Politics is in part about convincing people to do what is good for them. The premise of this book is that if growth is going to occur, it should be in much greener ways than it has in the past. Half the problem is that people tend to attach more value to near-term than long-term gains and losses. In economics jargon, we have *high discount rates,* meaning that, most of the time, we are likely to put more stock in what happens sooner rather than later. The other half of the problem is that some in society gain from any set of policy changes, while others lose. Change on nearly any issue creates winners and losers. This is why growth is a sought-after goal; aggregate growth generally is perceived as creating lots of winners and few losers. Growth critics disagree, for many reasons. Still, as the consensus on "growth is always good" testifies, they are a minority.

Respecting ecological limits and promoting policies, institutions, and relationships that make it possible to remain within them—*living a good life on a finite earth*—is difficult given these political problems of short-termism and narrow interests. Without a doubt, green growth creates losers, and they usually have a great deal of power. And they will act to protect their interests. It is rational for the coal industry to fight renewable energy, for farm interests to resist subsidy reform, and for poultry farmers on Maryland's Eastern Shore to oppose nutrient controls.

That these interests are incompatible with the long-term well-being of society at large is at the heart of the problem green growth aims to address. In practice, only if a green growth policy agenda is adopted and carried out—a topic of Chapter 6—will the concept matter.

This chapter considers the role of governance in a green economic transition. It begins with a definition of the term, which includes but is much broader than politics. Governance is an important but underrated concept in ecological policy. The traditional three-legged stool of sustainability encompasses ecology, economy, and society, but does not include governance, which is lumped vaguely under the social dimension. Partly because of this, I think governance is a fourth sustainability system that enables progress on the other three (Fiorino 2010).

After considering the governance concept, the chapter presents a brief overview of the evolution of ecological governance over the last half century. In remarkably rapid fashion, health and ecological problems, captured under the concept of environmental policy, emerged as issues in nearly all industrial countries. The United States was seen as a "pioneer" in the early days of this evolution, but is viewed in a less favorable light more recently (Jänicke 2005). The chapter then turns to research that aims to explain why some countries do better on ecological policy and outcomes than others. The last chapter looked at economic factors; this one turns to governance and political factors. I consider this research for what it tells us about how governance for green growth should look, and as a basis later for evaluating green growth prospects in the United States.

## SOME BASICS OF ECOLOGICAL GOVERNANCE

Governance is defined here as "a process of—more or less institutionalized—interaction between public and/or private entities ultimately aiming at the realization of collective goals" (Lange et al. 2013, 406). A few aspects of the definition are worth noting. First, governance exists only when it has purpose, that of the "realization of collective goals." Second, governance consists of more than just government. To be sure, institutions and processes of government are central to the concept of governance, but the interactions between public and private institutions and groups are relevant as well. Of course, much of what we call governance occurs outside of government entirely, so we speak of corporate governance, university governance, and so on. The focus of this chapter is on governance processes and policies where government is involved, while also including the broader issues of the "interaction between public and private entities."

A third aspect of the definition is of a "process" that is "more or less institutionalized." A process suggests something that is recurring, happens in stages, and reveals patterns over time. Institutions play a critical role in governance. Varieties among processes and institutions in different countries would be expected to influence both policies and outcomes. The immediate concern, of course, is with ecological governance—processes and institutions for realizing collective outcomes with respect to the relationships between humans and nature, and in the interdependencies among them. Ecology is a recent addition to the functions governments are expected to perform. Whether they currently are at the *core* of the expected state functions, on a level with established concerns like physical security or economic vitality, is a matter of debate.

Ecological governance tends to involve a larger number of scientific and technical issues and more uncertainty than do other policy domains, such as social welfare and economic policy. Ecological governance also involves a high degree of political conflict, in part due to scientific uncertainty but even more because it historically has forced hard choices between economic and ecological goals. Ecological governance takes many forms in modern society, from local management of common pool resources like wetlands and wilderness areas, to state or federal regulation of air and water quality, to global actions to protect the oceans or stratospheric ozone layer. In ecosystem governance, for example, there have been trends toward more adaptive management and away from top-down policy prescription (Layzer and Schulman 2017). In cities, sustainability advocates debate ways of collaborating with and empowering citizens, or even whether citizen engagement is necessary for a sustainability transition (Fiorino 2014b).

Because my concern in this book is with green growth nationally, in particular the United States, my focus in this chapter is national ecological governance.

What role do ecological issues play in the activities of modern states? How has this evolved in recent decades as ecological issues emerged on national policy agendas? How do patterns of governance at national and, to a degree, subnational levels affect the ability to adopt ecological policy and achieve results? Most central, what can research tell us about the prospects for green growth? My emphasis on the nation-state reflects its central and defining role in ecological policy (Duit, Feindt, and Meadowcroft 2016).

Part of this chapter's purpose is to examine ecological governance and what it means for green growth. Another is to set the stage for analyzing US capacities in Chapters 7 and 8. Before moving to explanations for ecological results, some historical and political analysis is in order.

One point to emphasize: the research examined in this chapter focuses on factors that affect capacities, policies, and outcomes in the environmental or, as I prefer, ecological domain. They do not address the more complicated issue of capacities for and success at green growth. Some studies look at policy capacities: "the abilities of a society to identify environmental problems and solve them" (Weidner 2002, 1342; see also Jänicke 1996 and Jänicke and Weidner 1997). Others examine relative degrees of policy success, either as measured by commitments and policies or actual ecological and health outcomes. Some specify particular indicators (e.g., emissions of air particulates, lost forest area, nutrients in water) as the dependent variable; others examine composite measures of sustainability. My goal is to use this research as evidence for identifying the governance qualities and capacities that are best suited to green growth.

Nearly all societies stress the growth side of the equation. I want to understand why some countries do well ecologically—despite the growth emphasis—and then propose qualities that make them well-suited to finding and carrying out positive-sum ecology–economy relationships. First is a discussion of the evolution of ecological governance and how economic and governance capacities and performance are related.

## The Evolution of Ecological Governance

In an essay on *Greening the State*, James Meadowcroft observes that "The constitution of the environmental domain as a distinct sphere of government activity is a comparatively recent phenomenon" (2012, 63). To be sure, conservation and wilderness protection was the subject of government activity in many countries, including the United States, in the late 1800s and early 1900s. Similarly, urban public health issues of sanitation, contaminated drinking water, and coal-related air pollution drew attention early in the last century (Andrews 2006). It was only in the second half of the 20th century that air and water pollution, waste, chemicals, and ecosystem damages came anything close to center stage in industrial nations like the United States, United Kingdom, Japan, Sweden, and Germany (Jänicke and Weidner 1997; Schreurs 2002).

The rise of environmental concern and government responses in the late 1960s and early 1970s were little short of remarkable. In a noted cover story in 1970, *Time* magazine described the newfound concern for the environment as a "national obsession." In the environmental decade of the 1970s, the United States enacted a series of major environmental laws, beginning with the National Environmental Policy Act of 1969 and Clean Air Act of 1970, and continuing with laws regarding water pollution, drinking water quality, endangered species, forest management, solid and hazardous wastes, and waste cleanup. President Richard Nixon created the Environmental Protection Agency in 1970 to administer the law and protect public health and the environment.

The emergence of environmental policy as a distinct sphere of governmental action and authority occurred in parallel across nearly all the industrial democracies. Among countries in the Organization for Economic Cooperation Development, Meadowcroft notes, an average of 0.8 pieces of major legislation were adopted between 1956–60; 2.0 between 1961–65; 3.6 between 1965–70; and 6.2 from 1971–75 (2012, 64). Between 1967 and 1976, two dozen countries created a national environmental agency or ministry, and most enacted a national framework law by the early 1980s (Jänicke and Weidner 1997, 316). By now, clearly, "states have become irreducibly enmeshed in the management of environmental problems and their politics is continuously marked by environmental controversy" (Meadowcroft 2012, 67). The rise of global climate change as an all-encompassing ecological, economic, and social issue has reinforced this engagement while also increasing the level of political controversy.

Although environmental governance evolved in different ways in various countries, there are similarities. Most experts view its evolution as consisting of two phases (Weidner 2002). The first was a period of managing pollution via regulatory strategies, with an emphasis on technical expertise, legal instruments, bureaucratic organization, and a reactive approach to problem solving. Problems were defined based on their visible manifestations or specific evidence, and solutions flowed from that conception (Fiorino 2001). The United States and Sweden, later joined by countries like Japan, Germany, and Great Britain, were recognized as the "pioneers" in this first wave of governance. A second wave may be linked to such events as the World Commission on Environment and Development (WCED), which made the concept of sustainable development part of the common currency, and the 1992 Earth Summit in Rio de Janeiro. It was influenced as well by the growing interest, at least in Europe, in ecological modernization theory discussed in Chapter 2. The themes of this second wave were policy integration, global issues, long-term focus, and a shift toward more collaborative regulation (Fiorino 2001; Chertow and Esty 1997).

The United States has not been viewed as a leader in this second wave of ecological governance. Second wave pioneers typically include Sweden, the Netherlands, Denmark, Japan, the United Kingdom, Germany, and later the European Union (EU), which strengthened and harmonized policy among its members. The emphasis on policy integration in this second wave (Jordan and Lenschow 2008) mirrored the themes of sustainability in integrating not only in the ecological domain (i.e., air, water, chemicals, habitat, and resources) but also economics, energy, transport, agriculture, housing, and so on. This second wave is more suited to the demands of green growth.

Where do ecological issues fit within the functions of the modern state? Meadowcroft identifies three traditional, core activities of modern states: to maintain internal order and protect against external threats; to pursue national economic prosperity; and to organize and deliver welfare services. To these activities of the *security state*, the *prosperity state*, and the *welfare state* he adds, as a consequence of developments from the 1960s onward, the *ecological* or *eco-state*. This fourth core activity occurs in the context of interactions with the other three. Indeed, the interactions among security, prosperity, welfare, and ecological goals have grown stronger in recent decades. Aside from concepts like green growth and economy that link economic and ecological concerns, we now speak of environmental security and environmental justice to recognize other interactions. At the same time, "the environment remains the most vulnerable of these core domains of state activity because it is the newest and least institutionally embedded" (Meadowcroft 2012, 76). Most observers of US politics would accept the validity of this point.

For a transition to green growth to occur, ecological issues and goals have to become part of the core business of the state. This involves an "environmental transformation of the state" similar to what happened in the last century in the welfare state (Meadowcroft 2005; Dryzek et al. 2002, 659). This transformation resulted from a working class moving against "unrestrained capitalism" (659). Similarly, environmentalism constitutes a movement against the excesses of unrestrained growth based on industrialization, consumption, and resource exploitation. In most countries, ecological issues remain in a tenuous second tier behind security and economic concerns. Especially in the United States, ecological policy is at the periphery, not the core. Ecology competes with economy but never achieves parity. In the United States, "policy discourse features an old-fashioned stand-off between economy and environment" (Dryzek et al. 2002, 667).

The trend toward incorporating ecology into the business of the state continues, and it is expanding beyond just the OECD countries. Sommerer and Lim define an environmental state as one "where government actively addresses negative environmental externalities of economic activities" (2016, 92). After observing that the Environmental Kuznets Curve "has been tested and confirmed in a number of empirical studies" (93), they turn to the question of whether emerging economies are moving in the same direction as the industrial democracies in adopting ecological policies. Their study covered 25 issues in 37 countries from 1970–2010. They examined the transitional economies of Eastern Europe and growth economies like Brazil, Russia, India, China, and South Africa (the BRICS), as well as the OECD subset (including less-studied countries like Israel). They assessed not actual performance but the adoption of policies for dealing with the 25 issues and the time of adoption. Newer growth economies were indeed adding environmental policies to their repertoires, and time lags between adoption in OECD and the other countries were falling. Policies among countries were converging, partly due to the spread of experiences from the established democracies like those in the European Union to the emerging economies.

Another study of the "environmental transformation of the state" looks at the evolution of governance in the United States, Norway, Germany, and the United Kingdom (Dryzek et al. 2002). Although slightly dated, it suggests factors that help in explaining US capacities in Chapter 7. All of these countries meet the definition of an environmental state, defined as one "that possesses a significant set of institutions and practices dedicated to the management of the environment and societal–environmental interactions" (Duit et al. 2016, 5). Where they differ is in the degree to which ecological issues are *incorporated into the core business of the state*. Germany is a leader in this respect, having linked ecological issues to core state politics and governance under the conceptual framework of ecological modernization. Norway and to an extent the United Kingdom follow while, in the United States, "environment and the economy remain cast in zero-sum conflict" (666).

Although the United States was viewed as a leader in ecological and health protection in the 1970s, those days are "distant memories" (679). In the United States, ecological issues have had some success and institutional embodiment, but at the periphery, not at the core of the functions of the state. Of the four countries analyzed, the United States has achieved the least in terms of integrating ecological issues.

So there is such a thing as ecological governance, as countries at various stages of economic development and with different types of regimes address problems arising from growth, industrialization, urbanization, and technology. It emerged first in the OECD-style countries; this gave it a particular cast, with "their privately-owned and market-mediated economics and representative political systems" (Duit, Feindt, and Meadowcroft 2016). Most of the research has been done in these countries, with recently more in others (e.g., Hochstetler 2012; Death 2016).

## The Political Economy of Ecological Governance

Central to assessing capacities for ecological governance are the interrelation-ships among politics and economics. The previous chapter examined the link-ages of economic growth and incomes to ecological protection. Although the overall weight of growth adds to the pressures on ecosystems and resources, it does have offsetting effects. One of these, key to explaining the relationships among growth, incomes, and ecological protection, is governance. Growth creates demand for ecological policies, as the EKC suggests, and improves the quality of governance.

The quality of ecological governance is closely linked to economic devel-opment, at least to a point. Much of the early research on the effects of rising incomes on policy capacities was conducted by a World Bank team. They found a connection of growth to ecological quality, and they attributed it to improved governance that comes with economic growth more than any direct effect of growth. They "highlight the importance of institutional development, with significant roles for degree of private property protection, effectiveness of the legal/judicial system and efficiency of public administration" (Dasgupta et al. 2001, 173). Later research reaffirms that "governance has strong, independent effects on environmental policy" (Dasgupta et al. 2006, 1598). This is echoed in other studies (Esty and Porter 2005; Weidner 2002; Povitkina 2015).

The benefits of governance are apparent on many issues. A study of defor-estation rates in Latin America, Africa, and Asia associated higher incomes with reduced rates of forest loss and attributes this largely to better governance (Bhattari and Hammig 2001). This study also concluded that people in high-income countries value public goods (biodiversity and conservation) more than those in low income ones, and structural change in advanced economies may reduce ecological pressures, but governance itself is critical in influencing ecological performance. Some quotes are instructive:

Improvements in political institutions and governance significantly reduce deforestation (995).

The relationship between income growth and environmental quality is not straightforward, but involves a complex feedback mechanism passing through various institutional channels affecting both market and political forces (997).

[I]mprovements in institutions that empower citizens through enhance-
ment of democracy, strengthening of individual freedoms and civil liberties,
and establishing rule of law will ultimately reduce pressure on environmental resources and lead to better conservation of forest land (1003).

[U]nderlying institutional forces are relatively more important for
explaining the tropical deforestation process than other frequently cited
factors like population and macroeconomic conditions (1006).

In sum, developing countries may flatten the EKC by improving sociopolitical
institutions (Munasinghe 1999); they need not necessarily go through a stage of
highly brown growth.

Another study of 142 countries examined the effects of growth on air quality,
water quality, terrestrial habitat protection, and biodiversity. The definition of
governance quality was based on indicators from the World Bank: (1) political
stability; (2) governmental effectiveness; (3) regulatory quality; (4) rule of law;
(5) voice and accountability; and (6) control of corruption.

In this study, Xiaomei Tan examined the effects of both GDP and governance quality and reached different conclusions for air quality, water quality,
habitat, and biodiversity. For air, she found incomes and governance both were
associated with positive outcomes. Quality governance related to rule of law,
voice and accountability, and regulatory quality was linked to better water quality. For terrestrial habitat, on the other hand, both GDP growth and governance
had negative effects: for such habitat "growth literally means diminishing of
wildernesses" (Tan 2006, 326). Neither growth nor governance mattered for
biodiversity. She concludes that growth leads to better governance, and "governance is the key to accelerate GDP's positive impact" (330).

Another illustrative study on incomes and governance examines air quality, the subject of much EKC research. This study is distinctive in including
both OECD (31 countries) and sub-Saharan African countries (47 of them). To
give an idea of the contrasts, average annual income in OECD countries was
then at about $30,000 a year and that for the African countries some $1,400.
The authors found that emissions decline with growth, as predicted, but that
the "turning points" (the income levels at which emissions started to fall) varied by pollutant and country groupings. The study analyzed trends in two air
pollutants—PM10 (particulates with a diameter of 10 micrometers or smaller)
and carbon dioxide. The first is a serious threat to human health and a priority
around the world, the second the major cause of climate change. Early studies found that turning points for near-term, salient pollutants like particulates
came at lower income levels than for carbon dioxide. It was the same here: the
turning point for particulates was one-tenth of that for $CO_2$ for both sets of
countries. The turning points in Africa were lower for both; it seems that policy

actions and changes in economic structure were occurring earlier in the growth process. They conclude that the pollution cuts (consistent with the effects of the EKC) are "due to local and national institutional reforms, such as environmental legislation and market-based incentives to reduce environmental degradation" (Sulemana, James, and Rikoon 2015, 6).

A review of this research demonstrates that the ecology–economy relationships discussed in Chapter 3 are greatly influenced by an intervening variable— the quality of governance. Some level of economic growth influences ecological governance capacity—identifying and managing health, resource, and ecological challenges. This may even out at some income level, so it does not mean that more growth continues to deliver better governance. But some growth matters for stable governance, administrative quality, and low corruption (Pellegrini and Gerlagh 2006; Lisciandra and Migliardo 2016; Povitkina 2015). It also matters for democracy, examined next.

## IS DEMOCRACY A DISADVANTAGE FOR ECOLOGICAL PROTECTION?

The last chapter looked at calls by many advocates for drastic, even radical changes in the economic systems of most countries, and certainly the United States. Growth poses major, often irreversible pressures on local, regional, and global ecosystems. In particular, climate change presents an existential threat to many people, especially in poor, vulnerable areas, but eventually to all of us. If capitalist systems cannot stop the progression of exponential growth then it maybe is time to move on to alternatives. Similar arguments come up in governance. If democracies are ineffective in forcing the action for mitigating climate change, maybe something new is needed. These concerns about democracy and climate are reviving governance debates from the 1970s.

### Critiques of Democracy

A theme in ecological writing of the 1960s and 1970s was that democracy could not protect the environment. One advocate of this view was political scientist William Ophuls, who called in the 1970s for "political institutions that preserve the ecological common good from destruction by unrestrained human acts" (1977, 151). Moving to a steady-state economy that respected ecological limits demanded centralized, expert-based governance that is "more authoritarian and less democratic" and "much more oligarchic" (162). "Certainly," he concluded, "democracy as we know it cannot possibly survive" (152).

In a 1974 book, *An Inquiry into the Human Prospect*, historian Robert Heilbroner wrote that human greed in the face of ecological degradation required monastic government combining "religious orientation with a military discipline" (1974). In 2010, scientist and environmentalist James Lovelock (inventor of the Gaia Hypothesis) said: "Even the best democracies agree that when a major war approaches, democracy must be put on hold for the time being. I have a feeling that climate change may be an issue as severe as a war. It may be necessary to put democracy on hold for a while" (Hickman 2010). Al Gore used the war analogy in *Earth in the Balance* (1993) but foresaw a mobilization of democracy, not a transition to autocracy.

That these claims gain attention, even if mostly in academic writing, deserves serious attention. Advocates of ecological autocracy compare our current climate failure to that of a nation—or more appropriately a world—at war, one engaged in an existential struggle. They may be right, but they should realize this will be a war without end; climate change will always be with us. Do we really want to chuck the benefits of democracy—accountability, participation, political freedom and liberty, even the foundations of economic well-being (Przeworski 1995)—in favor of authoritarian states with a cadre of benevolent ecological experts at the top?

The practical issues overwhelm the normative ones. Just how would this transition to ecological autocracy occur? Would voters and their representatives just hand over authority? How would these new regimes establish political legitimacy? If there actually is a regime change of this magnitude, do we really expect ecosystem quality and biodiversity to top the agenda? Political stability is a precondition for good ecological governance. Why would states unwilling to restructure their energy systems turn their institutions, values, and futures over to autocrats?

An irony about this thinking is that it is just what the political right claims is behind climate activism—that it is a plot to suppress freedom, markets, and liberty. Columnist Charles Krauthammer of the *Washington Post*, a leading conservative writer, proclaimed in 2009 that "environmentalism is becoming the new socialism, i.e., the totemic ideal in the name of which government seizes the commanding heights of the economy and society." In a revealing book on the critics of the scientific grounding of issues like smoking, acid rain, stratospheric ozone depletion, and climate, Naomi Oreskes and Erik Conway (2010) stress the role played by experts from the Cold War scientific establishment who see environmentalism as a path to totalitarianism.

## Evidence on Democracy

A major problem with calls for a post-democratic ecological autocracy is that the evidence does not support them. Aside from all of the normative and practical issues, research suggests that democratic systems have been no less and probably more successful at ecological problem solving. It is worth considering this research and what it tells us about governance.

The asserted advantages of ecological autocracy are that leaders committed to ecological protection have the power and resources to make tough choices, without worrying about such institutional niceties as voting, citizen preferences, legislatures, interest groups, and so on. Those favoring more democratic approaches, in contrast, see advantages in the need to compete in elections, appeal to voters' preferences, and be politically accountable. Democracy also promotes flows of information, open speech and discussion, and respect for individual rights and liberties (for the theoretical case see Congleton 1992; Neumayer 2002; Jänicke 1996; Farzin and Bond 2005; Winslow 2005; Fredriksson and Wollscheid 2007; Duwel 2010). Democracies tend to engage more on global issues, a positive for ecological performance, and are governed better, given their economic success, administrative capacities, and lesser corruption (Esty and Porter 2005; Pellegrini and Gerlagh 2006; Przeworski et al. 1995). Autocratic systems are accountable more often to elites that are less affected by pollution than the public, tend to operate in shorter time frames, and are generally less accountable. This is the theoretical case. What does the evidence tell us?

Many studies of democracy and ecology find positives for air quality. One of the first found "liberal democracies are more willing to regulate environmental effluents than less liberal regimes" (Congleton 1992, 421). Building on EKC research, a frequently cited study (Barrett and Graddy 2000) found that low-freedom countries may reduce pollution as much or more by expanding political freedoms as by growing incomes. Studying 46 countries, Margrethe Winslow (2005, 781) determined that "the more democratic a country, the less air pollution." Another study of 107 cities in 42 countries provides additional support for the claims that "the degree of democracy has a positive effect on air quality" (Bernauer and Koubi 2009, 1356). They found this especially to be the case in presidential (e.g., the United States) more than in parliamentary democracies.

In a study of transitional economies in Eastern Europe and Latin America, Kathryn Hochstetler finds that "countries that have opted for democratic political systems generally have better environmental protections than do authoritarian regimes" (2012, 200). This is partly due to better governance and less corruption in democracies. To the governance explanation, however, she adds one that bears on the discussion of green growth prospects in Chapter 8: "democracies are more likely to learn from the policy successes and failures of other democracies" and to feel transnational pressure. She warns, however, that she analyzes policy, not outcomes. The quality of democracy appears to matter in influencing climate policy and performance (Hanusch 2016).

Other research suggests democracies are better at making commitments than meeting them. Michele Battig and Thomas Bernauer analyzed climate policies in 185 countries, 1990 to 2004; democracies were more likely to commit to policies but were "ambiguous" with respect to delivering on outcomes. Democracies, the authors conclude, have "not been able to override the countervailing forces that emanate from the free-rider problem, the discounting of future benefits of climate change mitigation, and other factors that cut against efforts to reduce emissions" (303). This summarizes the challenges to democracy of accounting for long-term issues in the short term (Boston 2017).

One of the more thorough studies used five indicators of ecological degradation: carbon dioxide and nitrogen dioxide emissions; organics in water; deforestation; and land degradation. The results were consistent across all five, leading to the conclusion that "a rise in democracy reduces environmental degradation and improves environmental performance" (Li and Reuveny 2006, 936). Democracies had lower air emissions per capita, lower levels of water organics, and less deforestation and land degradation than authoritarian ones. Democracies appear to be better at controlling deforestation, although this is partly due to better governance that comes with high incomes, as mentioned earlier (Bhattarai and Hammig 2001). An effort to isolate the effects of democracy from income found "democracy is more powerful in explaining deforestation rates than income" (Buitenzorgy and Mol 2011, 66); as a result: "in reducing deforestation rates the emphasis should not only be on economic development but even more on democratization" (59).

Some scholars discern positive effects only with an accumulated "stock" of democracy: "democracy matters, but only in the long run" (Gallagher and Thacker 2008; Fredriksson and Neumayer 2013). Another nuance comes in a study finding that higher incomes are associated with better results on health-related pollution but not ecosystem quality, which is explained by more democracy. The effect of higher incomes on health indicators levels off while ecosystem quality continues to improve. The higher the incomes, the stronger are the positive effects of democracy on ecology. In this study, Andrea Duwel (2010) finds "the effect of democracy on less visible ecosystem quality gets larger as countries become wealthier and citizens develop post-material values" (26). This highlights an unexpected effect of incomes in democracies; ecosystems are valued more at the same time that income growth increases ecosystem stress.

Another study found that features of democracy—information, accountability, better subnational governance, respect for the law—increase intelligence in citizens, which leads to less deforestation, so that "Intelligence is the force that shapes formal rules and informal regulations such as societal trust, norms, and traditions" (Obydenkova, Nazarov, and Salahodjaev 2016).

It is fair to point out that the research does not uniformly support these positive linkages. Midlarsky, for example (2001), finds positive linkages of land protection with democracy but the opposite for water, deforestation, and carbon dioxide. Some types of democracy may be more effective than others. Similarly, Fredriksson and Wollscheid (2007) conclude that "democracies set stricter environmental policies than autocracies," but this "is primarily driven by parliamentary democracies" because they usually have fewer veto points and more legislative cohesion (383).

Of course, more autocratic approaches may be more suitable in other settings. Countries of East Asia (including China), many with recent rapid growth, may find more centralized, less democratic governance of ecological issues to be necessary. Mark Beeson anticipates a "coming of environmental authoritarianism" in parts of the world, with "a decrease in individual liberty as governments seek to transform environmentally destructive behavior" (2010, 276). In their rapid growth, East Asian countries engaged in "a fairly ruthless exploitation of the natural environment" that eroded not only quality of life but the ability to maintain high growth rates, just as advocates of limits to growth have claimed. This form of authoritarianism, "in which environmentally unsustainable forms of behavior are simply forbidden, may become not only justifiable, but essential for the survival of humanity on anything approaching a civilized form" (289). Beeson concedes that this response may not be limited to that region; he questions "whether democracy can be sustained in the region—or anywhere else for that matter—given the unprecedented and unforgiving nature of the challenges we collectively face" (289). This comports with the thesis that ecological issues demand alternatives to democratic governance.

Then again, another line of thinking calls for not less but *more* democracy. This is near-gospel in writing on sustainable development, part of the social dimension (Agyeman and Angus 2003; Portney 2013; Fiorino 2014b). In the writing on sustainable cities, the thinking often is that genuine change is not possible without a strong dose of participation and engagement. Although there are dissenters, belief in full democratic deliberation is common. John Dryzek, for example, calls for a transition to *ecological democracy*, with deliberation on values and a recognition of shared interests in "the integrity of the ecological base on which society depends" (Dryzek 2013, 237).

There are virtues to such arguments, and they are valid in many settings. Yet these arguments are unduly optimistic about the effects they may have, and the likelihood of deliberation leading citizens to embrace ecological protection (Arias-Maldonado 2007). It also gives too little regard to the realities of political power in large nation-states. Except on some local issues, societies are not governed by small groups of highly engaged, deliberative citizens but through institutions and interests within complex governance systems. Thinking about an ideal of citizen engagement and empowerment ignores many of the realities of large systems and the effects of existing distributions of political power. Still, as Nico Stehr argues, "Rather than lamenting the inconvenience of democratic governance," we should enhance democracy and "recognize our changing climate as an issue of political governance and not as an environmental or economic issue" (2016, 39; also see Stehr 2015). My answer in Chapter 8 is *more* and *better* democracy that leads to changes in distributions of political power, not ditching it due to ecological challenges.

## WHY DO SOME COUNTRIES PERFORM BETTER ECOLOGICALLY THAN OTHERS?

In 1993, political scientists Kent Weaver and Bert Rockman published a collection of studies on the question of whether institutions matter in governance. Of course they do, but it is difficult to predict how and when. This question has been asked in a variety of settings to explain national policies and outcomes. Intuitively, the effects of institutions on outcomes should follow certain patterns. Parliamentary systems, for example, may be expected to be more nimble and adaptable with their fusion of executive and legislative power than presidential, separation-of-powers systems with their many veto points. Relatively centralized, more unitary states (like France or the United Kingdom) would be expected to have better prospects for policy change than federalist ones (like the United States or Canada), where subnational units of government can frustrate national goals if so inclined. An active judiciary with a policy role may obstruct popular preferences as decided by the more political legislative and executive branches (Weaver and Rockman 1993, 1–34).

In theory, these are reasonable assertions. In practice, they do not hold up as well. In the late 1960s and the 1970s, as David Vogel documents, the United States moved more quickly to respond to public concerns about pollution than did Great Britain and Japan (1993). This may have been because public opinion in the United States was stronger, environmentalists were better organized, industry was slow to respond, or some other reason. The US system of checks and balances did have an effect, but it was in preventing a rollback from progress made in the 1970s. While the British and Japanese rolled back environmental protection under conservative regimes in the 1980s, divided government in the United States checked the Reagan administration's effort to deregulate, forcing them to use an administrative strategy—one that was largely unsuccessful in changing long-term policy.

Another institutional factor is whether a system is more unitary or federalist in structure. Federalism is the extent to which subnational units of government (states or provinces) exercise political power independent of a national authority. The United States, Canada, Switzerland, India, and Germany grant more autonomy to state or provincial levels and are more federalist; France, Japan, Italy, and Israel limit autonomy and are viewed as being more unitary in structure. Federalism could be an advantage, because multiple levels of government could build their own consensus on change, innovate more freely, inspire others with positive examples, or act when other levels do not. On the other hand, having greater autonomy below the national level could impede the adoption or implementation of strong environmental policies determined nationally.

Research and experience support both of these views. Martha Derthick's concept of *compensatory federalism* asserts that "federalism works when governments at one level of the system are able to compensate for weaknesses or defects at another level" (2010, 59). Evidence of this is found in US climate politics: state and local levels are more active and innovative than a federal government hamstrung by institutional barriers, polarization, and clashing regional interests (Rabe 2004 and 2016). This is a reversal from the 1960s, when inaction by most states led to the Clean Air Act and other laws. In both the 1970s and in climate action more recently, we could easily argue that federalism has had a positive influence on US environmental policy.

## The Effects of Veto Points

An interesting take on institutional factors is the effect of "veto players" on the capacity to adopt policies for mitigating climate change. Veto players are individual or collective actors (such as a court or a legislature) whose agreement is necessary to change from the status quo. Each veto player, Nathan Madden (2014, 571) observes, "acts as a barrier for policy adoption by increasing the number of actors whose consensus is necessary for policy adoption."

Veto players come in institutional and partisan forms. The seven institutional ones are federalism, bicameralism, presidential systems, single-member districts, initiatives/referenda, judicial review, and pluralism. The three partisan ones are divided government, a minority or single party majority, and having an anti–climate action party in power. Based on an analysis of climate policy adoption in 23 OECD countries between 1996 and 2010, Madden concludes that when there are more veto players fewer policies are adopted and those that are adopted consist more of incremental than major change (also see Ward 2008; Harrison and Sundstrom 2010).

If veto players make change from the status quo hard, the United States faces a tough road on climate. The United States is federal and presidential, with a bicameral Congress and single-member legislative districts (in the House of Representatives). It lacks a national process for referenda or initiatives (although some states have them); it has a tradition of judicial review. and is a poster child for political pluralism. Divided government is commonplace, with different parties often controlling the White House and/or houses of Congress. Contrast this with the United Kingdom, with one institutional veto player and without an anti–climate action party comparable to Republicans in the United States.

Something that may influence ecological performance is electoral rules and systems of representation. One study found no evidence overall that parliamentary systems perform better than presidential ones or that single-party governments do better than coalition or divided ones. Being more federalist or unitary does not matter, based on Lyle Scruggs' analysis of seventeen industrial countries. He does, however, find that countries with proportional representation (PR) and multi-member legislative districts do better than those with winner-take-all rules and single-member districts. PR systems may help to lower barriers for new and marginal parties in gaining seats. This explains much of the success of the first European Green Party in Germany, where PR voting in multi-member districts helped the party earn seats in parliament and gain influence.

These findings are echoed elsewhere. A study of 866 democracies found "environmental policies tend to be stricter under proportional systems" (Fredriksson and Millet 2004, 238). On the other hand, in looking at why countries ratified the Kyoto Protocol, Kathryn Harrison and Lisa Sundstrom (2010) find that although PR systems may amplify minority viewpoints, other factors were better at explaining why countries did or did not (including the United States) ratify Kyoto.

An illustration of the complexity of institutional issues is the story of climate policy in the United States. Until the second Obama term, the United States was seen as a laggard in climate action. To protect fossil fuel interests, the Bush administration took little action on climate mitigation. This changed in 2009, when President Obama committed to national cap-and-trade legislation for greenhouse gases. But it never happened. Although the American Clean Energy and Security Act (called Waxman-Markey) passed the House in June 2009, it never got out of the Senate.

So how did the Obama administration move on climate action? The proverbial veto points combined to precipitate change. Frustrated at the lack of federal action in the Bush years, twelve states (Massachusetts was the lead plaintiff) filed a lawsuit arguing that the EPA should regulate carbon dioxide and other greenhouse gases under the Clean Air Act. The case was heard first by the US Court of Appeals for the District of Columbia Circuit; it decided the plaintiffs lacked standing to make a claim and did not address the merits. The states appealed to the Supreme Court, which granted standing and ruled in their favor. The Court held 5–4 in *Massachusetts* v. *EPA* (549 US 497) that greenhouse gases may be pollutants under the Clean Air Act; if the EPA found that they endangered public health and welfare, it must regulate (Greenhouse 2007). In response, the EPA Administrator determined based on the evidence that greenhouse gases were pollutants endangering health and welfare and should be regulated, as the plaintiffs had asked (for a review of this and standards proposed see Eilperin and Mufson 2014).

Consider how this major policy change had come about: twelve states (all, by the way, reliably blue in presidential elections) made a claim on the federal courts to gain an interpretation of an existing law which even the Bill Clinton administration had decided in the 1990s did not apply to greenhouse gases. By a one-vote margin, the US Supreme Court ruled for the states two years before a Democratic president in favor of climate action came into office. After Waxman-Markey failed, the Obama EPA used this authority to issue standards for new and existing coal-fired power plants in 2014 and 2015. Congress had no role in this process, except in passing the Clean Air Act Amendments of 1990. So the very veto players that can block change combined to provoke it. Federalism (in the form of the states' lawsuit) interacted with separation-of-powers (via the Supreme Court ruling) to establish the authority for the Obama administration to act.

Of course, the rule on existing coal-fired power plants, the Clean Power Plan, was later challenged by a collection of politically conservative states, and President Trump issued an executive order in March of 2017 calling for EPA Administrator Scott Pruitt to dismantle it (Schlossberg 2017). Just as federalism and separation of powers grant authority, they may also take it away.

## The Patterns of Governance

In sum, it is difficult to determine the effects of specific institutional features. What do appear to matter more than any one such feature are overall patterns of governance. This finding has particular relevance for green growth. The issue is how governance systems deal with trade-offs among ecological and economic policy and the extent to which they can integrate competing interests. Political science distinguishes between more pluralist systems like the United States or Australia and more neo-corporatist ones (Germany or Sweden). Pluralist systems are competitive, adversarial, and fragmented; neo-corporatist policy systems are more consensual, centralized, and integrated.

Corporatist systems are more consensus-based, accommodating, and learning-oriented; they are better than more pluralist ones in fostering

long-term, collaborative relationships and "providing many incentives to sig-
nal intentions to cooperate to produce positive-sum outcomes" (Matthews
2001, 496). Pluralist systems favor "self-maximization and atomistic behavior"
(Mathews 2001, 496). Mary Matthews notes that a pluralist system "not only
imitates the market process; it can be driven by it" (497). Her link to markets
is apt. Economists Peter Hall and David Soskice (2001) distinguish *coordinated*
from *liberal* market economies in patterns of interactions among firms: "Nations
with liberal market economies tend to rely on markets to coordinate endeavors
in both the financial and industrial relations systems, while those with coordinated market economies have institutions in both spheres that reflect higher
levels of non-market coordination" (19).

Table 4.1 presents a classification of economically advanced democracies based on degrees of corporatism (Siaroff 1999). Strongly and moderately
strong corporatist countries include Austria, Norway, Sweden, the Netherlands,
Denmark, and Germany. Among weakly or outright pluralist countries are New
Zealand, Australia, Canada, and the United States. Some—Israel, Spain, and
Greece—do not fall clearly into any category. What is useful in Siaroff's study is
how it redefines the corporatist–pluralist dimension to one of being a more or
less integrated governance and economic system. He describes the core capacity of the more integrated systems as one of cooperation between government
and other socioeconomic interest groups "aimed at forging a consensus . . ."
(176). Integrated governance and economic systems exhibit a long-term pattern
of "shared economic management involving the social partners and existing
at various levels . . . and joint shaping of national policies in competitiveness-
related matters (education, social policy, etc.)" (189).

*Table 4.1* RELATIVE DEGREE OF POLICY INTEGRATION IN DEMOCRACIES

| Most Integrated | | | | Least Integrated |
|---|---|---|---|---|
| Strongly Corporatist | Moderately to Strongly Corporatist | Moderately Corporatist | Weakly or Somewhat Corporatist | Pluralist |
| Austria | Netherlands | Finland | Ireland | United States |
| Norway | Denmark | Belgium | New Zealand | Canada |
| Sweden | Germany (based on West Germany) | | United Kingdom | |
| | | | Italy | |
| | | | Australia | |

SOURCE: Siaroff 1999, 184

The relevance of these types of governance systems and their relationship to ecological performance is striking. Scruggs observes that "countries characterized by strong, centralized interest groups and a more 'consensual' approach to policy making . . . have enjoyed better environmental performance than countries where economic groups are less comprehensively organized and policymaking is less consensual" (Scruggs 2003, 123). Scruggs suggests three reasons for the relative superiority of neo-corporatist systems. One is that collaborative systems are better at using information. A capacity for "ongoing consultation with a variety of interests having specific knowledge of the area of regulation" generates better information about options, costs, and the impacts of alternative actions (142). Second, a higher level of trust and business engagement in policymaking leads to flexibility in implementation. Policymaking occurs more as a learning process than one of conforming to technical standards in the context of legalistic relationships. Third is the way business interests are organized in neo-corporatism. Business is more likely to frame choices broadly and be willing to work cooperatively in reconciling and integrating policy goals. Further, strong industry associations may reduce free-riding, educate members on innovative solutions, and recognize opportunities and trade-offs in alternative policies. Many other studies reach similar conclusions about neo-corporatism (Jahn 1998; Crepaz 1995; Matthews 2001).

A more recent analysis found that neo-corporatist systems adopted more stringent policies: "collective action problems inherent in environmental policy can be solved more easily in neo-corporatist 'closed shops' based on trust and long-term reciprocity (Liefferink et al. 2009, 92). Other recent studies support the case for corporatist systems and their ability to generate collective behavior by various interests affected by ecological policies (Ozymy and Rey 2013).

Qualitative studies take a similar view. In *The Politics of the Earth*, John Dryzek's "consensus picks" for greenest countries are Finland, Germany, Japan, the Netherlands, Norway, Sweden, and Switzerland. What do they have in common? All are "consensual democracies" that have strongly supported international action. In an analysis of sustainability in high-consumption societies, William Lafferty and James Meadowcroft (2000) also look to patterns of governance. Of nine countries, they classify the Netherlands, Sweden, and Norway as "enthusiastic" in their embrace of sustainability. They identify three factors to explain this orientation. One is active engagement with global governance. Second is "a relatively dominant social-democratic and/or consensual political culture" emphasizing social equity, an active state, and "neo-corporatist or negotiated modes of decision-making" (424). Third are "traditions of solidarity with the poorer countries of the world" in development assistance, support for global agreements, and other engagement. This is critical; Chapter 8 argues that green growth must occur as a *global* process.

These conditions do not exist in the United States: "It is well known that the United States has long maintained a skeptical attitude towards transnational governance" (Lafferty and Meadowcroft 2000, 425). US foreign aid focuses mostly on security interests; its engagement in global agreements like the Kyoto Protocol, Law of the Seas Treaty, Basil Waste Convention, and Convention on Biological Diversity is weak. In its governance style, "The United States, with its individualist, polarized, and highly litigious society, is far removed from a 'social-democratic' or 'consensual' political culture" (425).

It is worth clarifying just what consensual and integrating governance means. It does not mean the absence of conflict. Certainly the widely heralded National Environmental Policy Plans in the Netherlands were the source of political conflict in the 1980s, to the extent the effort nearly failed. Germany's renewable energy policies are contested, especially in the issue of phasing out nuclear power. It is not the absence of conflict or a reliance on lax, easy-to-agree-on actions that characterizes policymaking in these countries; it is their ability to frame issues in certain ways, engage key political and economic interests, and adopt socially beneficial policies.

In sum, I see two aspects of the capacity for green growth. One is whether or not a system can give sufficient priority—absolute priority in cases of critical, nonrenewable ecosystems and resources—to ecological values, especially when they conflict with economic ones. The second is to be able to identify and carry out positive-sum solutions rather than simply minimize zero-sums. The first is necessary for the second to work. Indeed, if a system is unable to give priority to ecological values, the second is almost beside the point. In my approach, these are mutually reinforcing relationships: having the second helps in placing ecological on the same level as economic issues; finding and applying positive-sums makes it easier to elevate ecological goals.

## GOVERNANCE FOR GREEN GROWTH

The neglect of governance and politics is an omission this chapter aims to correct. Green growth writing, examined in Chapter 2, does many useful things: it describes the problem (that of reconciling growth aspirations and realities with ecological limits); makes a case for the positive synergies; examines policy and analytical tools and strategies (e.g., market-based mechanisms or ecosystem valuation); and illustrates activity at both the global and national levels. It does not, however, grapple with the qualities of governance that matter in shaping the ability to adopt and carry out a green economic transition, nor does it look at the politics of how this could occur.

What can we learn about governance? To begin, national ecological gover- nance is a relatively recent addition to the functions of government. Given that research has, until recently, focused on OECD countries, there is less variation than there might be; surely the United States and Germany, for example, have more in common than do Germany and Pakistan in capacities and policy styles. Still, the variations are instructive. Institutional features influence whether pol- icies are adopted and implemented. But it is hard to say if some features matter more than others. There are too many variables among institutions and their interactions with short-term factors like public opinion, leadership, economic conditions, and global trends to draw clear conclusions.

A lesson of this chapter is that interrelationships among institutional issues are complex. Yet these are worth studying, not because we are going to redesign the institutions or restructure the core policy styles of countries, but because *knowing how institutions and policy styles affect ecological policy success allows us to devise better policy strategies for change and to take steps, however incre- mental or reformist they may be, to improve our governance capacities.*

Ecological issues still occupy a tenuous place on national and subnational agendas. This is nowhere more apparent than in the United States, where cli- mate and ecological issues are a partisan battleground. Indeed, in 2016 one of two main parties in the United States nominated a presidential candidate who called outright for the elimination of the Environmental Protection Agency (Milman 2016), and he was elected president of the United States. Of course, eliminating agencies is easier said than done, but that a candidate was even say- ing such things, and then would win the office, is revealing in itself.

My view is that we cannot think of anything like a *green state* existing until ecological issues are treated on the same level as economic ones and integrated into decision making. For now, countries like Denmark and Sweden come clos- est to doing that, but there are flaws in these and others. In the United States, California comes closest to being a green state on energy and climate; its poli- cies for water use, allocation, and efficiency are improving but still leave much to be desired.

This and preceding chapters suggest conditions associated with an ecologi- cal state, if not a truly green one. Some growth is necessary, but maybe not too much. Political stability, an effective legal system, administrative capacity, and low corruption help. Strong technology and science—products of growth—are needed to understand problems and devise solutions. Research suggests that active global engagement matters (Harrison and Sundstrom 2010; Recchia 2002), as do pressure groups/activists to promote visibility and accountabil- ity for ecological issues (Binder and Neumayer 2005; Bohmelt, Bernauer, and Koubi 2015). PR systems perform better, and perhaps federalist ones, with mixed evidence on the latter (Walti 2004; Poloni-Staudinger 2008). Regional associations like the EU support better ecological policies (Liefferink, et al 2009; Holzinger, Knill, and Sommerer 2011; Borzel 2000; Busch and Jörgens 2005).

Debates over the adequacy or wisdom of democratic institutions given the challenge of ecological degradation do matter. The issue is not that political systems around the world are about to be torn apart by climate scientists or aquatic ecologists storming the gates. Political instability is more likely to be driven by economic turmoil, anti-immigration sentiments, fear of terrorism, or other issues. Still, effects of climate change, water insecurity, ecosystem damages, and air and water pollution link closely with economics, immigration, and security concerns.

In my view, the weight of the evidence suggests democracy is likely to deliver better ecological governance and policies than more authoritarian systems. We can say with confidence that democratic institutions and processes are not less capable than authoritarian counterparts—that they can produce ecological policies (and perhaps outcomes, although these are hard to measure reliably) that are as strong and effective as other regime types. Of course, the increasing array of political, institutional, and cultural settings in which ecological issues now are being addressed—from China to Vietnam to Turkey to India to Indonesia— means other models are emerging that may or may not prove to be effective. For our purposes, democracy is the institutional form we are working with, and for many reasons should want to maintain, so understanding its capacities, strengths, and limitations helps in assessing our prospects.

The most important findings from the research lie in the differences between pluralist, competitive, and more adversarial political systems and the integrating, corporatist, consensus-based ones. On this point the research is consistent, even startling. I am not the first policy expert to draw attention to these conclusions. In an essay on "earth systems governance," John Dryzek and Hayley Stevenson (2011, 66) conclude that being corporatist and consensus-based is "a particularly robust predictor" of strong ecological performance. What is most interesting about this line of research is that it also offers lessons for understanding green growth capacities. The more integrating, consensus-based systems are more equipped for a green transition than are more pluralist, adversarial ones. The model for political pluralism, the United States faces particular challenges in adopting a green growth agenda. This is not fatal, but it has to be accounted for.

Closely related to economics and governance is inequality. This has come up before. It is central to ecological economics and the social critique of growth. A tenet of de-growth writing is that the rich have to give up much of their income so the poor can enjoy a reasonable quality of life within planetary limits. Inequality is part of governance: economic inequality is a product of politics, and it affects how institutions operate and the policies they deliver. Chapter 3 considered how growth and incomes affect policy and outcomes, and this chapter examined institutions and patterns of governance. The next chapter looks at economic inequality and its implications for green growth.

# Inequality and Green Growth

Imagine two countries, each with an annual GDP of about one trillion dollars. Both have a history of stable democratic politics. Both are guided by two parties, one center-right and the other center-left, that alternate being in power. In one respect, however, they differ. Starting at the same place in the middle of the last century, one has maintained low economic inequality while the other has steadily evolved into a society with high inequality. The contrasts are evident in their ratings under the Gini index, a metric for describing inequality. The first country's Gini is .35, a sign of low inequality; the second rates at just below .55, an indication of much greater inequality. Zero is perfect equality, a 1.0 is where all income goes to one person.

All other things being equal, as the economists like to say, which society would impose more ecological stress? Which is more likely to be wasting resources and damaging ecosystems? Both are equal in population density; the GDP is the same, as are incomes. In short, in our two hypothetical countries, we are controlling for everything but the level of economic inequality.

The answer is that we really don't quite know, at least for certain. The effect of economic and income growth over time is to increase ecological stress and bring us closer to breaching planetary limits. Although there are offsetting effects, discussed in Chapter 3, the net effect of growth in current policy scenarios is to add to the weight of pressures on the planet. Ecological economists give a great deal of attention to reducing inequality in a way that offsets a need for growth and distributes well-being more evenly. They may be even more right than we thought.

Several factors might lead us to predict that the more unequal of our near-twin countries would be more damaging ecologically. Some of these relate to the effects on economic behavior and incentives. Income differentials could lead to more consumption than might be expected in a more equal country. Economists have established that income differences lead to consumption of *positional goods* things valued for the status they confer rather than for their utility. We might expect more inequality to encourage attachment to positional goods. People may want to establish and display their status and demonstrate their position in a society. We might also expect higher income groups to assign less value to *public goods*—things that are shared by all or most everyone, and where a person's use does not exclude others. Wealthy people—and there would be *relatively* more of them in the less economically equal society—could meet their needs through private goods and thus have less need for the benefits of public goods that all may share.

Other factors that might cause inequality to impose more ecological stress are political and social. They are related to the economic factors, but worth distinguishing analytically. Their effects on ecological policy are informed by a social science literature on social trust and collective action. The literature suggests that high inequality may create low-trust societies in which it is difficult to establish and act upon common goals. Inequality increases social distance, a sense of "us against them," a resentment of the outsider. Ecological protection requires collective action: private interests and markets on their own do not give us clean air, protect habitat, or decarbonize energy systems. This overlaps with the point on public goods; the same factors that allow the affluent to insulate themselves from public goods (like private education and health care) could undermine societal support for ecological protection.

This is the more speculative chapter in the book. Although some aspects of the linkages between economic inequality and ecology have been studied and debated, others have not. Those receiving more attention are focused on environmental justice—also captured in terms of *climate justice, environmental equity*, and *eco-justice*, among others—which refer to a *disproportionate* distribution of environmental (both health and ecological) harms and benefits across societies. The concept of environmental justice emerged in the United States as a powerful merging of race, health, and ecology in history and politics (Baehler 2017). Although the issue has been one of both race and socioeconomic inequity, the term is used largely to refer to unfair distributions of ecological and health harm based on race and ethnicity. Not only do race and ethnicity dominate the policy debates, a meta-analysis of research in the field found that "environmental inequities based on these characteristics are ubiquitous" and class linkages are "substantially weaker" (Ringquist 2005, 241).

Of course, equity and fairness are only one side of the relationship; they focus on the effects of institutions and policies, as well as social and economic conditions, on the distribution of inequities in society. What about the other side of the question—the effects of inequality on the capacity to respond to ecological problems? That was the question at the start of the chapter. In terms of the themes of this book, the question is: *What are the effects of economic inequality on making a transition to green growth?*

While the first side of the environment–inequality relationships has received attention, the second has not. This is not to say there has been none. On ecological issues specifically, this chapter examines a modest body of research suggesting that inequality may serve as a barrier or inhibitor to ecological progress. This builds upon both the economic and social-political factors mentioned above in speculating about the effects of inequality. Beyond ecology, other research looks at how inequality influences capacities for collective action and support for public goods.

This chapter aligns closely with the three previous ones. Chapter 2 examined the more visible expressions of the green growth concept from such organizations as UNEP, the OECD, the WBCSD, and the World Bank. I would not say that economic inequality is ignored in those documents; after all, both UNEP and the World Bank give a nod to the need for *inclusive* green growth, meaning that growth should occur in ways that benefit all groups in society, in poor and developing countries as well as in the rich countries. Yet the effects of economic inequality on policy capacities barely earn a mention. Indeed, the WBCSD appears to value economic growth mostly to expand markets. This neglect of social equity has been a sore point for green growth critics.

Chapter 3 took on the economy–ecology relationship directly, arguing that it is more complicated than both the advocates and the critics of economic and income growth typically recognize. Of course, a major theme of ecological economics is the need for less inequality and more economic justice. This is why ecological economics should continue to influence the evolution of the green growth concept. The social critics of growth shed some light on the economic factors that may link inequality with increased ecological degradation, as is captured in such concepts as positional goods and status competition. Fred Hirsch's book on *The Social Limits to Growth* (1976) gave us a picture of ever-unsatisfied wants—of growth generating demands that are never quite met, because well-being becomes relative rather than absolute.

Another aspect of inequality central to ecological economists and other critics of growth is that poor countries have to grow to meet basic needs, but the planet is up against ecological limits. If stopping or reversing growth is the only way to remain within planetary limits, as many growth critics contend, then something has to give, somewhere. For growth critics, that "something" is excessive affluence and consumption; the "somewhere" is the rich countries, mainly our OECD cohort. A tenet of de-growth is that countries like the United States, Canada, and Sweden need to scale back while creating ecological space for poor nations in Africa and Asia to grow.

Inequality also builds upon the previous chapter's discussion of ecological governance and what it means for green growth. Some governance qualities seem to be more favorable to ecological protection and positive-sum ecology–economy relationships than others. What the last chapter did not investigate, however, are the underlying social conditions that also may affect a country's capacities. Among these are such factors as ideology, political culture, race and ethnicity, and social inequality. I consider these to some degree in the context of the United States in Chapters 7 and 8, but focus here on inequality as a factor that may influence both a society's ecological impacts and the potential for collective action to achieve green, or at least greener, growth. That some countries consistently ranking high in sustainability ratings—Sweden, Norway, and Denmark come to mind—are also countries with lower inequality is hard to ignore. Is inequality the missing link in explanations for ecological performance, or at least a part of it? Are their more consensual politics and cultural homogeneity part of an answer (Putnam 2007)?

The next part of the chapter gives a perspective on the extent, causes, and consequences of economic inequality, especially in the United States. This is a large topic, but worth reviewing to set the stage for what follows. This includes environmental (or climate or eco-) justice, which is the more visible side of ecology–inequity relationships and the effects of a green growth compared to a conventional policy agenda. The second and third parts of the chapter turn to the effects of economic inequality on political capacities to respond to ecological issues as well as to implement a green growth agenda. The second part reviews the still-limited empirical research on the effects of inequality on ecological performance. The third is on the theoretical case, looking at economic and then political-social explanations. The conclusion draws lessons for green growth.

## THE BIG PICTURE: INEQUALITY, SOCIETY, AND POLITICS

Inequality is a relative concept. One person's image of raging economic inequity is another's just society. A socialist calls for distribution of income and wealth, "to each according to their needs," while a hard-core capitalist sees inequality as an inevitable by-product of affluence and efficiency. Still, there is a good deal to be learned from patterns of economic inequality within and among countries. Inequality in the United States is higher now than at any time since the 1920s. In income, it is higher than in all but two of 35 OECD countries (behind Mexico and Chile, ahead of Turkey). In the distribution of wealth, the United States is the most unequal OECD country.

This chapter focuses on economic inequality, although a few studies examine the political form. There is more research on the economic inequality–ecology linkage, and we can address it more directly. To a large degree, differences in income and wealth determine variations in political power. This is evident in voting and other participation. So we get at both by studying economic inequality, which affects many social and political issues. Inequality is a big topic; this chapter looks briefly at conditions and trends in the United States and developed nations, mainly the OECD.

## Economic Inequality in Rich Countries

Economic inequality refers to distributions of income and wealth: "income is the cash that people earn every month through work, transfers, or rents; wealth is the money they accumulate over time in bank accounts and in assets, such as property and stocks" (OECD 2015, 34). A 2015 OECD report, *In It Together: Why Less Inequality Benefits All*, presents a snapshot of trends in the developed countries. "In most countries," it states, "the gap between rich and poor is at its highest level in 30 years" (15). Although attention has focused on the so-called one percent, including what Senator Bernie Sanders called in his 2016 campaign the "billionaire class," what matters more are declines in household incomes of the bottom 40% of the ladder. In the last three decades, those in the bottom 40% have benefited very little from decades of economic growth.

One way to describe income inequality is comparing the ratio earned by the top 10% and bottom 10%. In the 1970s, this was 7.1; it then grew to 8.1 in the 1980s and 9.1 in the 1990s. By the time of *In It Together*, the top 10% earned nearly ten times more than the low earners (15).

The Gini index/coefficient compares countries on a scale of 0 to 1.0. If income were perfectly distributed, the Gini would be 0; if all were concentrated in one person, it would be 1.0. The lower the Gini, the more equal the distribution. In the 1980s, the average Gini for OECD countries was 0.29; by 2013 it was 0.32, an increase of 10%; it rose in 17 of 22 countries for which comparable data are available. The lowest Gini coefficients (and thus the least inequality) are found in countries like Denmark, Slovenia, Norway, and Sweden; the highest are found in Chile, Mexico, the United States, Turkey, and the UK (OECD, 20). These growing disparities are largely the result of declining incomes among the bottom 40% in most countries. The United States has seen large disparities; since 1978 the Gini went up by 18%, although it grew in nearly all OECD countries. Indeed, a 2016 Stanford University report went so far as to characterize the United States as "the world champion of disposable-income inequality among rich nations" (Fisher and Smeeding 2016, 33).

Wealth is distributed even more unevenly than income. On average, according to the OECD, the 10% richest households have half the total wealth and the middle 50% nearly all the other half, leaving the bottom 40% with only 3%. Particularly striking is a statistic from the United States, where *Forbes* reported in 2014 that the six surviving heirs to the Wal-Mart fortune controlled more wealth than the bottom 30% of the population.[1]

Recent distributions in household incomes as measured by the Gini coefficient in selected OECD countries are listed in Table 5.1. It also lists poverty rates as of 2012. The Gini coefficients reflect household disposable income, so they adjust for redistributions due to cash transfers (e.g., unemployment or social welfare payments) and income taxes. These reduce income inequality by an average of 27% in OECD countries (OECD 2016, 3). Sometimes the Gini is calculated without adjusting for these transfers, in which case the coefficient for any country will be higher.

Other US facts are found in a 2012 Brookings report on *Inequality in America* (Dadush et al. 2012). Among the more noteworthy statements are the following (all page cites are from Dadush et al. 2012):

Table 5.1 Gini Coefficients (Household Disposable Income) and Poverty Rates in Selected OECD Countries (2007 and 2012)*

| Country | 2007 Gini | 2012 Gini | 2012 Poverty Rate |
| --- | --- | --- | --- |
| Mexico | .450 | .457 | 18.9 |
| United States | .374 | .396 | 17.2 |
| Israel | .360 | .365 | 18.6 |
| United Kingdom | .373 | .351 | 10.5 |
| Japan | .329 | .336 | 16.0 |
| Australia | .336 | .326 | 14.0 |
| Canada | .318 | .321 | 12.8 |
| France | .295 | .308 | 8.5 |
| Germany | .285 | .289 | 8.4 |
| Austria | .285 | .276 | 9.6 |
| Sweden | .259 | .274 | 9.0 |
| Denmark | .244 | .249 | 5.4 |

*Ranked in order of the 2012 Gini. A higher Gini signifies more household income inequality. The poverty rate is the percentage of the households with less than 50% of the median income in each country.

SOURCE: *OECD Income Inequality Update* (November 2016)

https://www.oecd.org/social/OECD2016-Income-Inequality-Update.pdf

Between 1979 and 2007, average real household income grew by 58%, but the median income rose only 19%, demonstrating that incomes were becoming more concentrated. (9)

As of 2010, US concentration of incomes at the top was the highest since the Great Depression; in 2010, the top 1% of tax filers garnered 20% of US market income; the top 0.01% earned 5%. (12)

Since 1970, there has been almost no increase in average incomes among the lower 90% of the income scale, with the US incomes at the upper and lower ends being more "polarized" than in any other advanced economy. (14)

After taxes and transfers, the poverty rate in the US stands as one of the highest in the OECD, second at the time of this report only to that in Israel. (28)

In 1980, the ratio of CEO to worker pay was 42–1; in 1990 it was 107–1; by 2010 it had grown to 325–1. (61)

There are many explanations for these trends. One is *skill-based technology change*. This refers to the growing emphasis on technology and knowledge, and the barriers for those lacking training and skills to being job-competitive. The direct effects of trade policies are modest compared to the effects of a shift to a service-based economy; the indirect effects of competition due to technology innovation resulting from open trade do seem to matter. Worth noting in the wake of the 2016 US presidential election is that immigration has had little impact on wages and inequality; indeed, "a large number of studies have indicated only a weak link between immigration and the wages of U.S.-born workers" (Dadush, at al. 2012). Other factors include the effects of "winner-take-all-markets" in which small variations in performance cause big income difference (as for elite athletes or entertainers) and the "financialization" of the economy—the "growth of the centrality of the finance sector in the operation of the economy and governing institutions" (57). The decline of unions does explain "a significant part of the rise of male wage inequality" (67).

Public policy has played a role as well. Tax cuts in upper income brackets led to a system that is far less progressive and in some ways more regressive, such as in the effects of state sales taxes, social security taxes, and rates on capital gains. In rich economies, the marginal tax rates for the highest income bracket fell from 59% in 1980 to 30% in 2009 (IMF 2015a, 22). On the other side of the ledger, income support since the 1980s has shifted strongly from the poor to the elderly; the proportion of total transfer payments going to the bottom income quintile in the United States fell from 54% in 1979 to 36% in 2007. And these trends are self-reinforcing: "increased income concentration at the top has been associated with the adoption of policies that favor the wealthy" (Dadush et al. 2012, 68). Indeed, the political dynamics are such that economic inequality reinforces political inequality, and so on, in a vicious cycle.

The basis for the OECD subtitle that "less inequality benefits all" is the finding on the economic and social effects of inequality. The OECD analysis found "consistent evidence" that inequality depresses growth. Increased inequality from 1985 to 2005 alone "is estimated to have knocked 4.7 percentage points off cumulative growth between 1990 and 2010, on average across OECD countries . . ." (15). Why these effects? It is because low-income groups are unable to develop needed skills: "the dominant mechanism through which inequality seems to affect growth is by curbing opportunities for the poor and lower middle classes" (26). Low-income groups do not fare well in gaining the education and skills needed to compete in modern economies. This comports with US studies showing that economic mobility has essentially been frozen in recent decades (Chetty et al. 2014).

Other analyses reinforce these findings (Sommeiller, Price, and Wazeter 2016; Ashkenas 2016). A 2015 report by the International Monetary Fund (IMF) quantified effects of inequality on growth. It found that a one percent increase in the share of income going to the top quintile will reduce GDP by 0.08% in the next five years, "suggesting that the benefits do not trickle down." On the other hand, if the income share of the bottom quintile grows one percent, GDP will increase by 0.38% over the next five years (IMF 2015a, 7). The main reason is that "Higher inequality lowers growth by depriving the ability of lower income households to stay healthy and accumulate physical and human capital" (8). Education and access to health care are important. Slower growth also results from less intergenerational mobility and spending: high-income groups spend a smaller fraction of their earnings, resulting in less aggregate consumer demand.

With respect to "intergenerational mobility," the evidence suggests it has not gotten worse, nor has it gotten better. A study of people born between 1971 and 1993 found that "children entering the labor market today have the same chances of moving up in the income distribution (relative to their parents) as children born in the 1970s" (Chetty, et al. 2014). The good news is that social mobility has not declined, despite the trends in income and wealth inequality. The bad news is that it is no better. Mobility is lower in the United States than in nearly any other rich country.

The OECD report recommends four policies to reverse these trends: remove barriers to fair pay and career growth for women; invest in and promote jobs with career tracks and a future, of "stepping stones rather than dead ends"; promote education and skills development, especially for youth; and design government tax and transfer policies for efficiently redistributing income.

The OECD and IMF reports go beyond ethical arguments and document the real-world effects of inequality in terms of lost economic growth. Given the ecological and social critiques of growth given in previous chapters, the irony is obvious. I return to this point in the chapter's conclusion. It is also worth noting another way "less inequality benefits all," one that affects capacities for ecological protection. This is that economic inequality is a political as well as an economic problem. On the state of the bottom 40%, for example, the OECD notes: "When such a large group in the population gains so little from economic growth, the social fabric frays and trust in institutions is weakened" (21). Likewise, the IMF report expresses concern over the erosion of trust and social cohesion, citing research that, under conditions of high inequality, "Conflicts are especially prevalent in the management of common resources where, for example, inequality makes resolving disputes more difficult" (IMF 2015a, 9; this is citing Bardhan 2005).

## The Social Consequences of Inequality

Inequality has other consequences. In *The Spirit Level*, Richard Wilkinson and Kate Pickett (2009) bring together the results of a large number of quantitative, peer-reviewed studies on the effects of income inequality on ten social problems: low social trust, mental illness, life expectancy, infant mortality, obesity, child educational performance, teenage births, homicides, imprisonment rates, and low social mobility. For each, "there is a very strong tendency for ill-health and social problems to occur less frequently in the more equal countries" (19–20). The severity of these problems was related not to average incomes in a country but their distribution. A similar correlation of inequality to social problems exists in US states. They conclude: "The problems in rich countries are not caused by the society not being rich enough (or even too rich) but by the scale of material differences between people within each society being too big" (25). Beyond a point, what matters are not absolute but relative incomes: "where we stand in relation to others in our own society" (25).

The explanations turn on the interactions among individuals and society, specifically in responses to stress induced by threats to status and self-esteem. Low social status is one of three major factors known to affect or reflect "the extent to which we do or do not feel at ease and self-confident with each other." (39) More inequality magnifies the awareness of social status and heightens anxieties about distinctions. Especially worth noting are that (1) inequality increases status competition and anxiety, and (2) it weakens community life and reduces trust. The first is an economic factor and the second a political factor that may affect the capacity for green growth.

The correlation between income inequality and the prevalence of social problems is striking. Overall, Wilkinson and Pickett conclude, "there is a very strong tendency for ill-health and social problems to occur less frequently in the more equal countries" (19–20). Indeed, how a country does in one outcome predicts its performance in others. If it does poorly in health, "you can predict with some confidence that it will also imprison a larger proportion of its population, have more teenage pregnancies, lower literacy scores, more obesity, worse mental health, and so on" (174). They reached similar results in the effects of economic inequality in American states.

Could this inequality effect spill over into ecological performance as well? They suggest that it could. Beyond its effects on social problems, high inequality "weakens community life, reduces trust, and increases violence" (45). It increases social anxiety, impairs social relations, and fuels status competition, all of which may reduce a country's capacity for collective action (51).

Other writers echo these conclusions. The OECD's *In It Together* refers to it in discussing how, with rising inequality, "the social fabric frays and trust in institutions is weakened" (21). Former World Bank chief economist Joseph Stiglitz stresses this phenomenon in *The Price of Inequality: How Today's Divided Society Endangers Our Future* (2012). He challenges the premises of neo-liberal economics and its growth-above-all strategy of low taxation, minimal regulation, and skimpy public spending. Growth was "the rising tide that didn't lift all boats" (4). The "trickle down" economics of the Reagan era is "discredited" (6). Inequality "may be at once cause and consequence of a breakdown in social cohesion over the past four decades" (65). On the economics and politics, he writes: "If the belief takes hold that the political system is stacked, that it's unfair, individuals will feel released from the obligations of civic virtue" (120). The "enormous erosion of trust in recent years" (123) hurts the economy, but "may have even more invidious effects on the functioning of our democracy" (126).

Later I explore how economic (and to a degree political) inequality affects social trust and, in turn, the capacity for collective action. I draw on Eric Uslaner's book on *The Moral Foundations of Trust*, which also reflects the arguments Stiglitz and others have made. Before moving to that discussion, here is another side of ecology–inequality relationships—inequality in the distribution of ecological goods and bads, or what is usually termed *environmental justice*.

## Environmental Justice

For the first few decades of the modern environmental movement (1970s and 1980s) the struggle over the core economy–ecology relationship was the name of the game. It was all about the supposedly inevitable conflicts between growth and efficiency on the one hand, and health and ecology on the other. The distributions of damage from pollution, chemicals, and waste, and the availability of amenities like greenspace or recreational options, were not part of the picture.

Environmentalism took on a third dimension in the 1980s, when a confluence of environmental and racial politics created a new movement. Referred to first as *environmental equity* and at times as *environmental racism*, advocates eventually took *justice* as the foundation of their case that minority and low-income groups had to bear more than their fair share of (that is, "disproportionate") risks from pollution and waste (Baehler 2017; Konisky 2017). The movement began with protests against landfills and other sites but expanded to include risks from lead and toxics, urban air pollution, contaminated fish, pesticide exposures, contaminated drinking water, and multiple, cumulative risks in industrialized areas (Ringquist 2006).

The environmental justice movement in the United States is directed in part at how decisions and processes are biased against minority and poor communities, causing disproportionate health and other impacts. This has led to calls for reforming core processes of standard-setting, permitting, inspections, and enforcement to remove bias. It is aimed at identifying and ameliorating adverse health impacts arising from socioeconomic conditions of minorities and the poor. Examples are the cumulative risks of living in communities with many industrial facilities; housing in which residents are exposed to lead in paint or drinking water; and exposures to urban air pollution. Many of these problems are hard to address; they are rooted in socioeconomic conditions.

That poor minority communities bear more than a proportionate share of harm from pollution and other issues should not come as a surprise. They also deal with lower quality schools, health care, and housing; more crime and unemployment; and less access to healthy food and economic options. They vote at lower rates than more affluent groups, participate less in political decision making, and have less influence. It would be hard to say the environmental justice movement has greatly reduced ecological inequities, given its economic and social basis. It has, however, increased awareness among regulators of the inequities, and it has influenced agency processes (permitting, enforcement) and analyses (risk assessments, cost–benefit analysis). More important, it has enabled minority communities to mobilize more effectively (for an interesting view on the sources of ecological inequality in society, see Freudenberg 2005).

Recent assessments illustrate environmental injustices that are prevalent. Air pollution from ultrafine particulates (of 2.5 micrometers in diameter or less, known as PM 2.5) is a high-concern health risk. Indeed, extremely high levels of particulate matter are causing major health damages in urban areas of growing economies like China and India, which include the most polluted cities in the world. Levels in the United States are much lower but still regarded as a major health risk. A 2012 study from the Yale School of Forestry and Environmental Studies (funded by the National Institute of Environmental Health Sciences) found that minority groups were exposed to significantly more harmful exposures from PM 2.5 than other groups in American society (Bell and Ebisu 2012). This was due not to higher levels of particulates but to the constituents in the particles. As one review of the study put it: "Tiny particles of pollution contain more hazardous ingredients in nonwhite and low-income communities than in affluent white ones . . ." (Katz 2012). Hispanics in particular, but also African and Asian Americans, were exposed to pollutants linked with higher levels of asthma, cardiovascular disease, and cancer. These same groups are more vulnerable to health risks because of the overall levels of social and economic stress in their lives.

There are international dimensions to environmental justice as well. Historically, a great injustice is that countries and groups contributing the least to climate-changing emissions over the past 150 years will suffer most. Critics claim that climate action undermines growth in poor countries. The evidence is otherwise. A World Bank report (2016, 2) concluded recently that "climate change represents a significant obstacle to the sustained eradication of poverty . . ." The poor are more exposed to negative "shocks" from climate change due to their exposure to natural disasters, diseases and pests, and crop failures (because of their dependence on agriculture); they are more vulnerable, because any losses are much more significant relative to their incomes and resources; and they have less financial and other forms of support to shield them from the worst impacts (2016, 4; Provost 2016). Vulnerability to disease alone constitutes a major impact: more pathogens mean malaria and diarrhea; crop failures cause undernutrition. Reduced economic productivity due to hotter weather, the report concludes "could reduce income by several percentage points" (10).

What effect would a green growth scenario have compared to a business-as-usual path? Does green growth have equity consequences that are better or worse than the current trajectory? My case is that, properly conceived, green growth can be a positive for ecological equity, for three reasons. The first is that a green transition—the prerequisite for long-term change—is far more likely, at least in the United States but elsewhere as well, under a green growth framing and policy agenda. Second, finding and implementing positive ecology–economy relationships is the best path to achieving the economic security that helps low-income groups while reducing ecological harm. Third, a green growth framing and policy agenda, if properly conceived, is most likely to reduce economic inequality and, as the rest of the chapter argues, create the political and social conditions that make a green growth path feasible in the long term.

## INEQUALITY AND ECOLOGICAL PROTECTION: EVIDENCE FROM RESEARCH

The discussion so far has considered the state of and trends in inequality in rich countries, economic and social consequences, and environmental justice. Although significant on their own, these topics set the stage for another side of ecology–economy relationships: *What are the effects of inequality on the ability to solve ecological problems?* Do more unequal societies face a steeper climb in getting to green growth? Does inequality affect political capacities for change?

A place to start is with the empirical research on inequality and ecology. For obvious reasons, this research overlaps to a great extent with that on economics from Chapter 3 and governance from Chapter 4. The goal of all this research is to determine what enables some countries to perform better than others, measured in terms of policies adopted or ecological outcomes achieved. Building on the EKC research, experts began to ask why countries at similar income levels were rated differently in their ecological performance. If some level of economic growth could in general enable countries to adopt more effective policies and achieve superior outcomes, why did some still do better than others? Of course, governance capacities, as argued in Chapter 4, are part of the answer. Still, is there something about economic fairness that helps in explaining the variations in ecological policy and performance? Does inequality matter?

Some of the research examines how small communities in developing countries manage *common pool resources*—goods or systems where it is hard or costly to exclude use, such as fisheries, irrigation, or forest systems. Such resources became central to the ecological policy field with publication of Garrett Hardin's 1969 essay on the *tragedy of the commons*. In this parable of ecological degradation, Hardin imagines a village where grass on the commons is shared by all, each with an interest in allowing their cattle to consume it, none having a long-term incentive or mechanism to sustain it. Pursuit of individual self-interest ruins the resource for all, and "the inherent logic of the commons remorselessly generates tragedy" (1968, 162).

Many studies examine local, small-scale situations where "the pursuit of individual material gain in exploiting the commons enters into conflict with the general interest" (Baland, Bardhan, and Bowles 2007, 1). The authors of this collection assert that inequality "does indeed inhibit mutually beneficial approaches to the governance of the commons" (8). Still, the effects of inequality on cooperative relationships vary by the setting and kind of commons being managed. The focus here is on the effects of inequality in large, complex governance systems, at a national or subnational level. The work on locally managed, small-scale commons is relevant, but more relevant is research at a national level.

Elisabetta Magnani (2000) examines how inequality affects environmental expenditures in affluent countries, looking beyond the effects of higher incomes. She finds a "positive absolute income effect and a negative impact of income inequality on environmental protection" (432). In brief, higher incomes are associated with more environmental spending, but high income inequality had the opposite effect. With spending as the dependent variable, it is not surprising that absolute incomes matter. More affluent societies should be more willing and able to commit resources to ecological protection. What also matters, however, is the relative income effect: this offsets positive effects of growth by shifting voter preferences away from ecological quality. She adds: "In high income countries, agents' relative incomes affect preferences over private goods and public goods," such as the environment (441). So the basis for finding that inequality reduces spending is that people value public goods less in more unequal societies.

A later study builds on this research but relies on a more dynamic model that accounts better, the authors say, for a growing economy (Kempf and Rossignol 2007). Their conclusions relate to how income distributions affect perceived trade-offs between growth and ecological protection. They find that the "more unequal a society . . . the more resources will be used to sustain growth despite its negative impact on the state of the environment" (54). Further, "the poorer the median voter, relative to the average agent in the economy, the more deteriorated the environment will be, sacrificed to more physical production . . ." (54) Putting it simply, higher inequality increases demands for economic growth, which in turn causes more ecological stress.

Not all of the research relies on the same mechanisms for understanding inequality and ecology. One study looks how income inequality affects the spread of green technology. Green innovations of various kinds—in renewable energy, battery storage, farming techniques, and so on—are crucial for green growth. This study concluded that affluent consumers have a positive effect on green consumer products, because they buy them and help drive markets. As they state it, although richer and more educated households "consume more and hence can have a worse impact on the environment, they also tend to buy environmentally-friendly products" (Vona and Patriarca 2011, 2202). Think of the early-stage markets for products like the Prius, Chevy Volt, or rooftop solar panels. Using measures like public research and development, turnover rates in ecologically oriented industries, and patent applications, they find, especially in rich countries, that the "more equal countries appear also as the ones having a comparative advantage in developing clean products and methods" (2210). As a result, high incomes support innovation in poorer countries, and greater economic equity enhances it in richer ones.

This variation in the inequality–ecology relationship also came through in a study linking inequality in high-income countries with lower carbon emissions.

As the authors put it, "the terms of the static trade-offs with global warming will tend to improve over time when there is growth with equity, and become more acute under an inequitable growth scenario" (Ravallion, Heil, and Jalan 2000, 667). Less unequal countries performed better than more unequal ones. A more recent climate study of the United States found that income inequality and carbon dioxide emissions "have a positive relationship in both the long- and short-run, suggesting that greater equality of income in the U.S. has a beneficial effect on environmental quality" (Baek and Gweisah 2013).

Several studies focus on political more than economic inequality, and they support the case for negative relationships. James Boyce (1994) stresses power inequities. The political dynamic is that the winners causing the ecological degradation (such as fossil fuel, industrial agriculture, and manufacturing interests) impose costs on the losers (e.g., minority and low-income groups). In this dynamic, political losers either do not know they are being harmed or lack the power to do anything about it. Boyce and co-authors expanded on this theoretical case in their empirical work. A 1999 study (Boyce at al.) found that states with less *political* inequality (Minnesota being the most equal) had stronger ecological policies than the more unequal ones (Mississippi being the most unequal). Their measure of state policies is deficient in many ways, so it is hard to know what to make of these findings, but this a part of the literature on inequality.

Other work finds that "greater inequality in the distribution of power leads to more pollution" (Torras and Boyce 1998, 155). In addition to the case that winners impose costs on the less powerful, this 1998 study emphasizes the role inequality plays in reducing support for public goods. Wealthier people may support public goods less because they can avoid ecological harm through access to private and semiprivate goods like "luxury housing, country clubs and vacation in relatively pollution-free places" (150; also see Boyce 2007 and Torras 2005).

Inequality has been found to be a factor in biodiversity loss. This is documented at a small community level in the research on managing common pool resources (discussed earlier). Less economic inequality creates the social capacity and economic conditions in which more cooperative resource management occurs. This "shows that inequality can thwart the collective action required for environmental protection" (Holland et al. 2009, 1305). At a national scale, Holland and co-authors found that, although a higher country-level GDP is associated with an increased number of threatened species, those "with higher socioeconomic inequity tend to have a greater number of species undergoing population decline" (1301). They conclude that, when there is high inequality, the wealthy are able to insulate themselves from ecological degradation; that can make it difficult to reach agreement and act on shared goals in a society.

Reinforcing this is another national study finding that "states with higher socio-economic inequity tend to have a greater proportion of species undergoing population decline" (Mikkelson 2007, 1306).

In sum, inequality not only is manifest in the distribution of ecological and health risks, as reflected in environmental justice, it may affect ecological policy and outcomes—what may be termed *ecological capacities*—in a society. As Susan Holmberg put it in the pro-environmental site *Grist* in 2015, "it is important to point out that the relationship between the economy and the environment goes both ways." She adds: "We've become more aware that environmental damage can be especially bad for poor people and people of color. What is less obvious is that high economic inequality—in the United States, we're almost at pre–Great Depression levels—is also bad for our environment" (Holmberg 2015). An obvious next challenge is explaining why.

## WHY WOULD ECONOMIC INEQUALITY UNDERMINE ECOLOGICAL PROTECTION?

This review of the research makes a plausible case that economic inequality may impair ecological policy capacities. The issue cannot be said to be settled once and for all; that is not how social science works. But the weight of the evidence *suggests* that inequality and ecology are at odds. I next look at why this may be so.

### Economic and Political Explanations

Economic inequality links with ecology in two ways. One is in promoting behavior that intensifies ecological degradation through resource-intensive consumption (air travel or larger houses), such as by increasing pressures for income growth. The second is in the political effects. Inequality may have consequences for the ability to take collective action that is needed for ecological protection and for attaching value to public goods like clean air or protected land.

The first set of linkages of inequality with ecology are economic, the second political. I distinguish them by an orientation toward either the *economic* or *political* system. The writing and research on the likely effects of inequality suggests the following economic explanations:

*When there is more economic inequality, overall growth rates have to be higher to satisfy public demands.* If growth is spread fairly among all income groups, those at the bottom feel they are making progress, and the prospects for their children to enjoy a better life are positive. If most income goes to the top, and relatively none is going to the bottom, there will be greater pressure to create a larger pie and hope that some of the benefits "trickle down" to the bottom.

The argument applies at both domestic and international levels. In the United States or most other countries, unevenly distributed growth (such as what has occurred over the last three decades) means that much more growth in GDP needs to happen for lower rungs of the economic ladder to benefit. Globally, inequitable growth leads to more growth overall, with the resulting stresses on planetary limits. The latter point is a mainstay of calls for negative growth in rich countries.

*Income growth beyond a point encourages unsustainable levels of consumption by linking it with status in society.* This is where ecological and social critiques of growth converge. Prosperity creates a desire for more affluence. Fred Hirsch viewed this in terms of the *social limits to growth* and its effects in improving human well-being. Part of this phenomenon is the role played by positional goods, like big houses, luxury cars, elite private schools, the latest electronic devices, and so on. Positional goods are valued for what they express about one's status in society rather than for their actual utility. As the Brookings report (2012, 25) put it: they are "goods from which consumers derive utility based on their consumption relative to that of others, rather than from the goods themselves." Such consumption is more likely to occur under conditions of high inequality "and in turn spurs a vicious cycle of ever-greater income inequality" (2012, 25).

Tim Jackson stresses this issue in his analysis of prosperity without growth. It also is related to the research on happiness. Carol Graham notes that, given a choice, most people would rather live in the higher income range in a society than a lower one, even if their absolute income is less. Another connection with happiness research goes to the prospects for upward mobility. People with prospects of moving up the economic ladder "are much more likely to invest in their own and their children's future" than those with lower prospects (Graham 2011, 43). A perceived lack of mobility depresses willingness to invest in the future, not only for education and saving for long-term goals but in investing in ecological protection. People with less mobility have higher discount rates: they undervalue long-term benefits in favor of short-term ones. This tendency exacerbates the governance challenges of short-termism presented in Chapter 4.

In comparison, political explanations for the linkages between economic inequality and ecological protection turn on the effects of skewed income and wealth distributions on the capacity to manage ecological problems. The focus here is not economic behavior but the realm of politics. Two explanations for how inequality undermines ecological capacities come to mind.

*Economic inequality leads to social mistrust that undermines capacities to solve such collective action problems as pollution, habitat destruction, and other ecological degradation.* The logic here is that economic inequality leads to social mistrust and distance, which in turn makes it difficult to agree on shared goals and to act for the general good. These linkages are established empirically in the social science literature outside of the ecological policy domain and are supported by some of the studies reviewed earlier in the chapter. This is not just an ecological capacity issue: it may be that the polarization and dysfunction in US politics is related to the pattern of rising inequality in recent decades. But our focus here is on ecological policy.

*Income inequality enables those high in income and wealth to insulate themselves from the effects of ecological harm, which reduces political support for ecological public goods.* In economic terms, the wealthy or highly affluent have resources to escape or manage negative externalities associated with air and water pollution, legacy risks like lead or old waste sites, land degradation, and so on. This is not unique to the ecological domain; the more affluent have the financial resources to avoid public schools, buy higher than generally available health care, live in neighborhoods with low crime rates and fewer social problems, and avoid many health risks. By not having to rely on public goods, the top of the income and wealth ladders have less incentive to promote policies that invest in and expand the availability of public goods.

Robert Reich describes this trend. The wealthy have "moved into office parks and gated communities, and relied increasingly on private security guards instead of public police, private spas and clubs rather than public parks and pools, and private schools (or elite public ones in their own upscale communities) for their children rather than the public schools most other children attend" (2011, 22/23). He adds: "The adjective 'public' in public services has come to mean 'inadequate'" (23).

*Inequality in income and wealth leads to skewed distributions of power, and higher income groups are able to impose health and ecological costs on the less powerful.* This is the case of James Boyce and colleagues. They argue that the wealthy do value ecological protection less than lower income groups. This is a questionable assumption. Indeed, Lyle Scruggs, author of a comprehensive analyses of national performance discussed earlier, is skeptical of the idea that "the wealthy and powerful systematically prefer more environmental destruction" (1998, 262). Environmental advocacy often comes from the middle and upper classes, he argues, who may prefer better ecological quality. He calls for research on "how income and power are related to preferences for public goods" (272) to expand our understanding of the role of inequality.

These are some ways economic inequality may promote ecological degradation. All may have merit. The effects of status composition and positional goods matter, especially if they fail to deliver more happiness or sense of well-being. People at opposite ends of the income spectrum may value public goods like ecological protection differently, although more evidence is needed. Skewed distributions of political power favor the beneficiaries of pollution over the victims, as the environmental justice literature shows.

## Zeroing In on a Political Explanation

In sum, there are many plausible explanations for why more unequal societies could have less of a capacity for ecological protection and, by extension, for green growth. Economists tend, naturally, to stress economic behavior. Certainly the effects of status competition and the role of positional goods matter. Affluence on its own plays a role, as some research suggests (Aamaas, Borken-Kleefeld, and Peters 2013; Bastien and de Haan 2009), but affluence along with high inequality in distributions of income and wealth may magnify these tendencies. Inequality also adds to growth pressures that, if not accompanied by efforts to reduce ecological impacts (such by conserving water), bring us closer to ecological and resource limits. Still, *untangling the effects of affluence from the marginal impacts of differing levels of inequality* deserves attention.

In this section, I focus on one of the political explanations that could be critical: high inequality generates social mistrust that undermines collective action. I begin with the evidence in Eric Uslaner's *The Moral Foundations of Trust* (2002). He goes in depth on issues alluded to in OECD's *In It Together*, Stiglitz's *The Price of Inequality*, and elsewhere: the effects of economic inequality on social trust and cohesion and thus on capacities for collective action.

It is first worth laying out some terminology. *Collective action* issues apply to situations in which two or more people work together for a satisfactory outcome (Ostrom 1990 and 2000). Themes in collective action writing are why and under what conditions people cooperate, even when there are short-term incentives not to; why they put the common good on a par with or above individual self-interest; and why they accept the benefits of collective action without contributing (free-riding). Collective action is critical for ecological protection, which requires that particular, short-term interests often must be subordinated to general, longer-term ones.

Katharina Holzinger offers a broad, simple definition of collective action as "the joint actions of a number of individuals which aim to achieve and distribute some gain through co-ordination or co-operation" (2003, 2). Protecting people from air and water pollution, mitigating climate change, keeping harmful chemicals off the market, protecting critical ecosystems—all require collective action. Collective action, as in instituting a new policy such as a carbon tax, creates winner and losers, and the potential losers may be expected to oppose the policy change.

The goal of green growth is to promote the general and long term over the particular and near term. The discussion now turns to the question of inequality and its effects on collective action.

A key distinction is that between *moral* and *strategic* trust in society. Strategic trust is based on experience; someone knows you delivered on your commitments in the past and trusts you to continue. Yet experience matters only when there is a relationship with and knowledge of others. For those of us who have argued for building more trust into the regulatory system, the concern is with strategic trust, where actors in recurring relationships are willing to share information and take political risks (Fiorino 2006). At a societal level, for most of the world, we lack such experience, and trust is based on something else. We cannot trust strangers based on experience, so trust rests on moral rather than strategic foundations. Trusting strangers means to accept them into our "moral community" in which we assume most people are good and well-intentioned.

"Moralistic trust is the belief that others share your fundamental moral values and therefore should be treated as you would wish to be treated by them" (Uslaner 2002, 18). In practical terms, moral trust is *generalized rather than particularized* and varies by background and world view. Generalized trust is based on optimism; it is reflected in positive expectations about the future, a sense of control over one's fate, and anti-authoritarian (non-hierarchical) values. These, in turn, are associated with factors like a nurturing family background and parents having high generalized trust. Collective experiences also shape trust. People coming of age in the civil rights era of the 1960s exhibit higher generalized trust, studies have shown; they shared an experience and a time when American society became fairer and more inclusive. Group experiences also affect trust, which is lower among groups that have faced discrimination.

The state of moral/generalized trust in a society has many consequences for governance and thus for ecological performance. Lack of trust tends to undermine capacities for collective action, political cooperation, and shared goals and purpose. Among the social and political benefits of higher trust levels in a society are an open, inclusive spirit sympathetic to those seen as being less fortunate; more support for redistributing wealth; a more responsive and efficient government; stronger legal systems; less corruption; and openness to free trade (Uslaner 2002, 218, 242). Trusting societies are more tolerant than low-trust ones, less xenophobic, stronger on women's rights, and more likely to support shared public goods like ecological well-being and quality.

Low trust fuels political polarization that affects the ability to deal with collective action problems, including ecological protection. The most important influence on trust, the evidence demonstrates, is fairness in the distribution of income. Low trust creates social distance; this in turn reduces optimism about the future and affects feelings regarding the ability to influence it. Based on an analysis of opinion polling and research on societal trust, Uslaner concludes that "*collectively* the level of trust in a society depends on how economic goods are distributed" (162). Income levels have no effect independent of income distribution. "What matters is not how rich a country is, but how equitable is the dispersion of income" (181). He concludes: "the more equitable the distribution of wealth in a country, the more trusting its people will be" (230).

Additional research by Uslaner and others confirms the relationships among economic inequality, social trust, and capacities for collective action (an example is Rothstein and Uslaner 2005). A great deal of evidence supports the conclusion that "the roots of generalized trust lie in a more equitable distribution of resources and opportunities in a society," and "inequality stands at the beginning of the causal chain" (Rothstein and Uslaner 2005, 44). Low-inequality states, such as Nordic countries, exhibit higher generalized trust and strong ecological performance: "*Inequality is the strongest determinant of generalized trust over time in the United States and across the American states*" (48; italics in the original). High-trust countries are more optimistic about the future and more likely to share among citizens a sense of common destiny and values, both of which are positives for developing consensus and acting on major societal goals (52).

In explaining causes of a "presentist" bias in public policy (a preference for the present over the future, and an impediment to ecological protection), Jonathan Boston finds "increasing evidence that the level of income and wealth inequality in a society affects inter-temporal preferences and the policy-making environment" (2017, 94). The kind of consensus matters: a consensus that "environmental 'goods' should regularly be subordinated to short-term economic imperatives will ultimately undermine a country's long-term environmental and economic sustainability" (2017, 93). With respect to the economy, he cites the evidence on how an increase in a country's Gini coefficient diminishes growth, and that "Slower economic growth, in turn, is likely to undermine social cohesion, reduce social capital and intensify political divisions" (94).

This research has several implications. Economic inequality as measured by the Gini is rising in many high-income countries, but the United States has shown a particular trend that may help to explain political polarization and gridlock, especially since the financial crisis and recession. This polarization extends across many policy areas, including health care and immigration, as well as ecological issues, with their status as public goods and the short-term/long-term trade-offs involved. With a weak sense of shared purpose, limited concern for the well-being of others in society, and lesser focus on longer-term issues, an increasingly unequal country like the United States faces challenges in dealing climate change, water security, habitat protection, and similar issues. Indeed, sharp party divisions on ecological issues may be, in part, a result of income disparities.

Another implication is that we should emphasize the forms growth takes, and not just the fact of growth itself. My view is that a no-growth or de-growth agenda is infeasible politically, risky economically, and socially unfair. Issues with growth should be addressed by changing its form and addressing its negative impacts, the ecological prime among them, rather than with a blunt no-growth agenda. The inequality–trust–environment relationship strengthens the case for making fairness in the distribution of incomes and wealth a part of the green agenda. Although inequality has been on the more radical green agenda for some time (e.g., Cato 2009), that was mostly for ideological and ethical reasons. There also is a case for reducing inequality on practical, empirical grounds.

Finally, the evidence on inequality and trust should be considered in policy research on ecological performance. The relatively strong performance of countries like Norway, Sweden, Denmark, and Finland may in part be a result of high trust, which in turn may be a result of low inequality. Although there is some evidence of a link between inequality and the environment, the mediating role of trust is relatively unexamined. Some forms of social capital may matter more than others. That some studies (for example, Dulal et al. 2011) find little correlation between membership in clubs and organizations and ecological performance is consistent with Uslaner's findings. The trust thesis also sheds light on the relationship studied so extensively in the EKC research, particularly on effects of democracy. It may be that trust reinforces democracy's positive effects. The positive effects of growth may well be affected by income distributions and fairness in wealth concentrations, not just their absolute levels.

The trust thesis also suggests a combination of cultural and social characteristics that may be associated with a capacity for ecological protection and the ability to create economy–ecology synergies. High-trust societies display more concern for the future and the sense that it may be influenced. In the United States, for example, the belief that climate change is occurring but not much can be done about it could be a product of those having low trust. High-trust societies are more open to women having a role in politics and society, which also supports ecological values. High-trust societies may be more open to using evidence, developing consensus on societal goals, and harnessing the collective action needed to achieve them. This chapter uses the analysis in Uslaner's book to make the case for reducing inequality as a path for greener growth.

The last word (for now) on the political effects of inequality is from Robert Reich in his 2011 book, *Aftershock: The Next Economy and America's Future*, where he wrote (3):

at some point inequality becomes so wide it causes a society to fracture. Average people become so frustrated and fearful they become easy prey for demagogues hurling blame at anyone or any group that's a convenient scapegoat. Politics disintegrates into name-calling.

Given the tone and results of the 2016 US presidential election, this is remarkably prescient. Political analyst Thomas Edsall (2016) makes a similar point on the outcome of that election.

## CONCLUSIONS ON INEQUALITY, ECOLOGY, AND GREEN GROWTH

The theme of this chapter is that economic inequality and its effects on ecological protection have been neglected. Reducing it may enhance prospects for green growth. Inequality matters not just in terms of the distribution of health and ecological harm in society, as captured in the concept of environmental justice; it also works the other way by diminishing performance and policy capacities. Some of the inequality effects relate to economic behavior, such as increasing pressures for growth or, more importantly, fueling status consumption via positional goods. Others affect social and political behavior in a society.

In sum, economic inequality may have pernicious effects on ecological quality. These effects are not distinct to ecology and health. Societies attaching low value to public goods and having weak capacities for collective action are unlikely to be particularly good at adopting clean energy; restructuring water, energy, transportation, agricultural sectors; or preserving habitat.

One issue coming out of the discussion in this chapter is the positive effect economic equity has on economic growth. This is primarily a result of opportunities in a more equal society to gain the skills and knowledge needed to succeed in modern economies. This may be a problem for anyone advocating growth limits for ecological purposes. But is growth a negative if it develops capabilities and allows people to flourish? Is growth that simply goes to high-income groups the same—ethically and practically—as growth that is distributed fairly across society? This is why I argue in Chapter 3 that we be neutral about growth: how and why we grow, with what effects, should be what matters and not the reality or facts of economic growth itself.

The irony of contemporary American politics, of course, is that opponents of green growth and ecological protection base their opposition on the negative economic effects, which the evidence demonstrates is highly questionable. Yet they ignore the compelling evidence that economic inequality in a society actually does impede economic as well as ecological prospects and performance.

Whether as a cause or an effect, inequality is rooted in socioeconomic conditions in a society. From a justice perspective, asking agencies to reduce disproportionate health and ecological impacts is like telling public school officials that they have to correct for all sources of inequity in their neighborhood. They can help at the margin, but the root causes are beyond their control. Similarly, achieving ecological protection and green rather than brown growth depends not just in ecological investments and strategies but also socioeconomic conditions. This is why, in the last two chapters, reducing economic inequality is part of the green growth policy agenda.

This chapter's theme is economic inequality, and indirectly political inequality. It did not deal directly with other forms, notably intergenerational and gender equity. This is a matter of focus, not of priority, because both are crucial. As for generational equity, trust is associated with optimism and concern about the future. As for gender, changes in the status of women link positively with ecology, beyond a leveling of birth rates in poor countries. There is evidence, for example, that having women in positions of power leads to better ecological policies and outcomes. One study found: "Our most consistent result is that gender inclusiveness is associated with cross-country differences in environmental performance" (Dulal, Foa, and Knowles 2011, 136). Women are more supportive of public health and ecology and more sensitive to social issues like equity. Indeed, in seven of eleven nations surveyed, the Pew Research Center (2015c) found that "women are more likely to consider climate change a serious problem, be concerned it will harm them seriously and say that major lifestyle changes are needed to solve them."

Where does this leave us with the two hypothetical countries that opened the chapter? Other things equal, we would expect the country with the low Gini, and thus much lower levels of economic inequality, to be more ecologically progressive and better suited for making choices that support a transition to green growth, for economic *and* political reasons.

Without a doubt, the unequal impacts of ecological problems are a major normative and practical issue. In this sense, inequality begets inequality: the larger exposure of the poor to climate risks, ecological degradation, harmful air pollution, and loss of crucial resources like water and topsoil means they will suffer not only now but in the future. What has been neglected is the other side of inequality—of the ways economic (and as a consequence political) inequality affects the capacity in the more economically developed countries to recognize, act on, and manage ecological issues. In the language of social science, my thesis is that economically unequal societies attach less value to public goods and are less capable of collective action. In everyday terms, shared goals, mutual trust, and cooperation are difficult to achieve in more unequal societies.

Although a green transition involves many economic, governance, and social factors, there still is the matter of what strategies, investments, and tools make up the green growth policy agenda. In many ways, it draws upon the standard ecological toolkit; it differs in others. The *policy agenda* for green growth is rich and dynamic and offers many options. It will help to examine it before moving to the politics of and prospects for green growth in Chapters 7 and 8.

# The Green Growth Policy Agenda

From the end of the Second World War until the break-up of the Soviet Union in the early 1990s, US foreign and defense policies were embodied in a framing concept known as the Cold War. The story line or mental map of the Cold War was that two dominant military powers in the world, the United States and Soviet Union, were engaged in a titanic, life-or-death struggle to make their ideology and worldview triumphant over the other. In symbolic terms, this was seen as a battle between democratic capitalism and authoritarian communism. In practical political terms, it was a confrontation of two alliances: the United States and its Western European, British Commonwealth, and Japanese allies on the one side, and the Soviet Union with its Eastern bloc and ideological affiliates on the other. At stake, among other things, was the support and future of so-called third world countries in Latin American, Asia, and Africa. Although the mutually assured destructive threat of nuclear weapons enabled the superpowers to avoid a direct hot war, despite close calls in Cuba and Berlin, regional proxy wars in places like Korea and Vietnam were fought.

The influence of the Cold War as a framing concept at a strategic and policy level is readily apparent. US foreign and military policy was based on a strategy of "containment" in which communist influence would not be allowed to spread. Defense spending and strategy were aimed at maintaining superiority over the Soviets in a constant arms race. Investments in education, space exploration, economic growth, and technology typically were justified on the basis of their role in winning the Cold War. Even the massive interstate highway system built starting in the late 1950s was justified on national security grounds. Intelligence and diplomacy were based on winning the struggle without direct conflict.

The Cold War was an especially powerful framing concept that guided US policy for five decades, until the collapse of the Soviet Union made it no longer relevant. In this case, as with any influential framing concept, that of the Cold

War played out in major ways in the worlds of policy, politics, and military competition. The concept thus may be seen at two levels: (1) as a framing that defined foreign and defense issues in the second half of the century, and (2) as a set of principles, goals, and relationships on which many policies and investments were founded.

The same may be said of any successful framing concept: it matters only if governments and other key actors in society use it as a basis for making decisions, directing investments, setting priorities, devising incentives, and planning for the future. Green growth is having some impact as a reframing concept. That major entities like the World Bank, OECD, and UNEP, and many national governments use it is a clear sign of its influence. This chapter focuses on green growth at a practical level—as a policy agenda, a menu of policy tools, strategies, principles, and indicators that translate the concept into ways of solving ecological and other problems.

For green growth to matter in the world of policy and politics, two conditions have to be met. First, strategies must exist for translating the framing concept into policy change. Second, those strategies must be adopted and implemented. This chapter considers the first condition. A rich set of strategies and policies exists for applying green growth in practice. Chapters 7 and 8 consider the second condition, of putting the policies into effect. This second one is far from being met. Overcoming the political barriers of particular interests and short-termism is a major challenge.

As the OECD stated in 2011, "what matters for the success of a green growth strategy is a well-defined framework for action and a consistent set of economic and environmental policy criteria" (2011, 13). I begin with a brief history of the ecological policy agenda in the United States. Next is a look at how a green growth agenda differs from a conventional one, then at the principles, tools, and indicators that make up the green growth agenda. The last section considers criticisms.

Three themes define this chapter. One is the array of strategies and policies available for green growth. In many ways, green growth builds upon conventional ecological policy agendas, with a reliance on ambient, technology, and performance standards and regulatory oversight. In other ways, it is distinctive. A range and variety of creative policy approaches are available—if they are used. To succeed, these should be combined creatively, respond to social and political conditions, and align with the settings in which they are applied (Howlett 2005).

A second theme is that many assessments of the aspects of a green growth agenda are colored by ideological bias, from both the left and the right. An illustration is carbon trading. Critics from the left often attack it, because it incorporates certain market principles in its design and operations, while they assert that market deficiencies are at the root of most ecological problems. Critics from the right assail carbon trading for its costs to society in the form of lost competitiveness, jobs, and growth. Both are mostly wrong and reflect a misunderstanding of carbon trading (and other forms of trading, for that matter) or a failure (often deliberate, to be sure) to consider the full range of effects in the use of such programs. If we are to sustain a reasonable quality of life while respecting ecological limits, we need to get past ideological and political biases and determine what works, is fair, and is politically and economically acceptable.

A third theme reflects a point made at the end of the last chapter: ecological policies, the subject at hand, are only part of the overall policy agenda for achieving green growth—the proverbial tip of the iceberg. As the preceding chapters argued, many economic, governance, political, and social factors affect ecological performance and the capacity for ecology–economy synergies. Economic development, the composition of the economy, cultural conceptions of happiness and well-being, patterns of policymaking, regime types, electoral rules and representation, the extent of economic and political inequality, levels of trust—all of these matter. Still, it helps to examine the policy agenda before moving on to politics of and prospects for green growth in Chapters 7 and 8. After all, the tip of the iceberg is still part of its structure.

## A BRIEF HISTORY OF THE ECOLOGICAL POLICY AGENDA

Much of the green growth agenda will be familiar to students of ecological policy. Many kinds of standards—ambient, technology, and performance—are staples in the portfolio. Often the most direct and effective approach to a problem is to specify a best available technology or an emissions rate (such as a limit on carbon dioxide emitted per unit of energy generated) and use legal authority to compel sources to meet them. What are known as *ambient standards* are pervasive in conventional ecological policies. They embody limits by defining science-based targets for protecting public health or ecological resources. US examples are the National Ambient Air Quality Standards (NAAQS) for protecting public health, and state Water Quality Standards for defining allowable levels of pollution consistent with uses of water resources.

As with a conventional agenda, substances, products, or technologies are banned or restricted. Some of these may be determined to be too hazardous to human health or ecological resources and taken out of commerce, or as much as is feasible. Examples historically are DDT (one of the first chemicals banned by the newly created US Environmental Protection Agency in the 1970s), asbestos, dioxin, and polychlorinated biphenyls (PCBs), all of which have been for the most part banned. Many policies correct or manage so-called legacy issues, such as abandoned waste sites, lead in drinking water supply lines, or cleaning up Department of Energy nuclear weapons sites around the country. The costs of fixing legacy problems are generally very high; avoiding them in the future is a priority in any policy agenda and is far more cost-effective.

What is termed *direct regulation* was a mainstay in the early years of ecological policy (Fiorino 1995; Portney and Stavins 2000). Embodied in such laws as the Clean Air Act, Clean Water Act, Resource Conservation and Recovery Act, Safe Drinking Water Act, Endangered Species Act, and others, these regulatory acts relied on a process of setting ambient, technology, or performance standards; monitoring compliance via inspections, reporting, and recordkeeping; and taking enforcement action when that becomes necessary. As suggested earlier, that model worked reasonably well, although far from perfectly. Some of the best results have been in air quality and point-source water quality, in cleaning up waste sites, and in preventing many new ones. There is less progress elsewhere, like for nonpoint source water and air toxics (Kraft 2015).

Whatever the results to date, it is misleading simply to extrapolate from the early policy success of the United States and assume the same model will work just as well in the future. The solutions of the 1970s are not necessarily the best ones for the future, given the changes that have occurred in problems, economic-political relationships, technologies, and governance (Fiorino 2006; Durant, Fiorino, and O'Leary 2004 and 2017). It makes sense to think of new governance capacities and tools needed for dealing with climate change, water security, ecosystem stress, and nanotechnologies.

A useful perspective is Daniel Mazmanian and Michael Kraft's depiction (2009) of three environmental epochs (which I view as policy or governance epochs). Each "is characterized by a dominant way of defining 'the' environmental problem . . . which in turn leads to a set of policy goals, the use of certain implementation strategies, and other features that must be considered together to capture the essence of an epoch" (7). Policymakers move from one epoch to another, although usually without "fully replacing them—along with the confusion and complexity such progression leads to" (2009, 7). Indeed, each epoch may be seen as an overlay on what already existed.

The first epoch, of *regulating for environmental protection*, began with the creation of the EPA and passage of the clean air and water acts in the early 1970s. The key aspects are a reliance on technology-based rules, fragmented definitions of problems and solutions, a focus on the end-of-pipe rather than the causes of pollution, and emphasis on legal compliance. Beginning in the 1980s, there came a second epoch based on *efficiency-based regulatory reform and flexibility*, in which policymakers aim for more cost-effective strategies, give attention to ecological as well as health issues, strive to prevent pollution rather than just control it, begin to incorporate emissions trading and other market-like incentive approaches, and seek collaborative ways to make decisions. Since the early 1990s, there has been a slow, still unfinished transition to an epoch of *sustainability*, which adopts a more holistic and global perspective, seeks to balance human and natural systems, aims for solutions on a broad or sectoral basis, and views the problems in the context of limited sources, sinks, and services and of future generations.

That each epoch is overlaid on the previous one is clear from experience. Despite the innovations introduced since the 1970s, regulatory strategies still dominate national ecological policy. The policy reforms of the 1980s, such as emissions trading and information disclosure, were overlaid on what already existed (Fiorino 2014c). As was discussed in the first chapter, the transition to sustainability is occurring largely at the local level, with little change nationally. If the findings of comparative research discussed in Chapter 4 are valid, it is fair to conclude that the fragmented, adversarial, and legalistic features of US policy, especially as they play out at a national level, pose formidable obstacles to adopting and implementing a green growth agenda.

A transition from the first to the second epoch is evident in the 1980s and 1990s. There was growing interest in new strategies and policy tools in the second epoch. This epoch emerged for many reasons. One was experience. Evidence of the costs of technology-based regulation and the difficulties agencies faced in anticipating the leading but still economically feasible technologies for controlling pollution led to new tools and analytical methods. When the Clean Water Act was revised in 1987, for example, difficulties in controlling nonpoint sources of pollution, such as farm runoff and urban storm water, led to the adoption of new strategies for those forms of pollution (Rosenbaum 2017, 221–226).

Other reasons for rethinking ecological policies were political and practical. In one of the cycles that have defined US ecological politics, a regulatory backlash set in, during the 1980s. At the same time, an awareness of changing problems and a need for new approaches stimulated policy innovations. Enthusiasm from the first epoch ran up against the political conservativism of the Ronald Reagan administration; worries about economic growth and energy; and a governing philosophy (neo-liberalism) focused on small government, low tax rates, and private markets (Layzer 2012).

Whatever the causes, there was a great deal of innovation in the ecological policy agenda during these years (Chertow and Esty 1997). The origins of emissions and effluent trading—by now standard elements in the green growth agenda—may be found in developments in air policy in the late 1970s and 1980s, all of which culminated in the acid rain allowance trading provisions of the 1990 Clean Air Act Amendments. Beginning as community right-to-know laws following the 1984 Bhopal chemical disaster in India, mandatory information disclosure made industrial firms inform communities of harmful chemicals stored on or released from their sites (Kraft, Stephan, and Abel 2011; Durant 2017). These were codified as the Toxics Release Inventory (TRI) in the reauthorized Superfund law (the authority for cleaning up old waste sites) in 1986. The concept of pollution prevention became prominent (Geiser 2004), as did consensus-based approaches and adaptive ecosystem management (Layzer and Schulman 2017).

The second epoch was a period of innovation in analytical methods as well. Concerns about the risks from chemicals, products, and technologies expanded in the 1970s and 1980s. Policymakers needed a way to differentiate among the more and the less serious concerns, both to set priorities and determine what protective action to take (Kraft 2017; Fiorino 1990). The practice of risk assessment—of estimating hazards times the exposures and evaluating human and ecological risk—was refined to meet this need (National Research Council 1983). Somewhat more controversially, methods for estimating and comparing costs and benefits also became prominent in ecological policy in the 1980s. In a series of executive orders, cost–benefit analysis was required for major policies with the direction that, when laws permit, the benefits should exceed the costs.

In sum, the notion of the first two policy epochs fits the evolution in US ecological policy nicely. A first epoch of direct regulation, legal instruments, technology requirements, and a focus on large, visible sources was followed by a second one of new problem definitions, diverse tools, and emphasis on risk and economics. Some experts are wary of many innovations emerging in this second epoch; others (including myself) see evidence of useful policy learning coming out of it (Fiorino 2001). The idea of a third, sustainability epoch defines a major, needed transition for ecological policy, but one that is yet to occur nationally. Although EPA tried (National Research Council 2011) to shift more to the sustainability epoch, it has had to contend with fragmented authorities, competing agency missions across government, and a lack of consensus for change.

Signs of a transition to the third epoch are found in many cities. Sometimes using the term *sustainability*, at times *smart growth, green growth*, or simply *quality of life*, cities like Portland (Oregon), Seattle, and San Francisco are joined by big cities like New York and Chicago and smaller ones like Boulder, Colorado and Santa Monica, California in moving into a sustainability epoch (Portney 2013). They reflect green growth in seeking positive ecology–economy outcomes and integrating housing, energy, transport, land, and water policies (Slavin 2011).

Several aspects of this brief history shed light on the green growth agenda. One is the continuity and change in US ecological policy over the last five decades. Regulation, often technology-based, was the strategy for the first epoch and remains prominent, while many policy and analytical innovations also were incorporated into the mix. Another lesson is how economic and political trends shape policy agendas; similar factors influence the evolution of the green growth agenda and its applications. Third, the variety of tools available and lessons from their use offer a rich green growth agenda. I turn now to what is distinctive about green growth.

## WHAT IS DISTINCTIVE ABOUT THE GREEN GROWTH AGENDA?

Do ideas matter for public policy? John Maynard Keynes once wrote that "Madmen in authority, who hear voices in the air, are distilling their frenzy from some academic scribbler of a few years back" (1936, 383) Most changes of consequence in ecological policy over the last half-century may indeed be traced to some sort of intellectual influence, even if the scribblers were not always academic, and those in authority not necessarily madmen. The concept of the *environment* was typically not used to refer to nature and human interactions with it until the 1960s. The 2009 Affordable Care Act in the United States may be traced back to debates from the 1990s. The intellectual roots of key aspects of the Cold War often are traced to diplomat George Kennan's famous "X memorandum" from *Foreign Affairs* in 1947. And of course, the intellectual anchor of modern economic policy goes back to Keynes himself.

Chapter 2 examined several sources of influence on the emergence of the green growth concept. These influences include academic thinkers in ecological modernization and ecological economics, among others, as well as the more applied analysis and strategic thinking in business and eco-efficiency. For some people, the Keynes of green growth may have been the authors of the *Blueprint* series; for others it may be someone more along the lines of Amory Lovins or, from the steady-state economy perspective, Herman Daly. Others might point to the recent, mainstream expressions from sources like UNEP, the OECD, and the World Bank. I draw upon many such sources in outlining the green growth agenda, stressing what is feasible in the US policy system.

What distinguishes a green growth agenda? How does it differ from standard approaches to organizing problems and solutions? Although it reflects much of the existing agenda, green growth differs in that it (1) adopts an alternative ecology–economy framing; (2) applies in a broader scope and longer time frames; (3) seeks integrated strategies; (4) focuses on the sources of problems; and (5) draws on diverse tools, including market-like tools applied by government.[1]

## Ecology–Economy Relationships

A green growth policy agenda differs most significantly from a standard one in *framing ecology–economy relationships*. The standard approach is based on the assumption of nearly unavoidable conflicts among two sets of goals. As a consequence, policy choices are structured around avoiding negative impacts of one kind or the other. Protect the environment, but without imposing unacceptable levels of economic harm. Pursue growth, business profitability, and economic success, but in ways that do not pose too much of a threat to human health and ecosystems. As presented Chapter 3, the objective is to avoid unacceptable outcomes rather than to seek outcomes for maximizing positive ecology–economic interactions.

In contrast, a green growth policy agenda seeks, but may not always find, positive relationships. Issues are framed to *maximize positives*, not to *minimize negatives*. Consider, for example, if UNEP's proposed 2% global GDP investment target actually were to be met. Such a redirection of resources, if well-directed and consistent over time, would deliver major benefits in terms of a greener economy and growth. The old approach takes the investment as a given; green growth looks first to investments as tools for achieving mutually beneficial outcomes.

This objective of seeking complementary or synergistic ecology–economy relationships is evident in policies associated with a green growth agenda. Energy, water, and material efficiency are obvious cases: less resource use, less pollution and waste, and lower costs. Eco-efficiency is an obvious enabler of green growth. Many critics on the left dismiss it as a partial fix that does not solve the long-term problem, given the reality of exponential growth. Still, a partial fix is better than none. A shift away from fossil fuel power sources to renewables like wind, solar, and geothermal offers positive-sum options. As prices of renewables fall, they compete with fossil fuels. If we account for social costs, the positive-sum is stronger. Shifting from nonrenewable to renewable sources reduces unhealthy pollution, cuts carbon, promotes new technology, creates new markets, and creates jobs with more labor-intensive investments.

In seeking to maximize positives more than minimize negatives, this agenda reflects thinking in the sustainability field. The best expression analytically is the OECD's *Guidance on Sustainability Impact Assessment* (OECD 2010). Of the ten steps in such an assessment, most critical is *identifying conflicts, synergies, and trade-offs*. "Once the potential impacts of a proposed policy have been enumerated," the *Guidance* directs, "the next step is to identify the major synergies, conflicts or trade-offs across the economic, environmental, and social domains" (22). Of course, conflicts and trade-offs exist. Still, green growth policymaking is designed around a search for potential ecology–economy and even social win–wins.

## Timing and Scope

Another difference between a green growth and a conventional policy agenda lies in the scope of and time frames for decision making. The typical approach, at least in the United States, relies on a narrow framing of decisions. Someone wants to build a road in a protected area: What are the impacts on habitat, species, and recreation? Should the road be built? Can it be designed and built in less ecologically damaging ways? Conversely, consider when an agency issues a rule limiting water pollution discharges: What are the economic effects? Does it mean less employment, higher costs, or firm closures? Decisions are framed narrowly as they emerge, not as part of larger strategic choices. It is harder to achieve positive-sum solutions when choices are framed narrowly and analyzed only in the short term.

Climate mitigation illustrates how scope and timing may enable positive-sum outcomes. A standard approach takes the existing patterns of power generation and consumer behavior as a given and seeks solutions within that constraint. This is typical in laws like the Clean Air Act: identify the source of problems—say, coal-fired power plants—and select the best technology for controlling them. An alternative is to adopt a broader scope by looking at the entire system of power generation and, through efficiency and conservation, reducing electricity demand. As for time frame, consumers may face near-term price hikes but realize long-term savings from energy efficiency.

Both the scope and time frame for decisions matter, but they present challenges. One is cognitive. The broader the range of variables being evaluated, the more complex and uncertain are the choices. Even more difficult are challenges of accountability. Politics does not deal well with long time frames, as fights over climate change reveal (Boston 2017). We have a general idea of the long-term costs and benefits of acting now to offset climate change later (Stern 2007), as well as of the benefits of renewable energy. Yet, justifying transition costs now for benefits later is a tough political sell, as Democratic politicians from the coal-reliant Midwest probably would agree.

## Policy Integration

Green growth differs in yet a third respect—its emphasis on policy integration. This is most obvious in ecology–economy issues, where green growth gets its meaning. Central to finding positive-sum synergies is a need to integrate—taking separate issues and combining them. At the highest level, green growth aims to integrate what historically have been the two separate and competing domains of ecology and economy. Governments have dealt with economic issues far longer than ecological ones, so this does not come easily (Lafferty and Hoven 2003; Jordan and Lenschow 2008).

US ecological policy is often described as fragmented, or the opposite of integrated (Davies and Mazurek 1998). This fragmentation extends well beyond ecology and economy. Economic and social issues combine with ecological ones in complex ways: Air pollution is a result of energy production and use, movement of people and goods, and making cars or steel. Water pollution is caused by construction, farming, energy production, and land use. Each involves a complex set of interactions among diverse economic sectors. Yet they are governed by different laws and a variety of agencies that often have competing policy agendas.

The reasons for this fragmentation are administrative and political. On the first, the practice in responding to complex tasks is to rely on bureaucratic organization. The ideal type of bureaucracy was defined over a century ago by Max Weber: hierarchy, rules, procedures, specialization, division of labor, and so on. The heart of a bureaucratic strategy is to break complex problems into small parts to make them manageable. Politically, especially in the pluralistic United States, strategies emerge incrementally as they are recognized, draw political support, and elicit a government response. Even in the environmental decade of the 1970s, ecological policy emerged piecemeal, as a series of targeted interventions, not as an integrated strategy. Despite these barriers, green growth aims for integration. Countries like the Netherlands and Sweden achieved a degree of policy integration in recent years; this is challenging in the United States.

## Sources Rather Than Manifestations of Problems

It is odd that in the green growth literature we rarely, if ever, hear mention of pollution prevention. This became an influential concept in the 1980s and was integral to the second epoch (Geiser 2004). It was incorporated into law in 1990 in the Pollution Prevention Act; many states enacted laws in pushing for prevention, Massachusetts and New Jersey being leaders. Pollution prevention is the best green growth strategy that rarely gets mentioned. It asserts that we should reduce pollution at the source rather than the point at which it is released. What is impressive about the concept for our purposes is that it may lead to many positive ecology–economy synergies.

Energy illustrates this point. A lot of money, technology, and effort in the last five decades have gone to cutting emissions to protect public health and welfare, as the Clean Air Act authorizes. Catalytic converters for vehicles, baghouses for particulates, scrubbers for sulfur dioxide—all such technologies take activities generating the emissions as a given, and control at point of release. This is classic epoch one policy. A more direct route is to focus on the original cause of pollution, such as power generated with coal. For economic and political reasons, that did not happen in the 1970s. Now, with a changing climate largely due to emissions from coal-fired power plants, public policy focuses much more on energy efficiency and renewable energy.

Other examples of large-scale pollution prevention abound. Lynn Mandarano offers a case study of green infrastructure in Philadelphia that not only addressed water quality issues due to combined sewer overflows but cut capital costs by $14 billion, 90% below an end-of-pipe solution. In combined sewer overflows (CSOs), high rainfall causes storm water discharges that overwhelm wastewater plants, leading to releases of untreated pollutants. A classic approach would require a complete physical separation of two systems—sanitary sewers and storm water—at a cost of $16 billion. The alternative selected was using green infrastructure with limited physical upgrades, which reduced construction costs. As Mandarano puts it (2011, 174), this meant "converting 34% of the combined sewer drainage area to greened acres using green storm water construction techniques, implementing stream corridor restoration and preservation projects and upgrading the water treatment plants to handle larger wet weather flows."

## Many Tools, Especially Market Mechanisms

Part of the transition from the first to second policy epochs was diversifying the suite of policy tools. This transition has been more dynamic than this brief review can convey and is documented elsewhere (Harrington, Morgenstern, and Sterner 2004; Jordan, Wurzel, and Zito 2003). The green growth agenda stresses policy diversification and innovation. A central tool is using government-created, market-like mechanisms to reflect the social costs of ecological harm.

This preference for market-like mechanisms is a defining feature of green growth. That markets should be used for ecological benefit is a matter of debate. Critics from the political right praise unfettered markets (as if there were such a thing) as solutions to all problems. For many from the left, markets cause harm and have no role in ecological policy (Sagoff 1988).

Market critics are correct to a point: unregulated markets create negative externalities like air and water pollution and fail to protect common pool resources like the Chesapeake Bay, the Great Lakes, or the Ogallala Aquifer. That is why governments intervened via regulation and other tools. This does not mean that government cannot use market tools like carbon trading or eco-taxes to promote ecological goals. This misconception or misrepresentation of markets comes through clearly in Naomi Klein's (2014) critique of cap-and-trade for greenhouse gases.

Both sides of this debate exhibit a fair amount of ideological baggage on the role of markets. As the authors of *Natural Capitalism* note, markets are "little more than a way of exchanging information about what people have and what they want" (282). They are a tool, like a hammer or screwdriver, which may be designed and used well or poorly. Of course, other tools also are part of a green growth agenda—information disclosure, performance standards, tax incentives—but the reliance on market-like tools, and with it an assumption that green growth can occur within the basic outlines of existing economic systems, assuming appropriate pricing, is a defining feature.

## ELEMENTS OF THE GREEN GROWTH POLICY AGENDA

The chapter so far looked at the evolution of US policy, how it shapes a green growth agenda, and the distinctions (more like shades of gray) between conventional and green growth agendas. This section turns to a third issue: What principles and tools define green growth?

This is a large topic and could occupy a book in itself. Indeed, it takes up major portions of the UNEP, OECD, and other reports discussed in Chapter 2. My goal for now is to start a conversation—to give a sense of the strategies and tools that are prominent in green growth thinking and make up John Kingdon's (1995) concept of the *policy stream*, discussed more in Chapter 8. The policy stream consists of the ideas, analyses, alternatives, and solutions that may be applied to any given set of problems. The *stream* notion suggests a steady flow of alternatives and solutions competing for attention; that some are more influential than others depends on such factors as economic and political contexts, the preferences and ideologies of those in power, the problems and issues drawing attention, and the interactions among events, ideas, and solutions.

A green growth policy agenda consists of three elements: principles, policy tools, and indicators (see Table 6.1 for a summary). The *principles* express the core ideas of and criteria for evaluating policy tools and their applications. *Policy tools* are mechanisms for changing behavior to achieve goals. They should reflect the principles and link them with desired outcomes. The *indicators* define the extent to which an agenda is fulfilled—its success or failure. This review is far from comprehensive. It does not aim to evaluate the specific policy tools and investment strategies for green growth. A large body of work exists on this, especially on the first two policy epochs (such as Portney and Stavins 2000; Jordan, Wurzel, and Zito 2003; or Tietenberg 2013).

Table 6.1 ELEMENTS OF THE GREEN GROWTH POLICY AGENDA

| | |
|---|---|
| **Principles**<br>*Criteria for guiding and evaluating policy choices* | Seek positive, even synergistic ways of linking ecological and economic goals |
| | Grant critical ecosystems and resources a *principled priority* in decision processes |
| | Aim for policy outcomes that deliver a net reduction in economy inequality |
| | Seek outcomes that increase options for family-supporting, career-oriented employment |
| | Create mechanisms for incorporating social costs/full-cost pricing into decision making |
| | Integrate institutions and policies as much as feasible across interrelated policy sectors |
| **Policy Tools**<br>*Mechanisms for changing behavior to achieve policy goals* | Mandatory performance standards |
| | Trading mechanisms |
| | Pollution taxes |
| | Payments for ecosystem services |
| **Indicators**<br>*Measuring whether goals are being achieved and strategies, policies, and investments should be adjusted* | Environmental and resource productivity |
| | Natural asset base |
| | Environmental quality of life |
| | Policy effectiveness |

## Principles

What principles should determine the specifications and selections of the policy tools used to deal with problems? What principles should guide decision making? In public policy generally, we may find examples of principles that guide decision making and the use of various policy tools. These include, as examples, the principles that policy tools or combinations of them should be *effective* in achieving goals; *equitable* in not harming or benefiting particular groups in ways that are seen to be unfair; *cost-effective* in achieving desired outcomes at the lowest or (more reasonably) at minimal cost; and *feasible* in gaining a needed level of political support. In ecological policy specifically, commonly relied-upon principles could be that strategies should be designed to reduce human health and ecological risks; should place authority at the lowest feasible level of governance to promote local control (an often controversial one); or be used only if the estimated benefits of an action are likely to exceed costs (even more controversial).

The discussion here is more focused on principles to guide decision making, use tools, and design indicators. Here are six principles for guiding a green growth policy agenda:

- Seek positive, even synergistic ways of linking ecological and economic goals.
- Grant critical ecosystems and resources a *principled priority* in decision processes.
- Aim for policy outcomes that deliver a net reduction in economic inequality.
- Seek outcomes that increase options for family-supporting, career-oriented employment.
- Create mechanisms for incorporating social costs/full-cost pricing into decision making.
- Integrate institutions and policies as much as feasible across interrelated policy sectors.

## LINK ECONOMIC AND ECOLOGICAL OBJECTIVES

This, of course, is a defining feature and core principle. Policies should be designed to seek and implement positive-sum outcomes. Examples presented at various points in this book include energy and water efficiency; wind, solar, and other renewables over fossil fuels; use of green infrastructure for achieving water and climate goals at less cost; or investment in smart grid or mass transit upgrades to promote employment, economic, and energy or water efficiency. In the short-term context of specific actions, trade-offs may be unavoidable, but the goal should be to seek and implement positive relationships.

## GRANT CRITICAL ECOSYSTEMS PRINCIPLED PRIORITY

A weakness in many current policies is that they give preference to short-term economic gains that benefit particular interests over the long-term viability of critical ecosystems. Critical ecosystems are defined in many ways; one is that of the Critical Ecosystem Partnership Fund (http://www.cepf.net/Pages/default.aspx). Certainly, ecosystems and resources that are seen to be irreplaceable, provide essential services, have aesthetic or historical value, or involve irreversible damage are included. The *principled priority* term is from William Lafferty and Eivind Hoven, who argue for moving ecological issues from the periphery to the core of policymaking, and that "The increasing recognition and acceptance of the fact that we are facing potentially irreversible damage to life support systems clearly implies that, as far as some environmental objectives are concerned, these cannot simply be 'balanced' with the objectives of other policy sectors" (2003, 11).

## AIM FOR OUTCOMES THAT REDUCE INEQUALITY

A normative issue coming through strongly in the sustainability literature but less prevalent in much existing green growth writing is reducing economic inequality within and across societies. This is central to ecological economics, both as a matter of justice, given the current and future distribution of ecological harms and benefits, and as one of constraining growth. As argued in Chapter 5, however, there also is a practical case to be made for reducing inequality that affects collective action and public goods. This may include eliminating risks that disadvantage low-income groups (such as lead in drinking water or vulnerability to climate change in poor countries) as well as creating economic opportunity.

## INCREASE HIGH-VALUE EMPLOYMENT

A critical distinction in green growth thinking is between *jobs* and *employment*. Like it or not, economies continually create and destroy jobs; consider the market for blacksmiths or elevator operators these days, or the prospects that technology will displace other jobs. In ecological policy, disputes over job impacts are standard currency, as the debates over Keystone XL or coal mining under the Obama administration's climate actions testify; they emphasize short-term impacts on specific groups rather than the long-term well-being of society (and of course the planet). The more appropriate emphasis is on economy-wide employment, particularly of family-supporting, career-oriented jobs (Jones 2008). A major justification for economic growth is generating enough employment to keep pace with population growth and to offset technology change; this principle not only addresses the social equity goal of promoting economic opportunity but can moderate the need for high growth rates.

## CREATE MECHANISMS FOR SOCIAL OR FULL-COST PRICING

This is central to green growth, which relies on market-like tools to correct market deficiencies. Some forms of ecological harm—air or water pollution—are not accounted for in markets; these are *negative externalities* in economics jargon (National Research Council 2010; Greenstone and Looney 2012). Many resources—water or tropical forests—are *common property resources* that are undervalued in market systems. Both need to be wrapped into decisions at many levels, from the individual and community to the national and global. Leading ways of doing this are carbon trading systems and a carbon tax

(Goulder and Schein 2013). Full-cost pricing also makes sense for water scarcity; low prices promote inefficient water use and fail to raise capital needed for investment and innovation.

### INTEGRATE ACROSS INSTITUTIONS AND POLICIES

Ecology–economy issues are only one opportunity for policy integration. Interactions across other policy areas also offer options for positive-sum relationships. Energy is an obvious case; its production, distribution, and use is a source of many ecological problems (Webber 2016). Agricultural practices are implicated in a range of water quality, ecosystem, and climate issues. Policies related to housing involve legacy risks (asbestos or lead) and current problems (radon or energy efficiency). As discussed earlier, administrative rationality builds on principles of division of labor, specialization, and hierarchy, and as a result is not well suited to cross-sectoral policy integration. This is one reason consensus-based democracies with capacities for interest group and policy integration may be better suited to a green transition.

## Policy Tools

Policy tools are mechanisms used to change behavior for achieving a given set of goals. Common tools that come up in public policy debates include regulations mandating the use of technologies or levels of performance, subsidies, tax credits or deductions, use or damage fees, revolving funds, restrictions or bans on products, grants and payments for defined beneficiaries, and many others. Ideally, these tools are used to pursue reasonably well-defined goals and are guided by principles like the above. In practice, the selection and application of policy tools emerges from a more incremental, piecemeal process resembling the "garbage can" model of organizational choice that will be described in Chapter 8 (Cohen, March, and Olsen 1972).

As suggested earlier, the green growth agenda builds on standard tools in ecological policy, some more than others. Tools from the first epoch play a role, but there is a preference for those from the second epoch, especially ones relying on market incentives. Other attributes of green growth tools are that they promote linkages among the ecological and economic policy goals as well as across other policy sectors and are aimed at more upstream sources of problems.

The test of the best fit of any policy tool to the objectives of green growth is that it reflects at least some of the principles proposed above. Again, these principles are offered as a way to start a conversation about a green economic transition in the United States and elsewhere. With these, as with any uses of a set of policy tools, three issues are worth keeping in mind: they are context

(1) and problem dependent, so what makes sense in one setting may not in others;
(2) more general principles still apply, such as effectiveness, equity, and efficiency;
(3) and some are more feasible politically than others. I suggest some policy tools in the green growth agenda, then offer brief illustrations of how they comport with the green growth policy principles.

### MANDATORY PERFORMANCE STANDARDS

Having government define standards of performance and ensuring that pollution sources meet them is a mainstay of ecological policy. Regulatory standards were the most relied-upon tool in the first policy epoch and still play a prominent role. In the second epoch, there was more emphasis on *performance* rather than *technology* standards, and they are applied at broader levels. Examples are clean energy or renewable portfolio standards for power generation and fuel efficiency standards for vehicles. More than half the states have mandated that a specified minimum of electrical generating power comes from renewables, such as wind and solar, or energy efficiency.[2] The Obama administration made Corporate Average Fuel Economy (CAFE) rules a centerpiece of climate action by increasing them to 54.5 miles per gallon (on a level with many European countries) by 2025.

An innovative use of performance standards applied broadly (that is, not to discrete sources but higher levels of aggregation, in this case states) is the EPA's Clean Power Plan (CPP), issued in October 2015. The Obama administration's first choice of an emission reduction plan, the Waxman-Markey bill that created a national cap-and-trade system, passed the House in 2009 but failed in the Senate. The fallback was authority granted in the *Massachusetts v. EPA* ruling in 2007, which held that carbon dioxide should be regulated under the Clean Air Act (CAA). Under the rarely used Section 111(d) of the CAA, the EPA set rate-based performance standards (pounds of $CO_2$/megawatts per hour) or mass-based (total) terms. The national target was set at 32% by 2030, but state targets varied depending on fuel use patterns and the potential for cuts. States could determine the best way to meet targets, with four options: improving plant efficiency, shifting to cleaner fuels (natural gas), expanding zero-carbon sources, or increasing energy conservation and efficiency. Each state also had interim targets for emissions cuts.

The CPP is an illustration of what I call *the new environmental regulation*. It sets targets, enumerates options for achieving them, grants flexibility in selecting the best path, and enables states to select the more economically and politically achievable strategy. Of course, the creative and innovative also stretches an agency's explicit legal authority, especially in a law nearly three decades old. More than two dozen states have challenged the CPP in the federal courts, although most remaining states strongly support it, in a political fight over coal use and climate action. Despite what many observers see as its clear policy, eco-logical, and economic advantages, the Trump administration set out in 2017 to dismantle it. The politics of green growth remain as a major challenge.

The green growth policy agenda incorporates this kind of regulatory inno-vation for more flexible, performance-based, and creative approaches (Fiorino 2006). It is captured in the goal of aiming for systemic innovation in pursuit of not *less* but *smarter* regulation in policy designs, business–government rela-tionships, and implementation strategies (Gunningham and Grabosky 1998).

## TRADING MECHANISMS

Given the theme of linking ecological and economic goals in positive-sum ways, tools that incorporate the social costs of pollution fit comfortably within the green growth agenda. These come in two main forms—emissions/efflu-ent trading and pollution taxes. In their objectives, market tools are no differ-ent from technology or performance standards: they force discrete sources to account for costs to society of the damages from pollution, which unregulated markets fail to do. They are simply different paths to putting a price on sources of harm and making sources accountable for their actions. Trading and taxes are two market-like tools for changing behavior. The difference is that trading caps pollution levels, but prices are uncertain; taxes establish a price, but the resulting pollution levels are uncertain. Both are widely used as ways of putting a price on carbon, but they also have applications to other ecological problems.

With trading systems, public policy creates artificial markets. Among the well-known trading systems are those in the EU (Emission Trading System, or ETS), California (linked with Quebec), and seven subnational, pilot systems in China, which committed to a national one by 2017 (World Bank 2014). The Waxman-Markey legislation that passed in the House in 2009 would have established a national cap-and-trade system for carbon dioxide, with the ultimate target (in 2050) of a nearly 80% reduction in emissions, consistent with the IPCC goal.

A promising—and challenging—use of trading is for nonpoint source water pollution. In the first policy epoch, the targets were sewage treatment plants and industrial dischargers. They were controlled with standards based on the best available, economically feasible technology. Technology controls and the other tools of conventional regulation were less suited to sources not trace-able to a discrete cause: fertilizer runoff, animal waste, sediment, urban storm water discharges, even air deposition from cars. No clear technology fix exists; they are hard to monitor and hold accountable. Yet these are the big remaining pollution sources; from a green growth view, they are far cheaper to control than highly regulated point sources. Reducing nitrogen from farm runoff costs a fraction per unit of the costs of new controls on a sewage treatment plant. Indeed, trading may be the only way to achieve needed levels of water quality.

In water quality trading, point sources in a watershed fund a range of best management practices (BMPs)—buffer areas around streams, planting of cover crops, fertilizer and animal waste reduction—among nonpoint sources to get more pollution reduction at less cost. The institutional and technical challenges to making this work broadly are significant, and there are equity and other issues to account for, but water quality trading is a serious tool that may play a constructive role in making nonpoint reductions politically and economically feasible (Selman, at al. 2009; Willamette Partnership and World Resources Institute 2015).

## POLLUTION TAXES

Even in the first policy epoch, experts called for direct mechanisms to put a price on pollution and hold sources accountable, as *fees* or *taxes*. In theory, the tax should correspond to the damages imposed on society; this leads to emission levels in which marginal social costs equal benefits. In practice, the actual fee is more likely to be based on judgments of what produces the desired changes in behavior (i.e., the lower emissions) and is politically and economically feasible. Fees and eco-taxes are used in many ways, including controlling air pollution and solid waste. A current focus is using them to cut carbon emissions, where they serve many purposes: to increase prices of fossil fuels, put renewables on a competitive footing, promote efficiency, generate revenue for clean energy investments, reduce deficits, train displaced workers, and redistribute revenue to consumers (Sumner, Bird, and Dobos 2011).

In 2008, the Canadian province of British Columbia adopted what may be "the purest example of the economist's carbon tax prescription in practice" (Murray and Rivers 2015, 2), covering some 75% of greenhouse gas emissions. It began at $10/ton and grew $5 in each of the next four years to $30/ton in 2012. To make it politically palatable, it was revenue-neutral. The proceeds were recycled back to businesses and households through lower marginal income tax rates. It has gotten favorable reviews; it cut fuel consumption and emissions by 5%–15% without negative job or economic effects and protected low-income groups (Murray and Rivers 2015; Porter 2016).

Another side of the pricing issue is subsidy reform. Subsidies are money paid to keep the price of a service or product low and are in themselves a distortion of market forces. They are used for purposes that promote ecological harm (fossil fuel, irrigation, or grazing subsidies) or benefit (energy efficiency, renewables). Built into historically brown economies are subsidies that, although adopted for reasons that made sense at the time, now serve to encourage inefficient resource use and ecological degradation. For example, publicly funded irrigation projects in the American west have supported economically inefficient and ecologically harmful water use for many decades (Reisner 1986). Annual US fossil fuel subsidies of some $6 billion are one part of annual global consumer subsidies of about half a trillion dollars in 2011 (IMF 2015b). Calculated post-tax (that is, counting the ecological and health damages from fossil fuel uses supported by the consumption subsidies), the annual costs came to some $4.2 trillion (5.8% of global GDP).

Related conceptually both to pollution taxes and subsidies are tax incentives. These use tax policies at various levels of government to encourage more ecologically driven investments and decision making. These have been most prominent in renewable energy and efficiency. As the Department of Energy describes it: "Government agencies, utilities and others offer a variety of tax credits, rebates and other incentives to support energy efficiency, encourage the use of renewable energy sources, and support efforts to conserve energy and lessen pollution."[3] At the federal level, for example, the Production Tax Credit and Investment Tax Credit are designed to promote the development and deployment of renewables. Tax incentives are more politically palatable than tools like a carbon tax or trading, because they do not directly raise the price of conventional energy sources but reduce those for renewables. At the same time, they appear to be less effective than taxes or trading, "play mostly an assisting role" to other energy policy tools, and are not the "primary drivers of alternative energy development" (Carley 2011, 277).

## Payments for Ecosystem Services

Another policy tool made feasible by the analytical method of ecosystem valuation is payments for ecosystem services (PES). Recall from Chapter 2 that valuation of ecosystem services is a means of quantifying the dollar value of vital services—water filtration, habitat protection, preservation of biodiversity, waste detoxification, and more—that natural systems provide. Historically, prices for such services have in effect been zero, given that they are not traded in markets. Attaching value to ecosystem services creates incentives for private and public actors to protect and restore them. The premise for PES is that "ecosystem services have quantifiable economic value, and that this value can be used to entice investment in restoration and maintenance" (UNEP 2008, 1). PES is a system in which beneficiaries of a service—a downstream town needing clean water or protection from flooding, or a government agency wanting to protect a landscape—compensate those controlling land or another natural resource. The obligation of those compensated may only be to preserve or not develop the land, or it may involve other actions, such as best management practices. What matters is that "the payment causes the benefit to occur where it would not have otherwise" (UNEP 2008, 3). It has to add value, be measurable and verifiable, and establish that the service is provided as a result of the PES agreement.

Payments for ecosystem services come in many forms. Some result from regulation, as when developers whose actions affect wetlands arrange funding for an alternative wetland of equal or better quality, a practice known as *wetland mitigation banking*. Often, private or nongovernment organizations purchase land outright to preserve it and the services it provides; some examples are the World Wildlife Fund and The Nature Conservancy. Conceptually, water quality trading is a form of PES, but it differs enough from other forms that it is treated as analytically distinct. The Natural Resource Conservation Service of the US Department of Agriculture uses PES through the Agricultural Conservation Easement Program, which provides financial support to landowners to preserve and restore land, wetlands, and habitat. Like any tool, PES can be used well or badly, depending on the design and application.

## Green Growth Indicators

A third element in a green growth policy agenda is indicators—ways of measuring whether goals are being achieved and determining if strategies, policies, and investments should be adjusted. Yardsticks like the Genuine Progress Indicator (an alternative to GDP) offer societal indicators of well-being, not just growth. Other, more finely-tuned indicators exist as well.

In many ways, green growth indicators resemble standard ecological ones, except in focusing on ecology–economy relationships. Eco-efficiency and the interactions among ecological, economic, and social factors are themes. One framework for green growth indicators is suggested by the OECD in its *Towards Green Growth* initiatives (OECD 2011; also see Global Green Growth Knowledge Platform 2013 and Dual Citizen 2014). It defines four categories of indicators: *environmental and resource productivity*, which measures efficiency in uses of natural capital; *the natural asset base*, focused on preservation of such assets; *environmental quality of life*, reflecting measures of human health and well-being; and a category for capturing *policy effectiveness* (investments, research and development) for delivering green growth.

Policy tools do influence ecological outcomes. For instance, the cost of wind energy has fallen by one-third in the last seven years, solar by even more, making them far more competitive with fossil fuels. The US Energy Information Administration (EIA) estimates that renewable energy sources overall may surpass coal by the late 2030s (DOE/EIA 2017). Indeed, between 2030 and 2040, solar could represent more than 50% of new generating electrical capacity in the United States (72). These trends, the International Energy Agency states (2017), have been "sustained and supported" by government policies, which largely "will determine where we go from here." In the United States, these policies include federal and state tax credits and the state Renewable Portfolio Standards. The key now is to build upon the steady progress in the generating sector and promote policies that expand efficiency and renewables in buildings, transportation, and manufacturing.

## INVESTMENT STRATEGIES: A GREEN NEW DEAL

Another green growth strategy is reorienting investments. In market systems, capital flows drive the economy and, over time, influence distributions of political power. A green growth theme is making planned and systematic investments in green economic sectors and activities, such as clean energy or water technology (e.g., for nutrient recovery technology).

One way to frame this redirection of investment is in terms of a *Green New Deal*. The term *New Deal*, of course, comes from policies adopted under President Franklin Roosevelt for bringing the nation out of the Great Depression in the 1930s. The strategy was to inject public funds into the economy to stimulate demand for goods and services and put people to work meeting that demand. This idea was revived for ecological ends in the wake of the 2008 financial crisis. The idea, as an economist in the UNEP green economy process describes it, was to devise "new and bold measures that not only stimulate economic growth and employment opportunities but also move the world economy further along the path of more environmentally sustainable development" (Barbier 2010, 27). Stated simply, "There is a need to 'green' the world economy as we revive it, not rebuild the old 'brown' one" (Barbier 2010, 27).

The financial crisis led many governments to enact macro-economic policies to counter negative growth and rising unemployment. The recession was a period of unintended de-growth; the US rate fell by 3.8% in the fourth quarter of 2008. As did other countries, the United States adopted a financial stimulus to kick-start the economy. This was a classic green growth opportunity: create positive-sum synergy by stimulating job creation and investing in green economic sectors.

The analysis firm HSBC Global Research collected data on economic recovery plans from some 20 countries early in 2009. These countries authorized investments, most to be made in 3–5 years, of some $2.8 trillion (all numbers are in US dollars). Of this total, about 15% ($430 billion) was associated with spending aimed at "stabilizing and then cutting global emissions of greenhouse gases" (including related water and waste investments). The primary US economic stimulus package was the American Recovery and Reinvestment Act of 2009 (ARRA). It injected $787 billion into the economy, of which $492 billion was in the form of new spending and $295 billion consisted of tax cuts. Of this total, $94 billion, or 12%, was directed at climate-related green initiatives. Although the United States was second only to China in total spending, it was below not only China but South Korea, Germany, and France in the percentage going to green initiatives.

Of the 20 or so countries, only the United States made a major investment in renewable energy, at $23 billion. Other stimulus categories were $52 billion to energy efficiency (half to buildings and half for grid, rail, and vehicle projects); $4 billion for carbon capture and storage; and $16 billion for water restoration, flood protection, and rural drinking water (HSBC 2009, 36–37). The initial ARRA proposal was an $825 billion stimulus, with $151 billion for green initiatives, but this was scaled back. Given this change, an original estimate of 3 million jobs created was cut to 2.5 million. Of these, 48% came from infrastructure spending, 30% from information technology, and 16% from energy employment. Consistent with findings in Chapter 3, HSBC found "that energy-efficiency improvements and green power investments have lasting employment benefits" (37–38).

Did the ARRA constitute a Green New Deal? It might have, had it been larger and been sustained over time. The ARRA amounted to about 0.7% of US GDP. In Sweden it was 1.3%, and in China and South Korea 3.0%, the highest among all countries (Barbier 2010, 65). If we were to heed UNEP's call for annual green investments of 2% of GDP, the US figure should be about $360 billion (2% of annual GDP, about $18 trillion in 2016), and it should be on an annual basis. The 2% would include public and private spending; a great deal of innovation comes out of the private sector, so federal investments alone give an incomplete picture. In this sense, an influx of nearly $100 billion, almost all of which was to be spent over five years, was a major shot in the arm to greener growth. What matters in the long run, however, is continuity.

One assessment of the clean energy provisions of the US stimulus found that "Overall, from a holistic perspective, our findings suggest that the stimulus programs had a positive effect on the RE [renewable energy] sector" (Mundaca and Richter 2015, 1184). If sustained over time and combined with an economy-wide carbon cap-and-trade system, as the Obama administration intended, it might have been transformational. On its own, although the stimulus "will no doubt have long-term impacts, and has set the stage for a green energy transition, the impacts of the RE stimulus are not in and of themselves enough for the large-scale transformation needed" (2015, 1184).

The most effective strategy is to use investments to complement policy tools, and vice versa. The energy portions of the ARRA would have had far more impact if applied in tandem with a system for incorporating the social costs of carbon through a cap-and-trade system or a carbon tax. Not only are the two sets of actions mutually reinforcing—attaching valid prices to ecological goods and bads draws capital by lowering investor risk, improving rates of return, and creating investment incentives (see D'Alessandro, Luzzati, and Morroni 2010)

## EVALUATING THE GREEN GROWTH POLICY AGENDA

This book argues that far greener growth is economically and technologically feasible. The main barriers are political and social. One series of analysis concludes, for example, that a transition to an electricity system powered entirely by wind, solar, and water is economically and technologically feasible in the 2030–2050 time period, with the right policies and investments (Jacobson and Delucchi 2009). Whether absolute, durable, long-term green growth—meeting human aspirations within ecological limits—is feasible without rethinking our definitions of progress and well-being is doubtful. Still, major gains are likely, even with the current growth trajectories. Calls for no or negative growth are insufficient ecologically and doomed politically.

A green growth agenda is not the full answer, but it is a large part of it. Still, it is worth looking at some criticisms and responses.

*It relies too much on technology.* Critics often assert that green growth depends too much on technology innovation as the path for sustaining growth within ecological limits. While it is true that technology plays a central role, especially by increasing the eco-efficiency of products and services, it is not the only instrument for getting to a green or substantially greener economy. Energy conservation and efficiency, for example, involve changes in behavior or modifications in insulation, lighting, and building design that are low on the technology scale. Reducing deforestation or overfishing, shifting to low-input and low-tillage agriculture, increasing mass transit, cutting fertilizer use, and preserving habitat from development requires little in new technologies, but demands changes in behavior and policies. Greener consumption through product redesign, reduced packaging, or selling services rather than goods is not based on technology.

Nonetheless, technology is central to green growth. Innovation in renewable energy, energy and water efficiency, water treatment and monitoring, land management and use, and the like depends on the ability to apply existing and develop new technologies. Is this a weakness? After all, technology played a major role in creating the brown economy, with fossil fuels, habitat stresses, industrial agriculture, and synthetic chemicals. Should we not use new technologies to undo the negative effects of previous ones? To be fair, for many critics the issue is not whether technology matters but that there are risks in assuming that technology change alone be enough. That is a fair issue and the reason many of us reject the narrow, eco-efficiency version of green growth in favor of one incorporating changes in economic structure, investments, and policies.

*It relies too much on markets.* A core premise of a green growth agenda is that market-like tools can be used to mitigate and resolve ecological problems. This reliance on market-like tools is viewed skeptically by critics. After all, market imperfections created the problems in the first place. Absent government action, people are not held accountable for pollution (a negative externality) or for misusing shared resources for private gain (the tragedy of the commons). For critics, it makes little sense to use institutions that create the problems in the first place to fix them later.

It helps to clarify what people mean in referring to the role of markets in ecological policy. Green growth advocates do not call for free-market environmentalism in which common pool resources are put on the auction block and sold to the highest bidder. The goal is not to enable the Koch brothers to own Yellowstone or Yosemite, even though a free-market environmentalist might be fine with that. In green growth terms, government may promote ecological well-being by simulating market conditions and creating artificial markets. The idea is not to turn public goods into private ones but to find better ways of protecting and expanding public goods, like a functioning climate system or quality wetlands. In creating a cap-and-trade system for air or water pollutants, for example, the goal is not to turn ecological decision making over to markets but to use markets to define paths to achieving positive ecology–economy outcomes.

The debate often is framed as a matter of using regulation (such as technology standards) versus markets (e.g., cap-and-trade). The flaw in this framing is that cap-and-trade *is* regulation, with a different set of design characteristics. When California launched its state-wide cap-and-trade program for carbon dioxide in January 2013, it imposed comprehensive regulatory obligations on utilities and other sources covered under the law. Instead of imposing technology standards on them, or specifying an emission rate all of them had to meet, it set a state-wide cap that declines annually. Sources had to have credits or buy them at quarterly auctions. It was regulation, but with an artificial market for carbon emissions.

*It stresses instrumental/utilitarian over moral/ethical values.* A related criticism is that green growth relies too much on selfish motivations and too little on cultivating and invoking respect for ecological values. This is expressed by Mark Sagoff, who prefers to motivate people through their values rather than their market preferences—as *citizens* rather than as *consumers*. He asks, about Americans (1998, 141): "Why is it so difficult for them to say that one may allocate resources not always as a perfect market would but on substantive, normative, and frankly ethical grounds?" For a start, his stated assumption that

Americans "generally share the ideology of environmentalism" (141) and share reliably green values is questionable. Despite expressions of modestly pro-ecological views in surveys, usually based on hypothetical choices having no real consequences, actual behavior as revealed in voting suggests that bread-and-butter issues of income and job security usually take priority. The 2016 elections outcomes did not demonstrate a generally shared ideology of environmentalism, although, to be sure, ecological issues were low on the agenda.

Even more to the point is whether incentives and values necessarily are at odds. Using prices or tax policy or cap-and-trade to incorporate the social costs of carbon and other pollution, or full-cost water pricing to promote efficiency and generate revenues for investments in smart metering or leak detection, does not have to undermine the ethical case for ecological protection.

Another ethical criticism of the market-like tools that comprise the green growth agenda is that, if poorly designed, they are unfair to low-income groups. Air and water pollution trading certainly can have that effect if they lead to a shift in pollution concentrations from high-income to low-income areas. Because low-income groups pay a much larger share of their incomes to energy and transportation than do high earners, solutions like a carbon tax can impose disproportionate burdens on the poor and near-poor, and this is why program designs matter (Stone 2015; Williams and Burtraw 2015). Funds raised from market-like programs can be used to reduce inequality; but this has to be built into policy designs, for both carbon/water trading systems and pollution taxes.

Of course, this agenda also is the subject of critical commentary from the political right, but based more on opposition to ecological policies generally than green growth specifically. Indeed, in the days when there was more of a conservative–liberal political consensus (into the 1980s), the center-right in the United States actively promoted market-like tools (McCauley, Barron, and Coleman 2008). Republican President George H.W. Bush supported what many consider to be the most significant regulatory law in US history, the 1990 Clean Air Act Amendments, because of the cost savings gained through acid rain trading. Even today, many conservatives see a carbon tax as an effective and efficient way to cut carbon emissions—once they accept the need to cut them.

## FROM POLICY AGENDA TO POLITICS

Nearly half a century of ecological policy generated a rich agenda of strategies and tools. Most of the foundation for the green growth agenda is found in the first two policy epochs, with influence from the third. The second in particular—with emphasis on market-like tools, policy integration, ecology-economy linkages, and collaboration—set the table for green growth.

I opened the chapter with three themes. One was the richness and variety of the policy agenda. A second was the reaction of various critics to a policy agenda weighted in favor of market-like instruments. From the left, the worry is that the very institutions that gave rise to ecological degradation now are being used to avoid or reverse it. As I argued above, however, market-like mechanisms like fees and trading use artificial markets or policy-induced social cost pricing to overcome deficiencies in existing institutions. Like other tools, markets may be used for better or worse, as good or bad policy. A core principle of a green growth policy agenda is to get past ideological biases and determine what works and in what form for achieving the desired policy goals. The design and operation of market tools is critical to their success. From the right, of course, the ideological bias is that unregulated markets work perfectly fine and will solve any problems of inefficient resource use and ecological degradation, so why intervene at all?

A third theme was that specifically ecological policies matter, but broader social and economic ones do as well. Ecological issues are intertwined with economic, housing, land use, transportation, energy, and a range of other issues. Ecological policies are but the tip of the iceberg. What lies below the surface matters, for two reasons: building a green growth coalition, and devising policy strategies that enable us to carry out the economic and political transition.

So what John Kingdon calls the *policy stream* is full of ideas, options, and proposed solutions, and the green growth literature still is generating more. Our experience with market-like tools and green investment is growing, and policy experts are documenting and evaluating what appears to be working, what is not, and in what contexts. A green economy is economically and technical feasible; it offers the distinct prospect of not only an ecologically benign but a fairer, more fulfilling, and more satisfying life than does an old-style brown economy. And yet, as the advocates of green growth constantly remind us, *the political barriers are formidable.*

The last two chapters turn to these barriers and their relevance in the United States. Chapter 7 picks up on evidence and arguments from earlier ones, particularly Chapter 4, regarding the factors that influence a country's capacities for ecological protection and green growth. Chapter 8 looks at prospects for a green economic transition in the United States and the conditions under which it might occur.

# Prospects and Politics
# in the United States

Chapter 4 examined explanations for variations in ecological policy and performance across countries, drawing upon a large and growing literature. It considered factors that help in explaining why some countries do better than others in keeping air and water clean, protecting habitat and species, using water and materials efficiently, and promoting other ecological goals. To summarize, Chapter 4 suggested that strong ecological protection is associated with the following:

- a moderate level of income and GDP, at least enough for stable and capable governance, public demand for health and ecological protection, and having resources for responding (although this varies by indicator, and the positive effects may diminish during growth)
- effective governance: administrative competence, rule of law, and low corruption
- democracy, with political accountability, free flows of information, and the associated positive effects on governance
- the ability to establish some level of consensus on major social and economic goals
- being able to link across not only ecological and economic but other policy domains, as reflected in the capacities of the more integrated and neo-corporatist political systems
- high levels of engagement in global problem solving, especially on ecological issues
- relatively low economic inequality, which may affect the capacity for collective action

Other explanations are harder to evaluate because of complex interactions among institutional factors, differences in indicators used in research, or variations in problem and political context.

For example, the presumed advantages of parliamentary systems do not necessarily lead to better ecological protection. A nimble parliamentary system may be as likely to adopt less stringent or ineffective policies or to undo existing ones as it is to adopt ecologically friendly ones. The research does not suggest that parliamentary systems are better in their ecological performance than systems like those in the United States. The capacities of federalist versus more unitary systems also are hard to evaluate. Based on the research, there is no clear evidence that unitary systems are better or worse, although one study (Walti 2004) identifies interactions among neo-corporatism and federalism. My own assessment of the United States suggests that federalism increases the number of points at which innovation may occur, as is evident in recent state-level climate policies, and it has been a net positive in terms of better ecological policies, especially in climate and energy.

One factor that does seem to matter in the comparative research is electoral systems, especially the effects of proportional representation and multi-member districts (e.g., Germany) compared to majoritarian, single-member districts like those in the United States. If this is the case, two reasons are likely. One is that the former offer opportunities for small parties asserting specific positions to gain access to political decision making and influence policy agendas. An example is the role the Green Party has played in German ecological policy (Uekotter 2014). Another effect of proportional representation is that it offers more than binary choices. Elections may produce legislators with varied and moderate positions.

What may matter more—in facilitating better ecological policies and positive-sum outcomes—are the patterns of policymaking. Recall the observations of researchers:

> countries characterized by strong, centralized interest groups and a more 'consensual' approach to policy making . . . have enjoyed better environmental performance (Scruggs 2003, 123).

> . . . corporatist institutions are more adept at implementing policies that serve the broader interests and effectively overcome problems of collective action (Matthews 2001, 495).

> . . . collective action problems inherent in environmental policy can be solved more easily in neo-corporatist 'closed shops' based on trust and long-term reciprocity (Liefferink et al. 2009, 92).

This chapter considers the prospects for green growth in the United States. It draws upon the analysis in earlier chapters, especially Chapter 4. It begins by assessing the United States. Although viewed by many as a leader in the 1970s, evaluations of US national policies and performance have become less favorable since then. The chapter then turns to the capacities for both (1) high levels of ecological performance and (2) the ability to undertake a durable green growth path. The United States is assessed in two categories: *structural factors*, the institutional features hardwired into the policy system; and *political factors*, which vary over time based on trends, events, shifts in opinion, and changes in governing coalitions. The third part of the chapter looks at expressions of the green growth concept in US politics and policy. This leads to the outline of a political strategy in Chapter 8.

## HOW DOES THE UNITED STATES COMPARE IN ECOLOGICAL PERFORMANCE?

Some countries are better at achieving collective goals than others. Some have a more consistent and stronger record of political stability, accountability, and responsiveness than others. One may have more successful foreign policies and global influence, while another is better at delivering that Holy Grail of societal goals—prosperity with GDP and income growth.

Why some countries are better at delivering economic prosperity (defined here as growth in GDP and incomes but that should also include notions of economic vitality and security) than others is a topic that has engaged social scientists for years. Some explanations go back to the early 20th century: German sociologist Max Weber attributed the economic success of the northern European countries to cultural factors in *The Protestant Ethic and the Spirit of Capitalism* (originally published in 1905). Since then, a range of social science literature has tried explain why some countries are more able than others to make citizens richer, including the book on *Good Capitalism, Bad Capitalism* that I used to introduce the opening chapter.

For much of the last century, the United States was viewed as a global leader in generating higher incomes, with some company from other parts of the industrialized world. Japan and what was then West Germany, for example, achieved high growth in the years after the Second World War. More recently, the Asian Tigers of Taiwan, Singapore, South Korea, and later China impressed the world with their rapid growth. Now countries elsewhere in Asia and Africa have joined the high growth club, while income and GDP increases in the earlier industrializers have leveled off. Even China's prodigious growth rates have slipped. As economies mature, growth rates slow or, in ones like Japan or

Russia, at times are negative (PWC 2015). What matters for now is that economic growth is a priority of nearly all counties, a variety of indicators exist for measuring economic success, and a range of institutional, cultural, and policy factors offer explanations.

A trend that many in the United States find disconcerting is slower growth rates. Here is where the effects of economic inequality are a double-edged sword. I already discussed the findings of the International Monetary Fund and others on ways that inequality—largely through poor education and training of low-income groups, but also from lost demand that slows economic activity—may undermine growth. That may be good news to growth critics; other things being equal, it may lead to less ecological stress. The other edge of the sword is that slower growth rates can increase dissatisfaction with political regimes, heighten perceived conflicts among ecological and economic goals, and reduce funding for investments in clean energy and other public goods critical to green growth. The key to ecological success may be *equitable growth rather than no growth*.

There is little reason to doubt countries' commitments to growth, although their ability to achieve it may vary. What about commitment to and performance in ecology and environmental health? Chapter 4 examined evidence on causes of variations in national performance, beyond the economic factors reviewed in Chapter 3. This chapter uses it and other evidence to compare ecological performance in the United States to other countries, especially the economically similar ones.

Measured against the environmental conditions existing at the middle of the last century, the US has made progress, especially given that the big drivers of ecological harm—economic scale, population, mobility, and land use—increased. The most impressive and reliably tracked results are in air quality, as discussed in Chapter 3. Information on water quality is less consistent and available, for many technical and resource reasons, but there have been big reductions from point sources like sewage treatment plants and industrial facilities. Less progress was made in reducing nonpoint sources—run-off from agricultural lands, urban storm water, run-off from forest lands, air deposition from vehicles, leaking septic tanks, and the like. The United States has invested effort and money in cleaning up existing hazardous waste sites through the Superfund program and preventing future ones under the Resource Conservation and Recovery Act. As for pesticides and chemicals, it is hard to assess progress, but many harmful substances—among them lead, asbestos, mercury, and cadmium—have been greatly reduced, yet with many remaining risks.

This kind of information gives us a snapshot of how the United States is faring over time; even more revealing is how it compares to other nations, especially economic counterparts. When it comes to cross-national comparisons of environmental performance, the most comprehensive and reliable set of measures is from the Environmental Performance Index (EPI), compiled and updated every other year. The most recent EPI (Hsu et al. 2016) assesses performance in two categories—environmental health and ecosystem vitality. Within these are nine issue areas and 20 indicators. The issue areas are the health impacts of pollution, air quality, water and sanitation, fisheries, forests, agricultural impacts, biodiversity and habitat, water resources, and climate and energy. Like all rich countries, the United States does well in environmental health indicators; richer societies have resources to provide safe drinking water, health care, and sanitation. Where wealthy countries vary is in ecosystem vitality. The EPI notes: "To a large extent, economic gain and the creation of wealth are tied to the exploitation of ecosystems" (Hsu et al. 2016, 93).

The US ranking for 2016 was 26th out of 180 countries evaluated. Of course, it does well on the health impacts of pollution and on clean water and sanitation, ranking 19th and 22nd It is in the middle on air quality at 43rd (based largely on fine particulates and indoor air); water resources (42nd); agricultural impacts (40th); and climate and energy (44th). Its weakest areas are fisheries (84th); biodiversity and habitat (90th); and forests (change in forest cover) at 105th.

As usual, the top spots are occupied by small, northern European countries: Finland, Iceland, Sweden, and Denmark. Following them are some surprises: Slovenia, Spain, Portugal, and Estonia. The two largest by population and probably largest economies by 2050 rank 109th (China) and 141th (India). Because the indicators are revised year-to-year to incorporate new criteria, methods, and data, comparisons over time are difficult. Some nations moved up recently (Australia and Ireland), others down (Germany, Switzerland, or Norway). It should be noted that the EPI considers some factors that may be unaffected by policy (such endowments as forest cover or biodiversity, for example), so it reflects government action but somewhat imperfectly. Table 7.1 gives a sampling of countries with their rankings overall in selected issue areas.

The Climate Change Performance Index (CCPI) offers another data-driven assessment of, in this case, a specific category of ecological performance. Updated annually for the last several years, the 2016 version assessed 58 countries on the basis of several climate-related indicators: current emission levels and trends, the state of carbon efficiency and trends, share of renewables in the energy supply, and policy ratings by some 300 experts around the world (Germanwatch 2016). In the 2016 assessment, the United States ranked 34th of 58 countries. It did not fare well on the current state of emissions but did compare well (and had moved up in the rankings) on emission trends and *especially* in the policy ranking, rising from 35th to 12th in the previous year, based on the Obama administration's ambitious climate policies. Among its

*Table 7.1* SELECTED COUNTRY RANKINGS: ENVIRONMENTAL PERFORMANCE INDEX

| Country (overall rank) | Air Quality | Climate and Energy | Biodiversity and Habitat | Water Resources | Forests |
| --- | --- | --- | --- | --- | --- |
| Sweden (3) | 22 | 10 | 57 | 12 | 107 |
| Denmark (4) | 57 | 24 | 17 | 13 | 96 |
| United Kingdom (12) | 62 | 30 | 12 | 4 | 94 |
| Singapore (14) | 54 | 5 | 118 | 1 | Not ranked |
| United States (26) | 43 | 44 | 90 | 42 | 105 |
| Germany (30) | 137 | 52 | 1 | 5 | 51 |
| Russia (32) | 73 | 31 | 113 | 24 | 67 |
| Japan (39) | 104 | 88 | 38 | 35 | 20 |
| Brazil (46) | 32 | 92 | 40 | 58 | 83 |
| Indonesia (107) | 92 | 41 | 83 | 128 | 109 |
| China (109) | 179 | 62 | 97 | 55 | 53 |
| India (141) | 178 | 79 | 135 | 101 | 31 |

SOURCE: Hsu et al. 2016

OECD peers, the US ranked 21st out of 32 countries. The top climate performers in 2016 included Denmark, the United Kingdom, Sweden, France, and Morocco. At the bottom were Russia, Canada, and Saudi Arabia, which took last place on the list. It is worth noting, but unsurprising, that President Obama got no credit in the media or anywhere else for the major US gains in climate policy—further evidence of the prominence of economic indicators. Given the 2016 election results, we may expect the policy ranking to fall rapidly in the next few years, even if performance does not in the near term.

Although probably the most complete and systematic, the EPI and CCPI are only a few of many assessments of ecological performance and policy. In many, the United States fares even worse than it does in the EPI. In a study of trends in 17 Western democracies from 1970–1995, Lyle Scruggs (2003) ranked the United States thirteen out of seventeen for his five ecological indicators. In a study of 18 OECD countries, Detlef Jahn (1998) places the United States among the negative, not the positive performers. Two more recent studies compare countries on the number and stringency of policies rather than conditions or trends. They see policy as a better metric for what countries actually do to protect health and ecology than conditions, which are shaped by factors (population density, transboundary pollution, economic composition, and so on) beyond a government's control:

> One policy comparison (Liefferink et al. 2009) places the United States at the bottom of a list of 24 countries in number and stringency of policies adopted. Its rankings actually fell over the years. In number of policies adopted, the United States fell from 10th place in the 1970s to 24th in 2005; in stringency, it declined from 9th to 24th in the same period. In both, the United States slipped in each of the four successive time periods studied since 1970.
>
> A more recent study (Holzinger et al. 2011, 37) also used measures of policy adoption and stringency. The United States rated 23rd out of 24 countries in the most recent year in their assessment (2005). This was an almost linear decline from being 11th in 1970, 8th in 1980, 12th in 1990, and 17th in 2000, just in front of Mexico.
>
> In a ranking based on the signing and ratification of 15 major environmental treaties between 1996 and 1997, the United States placed last among 19 countries (Recchia 2002).

These quantitative assessments are consistent with qualitative research. Although the United States was viewed generally, and with good reason, as a global leader in the 1970s, along with countries like Sweden and Japan, it is seen as a laggard recently. One comparative study asserts "the pioneering US role in environmental policy [is] now a distant memory" due in part to "an old-fashioned standoff between economy and environment" (Dryzek, Hunold, and Schlosberg 2002, 667). Another found that "there is still no clear, explicit and continuing nationwide commitment to sustainable development" in the US, partly due to "the widely recognized fragmentation in policy structures" (Jordan and Lenschow 2008, 283–284). Another observes that "the EPA has in recent years been systematically diminished in its environmental policy capacity" (Andrews 1997, 39). Although a leader in the 1970s, one scholar observes, the United States "has not been among the forerunners for the past decade" (Weidner 2002, 1351). In *The Politics of the Earth*, Dryzek's "consensus picks" for greenest countries include Finland, Germany, Japan, the Netherlands, Norway, Sweden, and Switzerland (2013, 165). Once part of that elite, "since the 1980s, the United States has fallen behind, stuck in a stand-off between supporters and opponents of the laws and regulations established around 1970" (166).

Of course, these are national assessments and obscure what is happening at a state level. Indeed, there is ample evidence for viewing many states as the "new heroes" of environmental problem solving, as Barry Rabe has put it (2016,

34). To take one example, if there were an exclusive club open to the climate action elite, California would be a member. Building on the Global Warming Solutions Act of 2006, California has articulated a vision of reducing greenhouse gas emissions to 40% below 1990 levels by 2030. Among its specific goals are increasing renewable energy production by 50%, cutting oil use from vehicles 50%, doubling energy efficiency in existing buildings, and cutting emissions of short-lived pollutants (climatechange.ca.gov). The state's economy-wide carbon cap-and-trade system, a "backstop" for other policies, now covers some 85% of in-state emissions. California already has linked its cap and trade system with Quebec and is considering links with Ontario and some US states. Demonstrating the state's long-term commitment, the California legislature in 2017 extended the provisions of the climate law to 2030 with a two-thirds majority in both houses (Nagourney 2017).

The potential for regional collaborations among like-minded states is illustrated by the Regional Greenhouse Gas Initiative (RGGI), a carbon cap-and-trade system operating in nine northeastern and mid-Atlantic states. Founded in 2005, RGGI requires defined categories of sources of carbon dioxide to obtain, through quarterly auctions, sufficient allowances to cover their emissions over a three-year period. The proceeds from the auctions are invested in such "consumer benefit" programs as energy efficiency, consumer help with utility bills, renewable energy support, and other climate- and energy-positive activities (rggi.org/rggi).

That some states are leaders means that others are lagging. A Pilot State Eco-efficiency Index developed by the Center for Environmental Policy at American University found wide variations among states on various ecological indicators. Performance indicators from readily available data were normalized by Gross State Product (the state-level equivalent of GDP) to determine the ecological impacts of generating a given unit of income in the state. High performers usually were states that had shown up as leaders in other rankings—New York, California, Massachusetts, Connecticut, New Jersey, and Maryland; lower performers included states like Oklahoma, Alabama, West Virginia, and Wyoming (Fiorino and Frost 2016). A subset of rankings that is focused on health-related air emissions, carbon dioxide emissions, energy efficiency, and VMT (vehicle miles traveled) revealed similar patterns: top-performing states deliver a high quality of life with much less ecological impact; at the other end of the scale, low performers impose a climate/energy tax on other states through their poor eco-efficiency. Table 7.2 presents the 2016 assessment of selected states in their air, climate, and energy performance.[1]

Policy rankings by Barry Rabe (2016) and the American Council for an Energy-Efficient Economy (2015) reach similar results. Most of these low-performing states also led the litigation against the Obama administration's

*Table 7.2* HIGH, MIDDLE, AND LOW RANKING STATES IN THE
AIR, CLIMATE, AND ENERGY INDEX*

| State | ACE Index Score | CE Index Rank |
|-------|-----------------|---------------|
| New Jersey | 47.04 | 1 |
| California | 41.36 | 2 |
| Connecticut | 36.17 | 3 |
| New York | 36.03 | 4 |
| Rhode Island | 30.49 | 5 |
| Michigan | 10.07 | 23 |
| Wisconsin | 9.99 | 24 |
| Maine | 9.87 | 25 |
| Georgia | 9.60 | 26 |
| Minnesota | 9.34 | 27 |
| Mississippi | 4.17 | 46 |
| Alaska | 4.00 | 47 |
| Montana | 3.38 | 48 |
| North Dakota | 3.35 | 49 |
| Wyoming | 2.20 | 50 |

*Sampling of state performance on four indicators: air emissions,
energy consumption, greenhouse gas emissions, and vehicle miles
traveled. A higher score signifies better performance. For more
detail, see Fiorino and Frost (2016).

SOURCE: Center for Environmental Policy, American University

Clean Power Plan and on many other ecological policies. In 2017, one of the
leading challengers to the Clean Power Plan and other environmental initiative,
Oklahoma Attorney-General Scott Pruitt, became the administrator of the federal Environmental Protection Agency. So the states vary tremendously in their
policies and performance. Policy and performance at the national level depend
on which governing coalition of states is able to gain sufficient power.

If we ask why the United States nationally has not maintained its status as
an environmental leader in recent decades, we can expect to hear a variety of
answers, all of which may be true to a degree. Has it been

- the political power of the well-entrenched fossil fuel and agricultural
  industries?
- a political culture that historically has been skeptical of
  governmental power?

- the pluralist, adversarial nature of the American policy system?
- electoral rules that magnify rather than moderate political conflicts?
- the effects of increasing economic and political inequality?
- a public that places low value on ecological relative to economic concerns?
- the political right's hostility to nearly any form of public goods and collective action?
- the corrosive effects of money in a "rigged" economic and political system?

All of these factors have been cited at one point or another for explaining short-comings in US policy and performance. All may have validity, although some more than others. That the fossil fuel industry enjoys impressive political power and has impeded innovation in energy and climate policies is readily appar-  ent. Indeed, in his study of US federal and state climate policies, Roger Karapin concludes that there "is much evidence that a large domestic fossil fuel industry adversely affects climate policy" (2016, 227; also see Dolsak 2001). By design, change is difficult in the American policy system, with its separation of powers and multiple veto points. Looking at the US system for nominating candidates and the ways state and federal legislative districts are apportioned, it is not hard to argue that it magnifies more than moderates political conflict. To be sure, economic growth is highly valued in American society and has often overrid-den ecological concerns. To many of us, there is little doubt that inequality is a source of mistrust and political polarization that makes collective action diffi-cult. Add to all of this the effects of money in politics, lack of confidence in gov-ernment and other institutions, highly polarized and adversarial politics, and the economic insecurities of recent years, and there are plenty of explanations.

The next section brings together evidence on some but not all of these. Rather than present them as reasons for an apparent relative decline in policy and performance, they are presented more positively as factors that may influ-ence and enhance green growth capacities.

## WHAT ARE THE CAPACITIES FOR GREEN GROWTH?

Three conclusions from the previous section help in assessing US prospects for green growth. First, the United States does not rank among the best or worst countries, although it does compare unfavorably to many of its economic peers. Second, it has moved from a position of leadership to, at best, the middle of the pack or even to that of a laggard since the environmental decade of the 1970s. Third, middling and varying performance nationally obscures a great deal of variation among the states. Indeed, some American states on their own would rank as global ecological leaders.

All of this serves as a backdrop for a third question examined in this chapter: What are the prospects for green growth—for an economic transition that moves the United States nationally from being (at times) *ecologically sensitive* to *ecologically driven*? This raises more specific issues: Do institutional barriers get in the way? Does the United States have assets or liabilities when compared to other countries? Can ecological goals, as discussed in Chapter 4, be a core activity of the state?

I begin with a brief case illustrating some of the factors that affect progress on ecological issues—patterns in the development of wind power in the United States and Germany. I then turn to two sets of factors—structural and political—for assessing national capacities for progress in ecological protection and green growth in my time horizon of the next three decades.

## Wind Power in the United States and Germany

A useful window into the explanatory value of policy theories discussed in the next chapter is Roger Karapin's story (2014) of wind power in the United States and Germany over the last four decades. Although the two countries rank second and third (behind China) in installed generating wind capacity, neither is a leader in the percentage of electricity generated by wind. At 8% for Germany and 3.5% for the United States, both are below Denmark (30% at the time), Portugal (20%), Spain (18%), and Ireland (18%). Although both the United States and Germany expanded their wind capacity, that process unfolded in different ways. Germany outperformed the United States in the 1980s and 1990s, only to slow down after 2004. In contrast, the United States showed an initial burst in wind power in the late 1970s, led by California, then went into a stagnant period until 2004.

Karapin draws on two sets of factors in explaining wind power development in the two countries. *Structural factors* cannot be altered in the near term. They include constitutional and other relatively fixed institutional features as well as economic composition (like the influence of fossil fuel interests or wind generating resources), policy style (the pluralist–neo-corporatist dimension), or such cultural factors as attitudes about the role of government. *Political factors* are variable, and change near term along with shifts or trends in political power, public opinion, interest group mobilization, priorities on the policy agenda, and other such factors.

Karapin analyzes four structural factors: electoral systems, patterns of interest group interaction (pluralist or neo-corporatist), fossil fuel endowments and influence, and dependence on manufacturing. The first two are institutional; the other two relate to economic composition. Especially relevant for my purposes are the distinctions between pluralism and neo-corporatism. The first is "marked by fragmentation of business interests and an adversarial relationship between business and government, and hence relatively unstable or uncertain environmental policies" (115). In contrast, the second is defined by a "relatively centralized and concentrated representation of interests, cooperative relations between business and government, and more stable policies that are more smoothly implemented by economic actors" (115). This is the neo-corporatist and more integrative policy style that was considered in Chapter 4.

In structural terms, the United States and Germany differ: the first is pluralist, the second more neo-corporatist; the United States possesses large fossil fuel resources, while Germany's are limited; and the German electoral system is based on proportional representation with multi-member districts, which the research suggests is associated with better ecological performance. Did these structural factors make a difference? To a degree they did, Karapin concludes. Especially in the 1993–2004 time period, when Germany made major advances, "its proportional-representation electoral system and cooperative business–government relations were major underlying causes of renewable-energy policies" (135). In the United States, progress was more difficult due to its winner-take-all electoral system and the adversarial relationships among government and business, as well as opposition from the fossil fuel sector.

The United States was a leader in wind power development in the 1970s, lagged well behind Germany in the 1990s, and then began to catch up in 2004 and since. Why the slowdown in the 1980s and 1990s? Although structural factors played a role, a variety of political and economic trends explain wind power stagnation in the United States in those years: big declines in fossil fuel prices, failures in early wind technologies, and the rise of conservative leaders (most prominently the Reagan administration) and a neo-liberal governing philosophy hostile to intervention in markets and less concerned about ecological issues. In Germany, on the other hand, a strong "advocacy coalition" formed around renewable energy (made up of environmentalists, the Green Party, unions, religious organizations, and moderate parties). Reinforcing this were the events like Chernobyl nuclear disaster and evidence on climate change and stratospheric ozone depletion.

The explanations for a wind power revival in the United States after 2004 are varied, but state leadership is a big one. Here is a situation where the structural/institutional factor of federalism, combined with the many points of access for ideas and interests in a pluralist system, contributed to green growth innovation. Awareness of climate threats led states to adopt policies on clean energy, climate mitigation, and energy efficiency (Rabe 2004 and 2010). In an illustration of compensatory federalism, many "state governments responded by developing climate policies to compensate for the lack of federal leadership" (Karapin 2014, 133). Reinforced by high energy prices and the popularity of renewable energy, even conservative states like Texas adopted renewable portfolio standards that promote more rapid development of wind power.

This framework later was expanded to explain causes of climate policy in California and New York as well as at the federal level in (Karapin 2016). Again, Karapin distinguishes structural factors (institutional features, strength of fossil fuels, interest group pluralism, electoral rules, and "a political culture hostile to regulation") and process or political factors made up of "short-term political interventions, processes, and events" (2016, 9). Issue framing also presents a political factor, one that is relevant to my case for devising positive linkages among ecological, economic, and other goals in coalition-building. Karapin concludes that "arguments about the co-benefits of climate policies often were important in gaining broad support for them" (249).

Karapin offers an approach for and introduction to my next section, which proposes two categories of factors for evaluating green growth capacities in the United States. *Structural factors* are institutional and other features that are relatively fixed—some more than others. They include the configuration of power, such as whether it is based on a fusion (parliamentary) or separation of powers, unitary or centralized, proportional versus majoritarian electoral rules, and related issues discussed in Chapter 4. *Political factors* are the second kind. Obviously these factors interrelate: institutional rules of the game influence electoral outcomes; electoral outcomes shape policy capacities; government performance influences public opinion. Some factors are less fixed and more subject to short-term political control than others; public opinion and election results are more variable than constitutional provisions. Each of these factors was examined in Chapter 4. This chapter applies them to the United States and its capacity for adopting a green growth policy agenda.

My approach to this issue is based on the concept of a political system's capacity. A standard definition of capacity (from merriam-webster.com) is "the ability to do something." Does the United States have the ability as a policy system to embark on a durable and effective set of ecological policies under the concept of green growth?

## Structural Factors

These are the hardware of a policy system—factors that are not amenable to or are hard change. Many radical critiques of US ecological policy ignore them by calling for transformative change without actually getting into how that change might occur, given institutional and other fixed forces. The core features of governance are set out in constitutions, legal precedent, designs of institutions, and so on, and are not easily changed, if they can be changed at all. In addition, factors related to the composition of the economy, geographic and demographic features, and political culture are fixed in the short or medium term. In assessing capacities for ecological protection and green growth, this part of the chapter focuses on institutional factors and the political economy of having a large and politically influential fossil fuel sector. Other factors are relevant, like a political culture emphasizing individualism and skepticism toward government activism, but are beyond the scope of this book. They are worth exploring more in other research.

My consideration of the evidence on the institutional characteristics of the US policy system suggests it is a mixed bag. There is no doubt that change and innovation are more difficult in presidential systems with multiple checks and balances than in parliamentary ones. That, after all, is the idea. But are parliamentary systems necessarily more ecologically protective? Evidence reviewed in Chapter 4 suggests only a slight preference for the ecological performance of parliamentary systems, and that is subject to caveats. Perhaps we should simply say that they are better at translating public preferences—when those preferences are clear and compelling—into ecological policy change and innovation than systems based on separation of powers.

Evidence on the advantages of neo-corporatist/integrating over pluralist/adversarial systems is more compelling. That countries like Germany, Sweden, Finland, and Denmark consistently rank better on ecological performance assessments may be due partly to the patterns of interest group interaction and the ability to reach agreement on major societal goals. These characteristics also should bode well for green growth capacities, with options for positive-sum ecology–economy outcomes more achievable than in adversarial systems pitting ecological against economic goals in a series of zero-sum choices. A range of quantitative and qualitative evidence supports this conclusion. From an institutional perspective, these limitations in pluralist systems— including and especially the United States—are a factor explaining green growth policy capacity.

In his chapter in *Do Institutions Matter?* David Vogel (1993) describes how the multiple veto points in the United States protected ecological programs when the Reagan administration set out to undo the legal architecture of the 1970s. Many studies conclude that a system with multiple veto points makes change difficult, but this same feature also broadens access for different interests.

Two brief cases illustrate the mixed effects of multiple veto points. One is the story of how the EPA came to issue its 2015 Clean Power Plan for reducing coal plant emissions in electricity generation, briefly mentioned in Chapter 6. In the early 2000s, 12 states and several cities, with Massachusetts as lead plaintiff, brought a suit against the federal government arguing the EPA had to regulate carbon dioxide under the Clean Air Act. The Court of Appeals for the District of Columbia rejected their claim, not on the merits but because Massachusetts had not demonstrated the particular harm that entitled it to standing before a court. On appeal, the Supreme Court disagreed in a 5–4 ruling; it rejected the EPA's position that it lacked authority, ordered it to determine if the emissions endangered "public health or welfare" and, if so, to regulate them under the Clean Air Act (*Massachusetts* v. *EPA* [549 US 497], 2007).

The *Massachusetts* ruling was issued less than two years before Barack Obama came into office. He wanted to do something about the causes of climate change, both to put the US on a new trajectory and to build a case for international action. The first choice for doing this was the American Clean Energy and Security Act, better known as Waxman-Markey after its House sponsors, Henry Waxman and Ed Markey (for a summary, see Center for Climate and Energy Solutions).[2] It would have established a national cap-and-trade system, leading to a nearly 80% reduction in emissions by 2050, as well as a clean energy standard, a portfolio of clean energy and economic assistance funding, and other measures. The bill passed the House by seven votes in June 2009 but never made it through the Senate. As threatened all along if a comprehensive bill like Waxman-Markey failed, the administration went to a fallback strategy of issuing coal-plant standards under authority from the *Massachusetts* ruling (Hulse and Herszenhorn 2010).

Issued in the fall of 2015, the Clean Power Plan (CPP) was an innovative strategy for cutting emissions. Rather than regulate emission sources directly—in this case applying it directly to coal-fired generating plants—the strategy was to push states to achieve a 2030 emission reduction target. As I described in the last chapter, states had flexibility in determining how to reduce emissions and could select from among four policy options for meeting the targets.

The typical veto points became action points; they precipitated rather than blocked policy change. Although the failure of Waxman-Markey in the Senate may be attributed to institutional factors—the 60-vote rule for overcoming filibusters or allocating two Senate seats per state, for example—it was the combination of judicial review and state-driven litigation that made the CPP possible. Of course, since then, more than half of the states have sued the EPA from the other side, claiming that the Plan exceeds the federal government's authority under the Clean Air Act.[3] The Supreme Court even issued a stay on further action under the Plan while the Court of Appeals for the District of Columbia ruled on the merits (Adler 2016; Magill 2016).

A second case on structural factors draws on the contrasts between the United States and New Zealand—a far smaller democracy presenting many institutional contrasts with the United States. As every successful graduate of American Politics 101 knows, the United States is the poster child for pluralism, a system in which power is decentralized and interest groups compete in an often adversarial fashion to influence policy. Indeed, it is replete with veto players (Madden 2014), where there exist many actors whose agreement is needed for a departure from the status quo. Of Madden's seven veto players— federalism, bicameralism, a presidential system, single-member legislative districts, initiatives/referenda, judicial review, and pluralism—the United States exhibits six at a national level (all but initiatives and referenda, which do exist in some states). The United States also displays two of Madden's three partisan veto points: divided government for most of the last several decades and an anti–climate action party in the form of the national Republican Party, one of the few major parties in the developed world that rejects a need to mitigate greenhouse gas emissions.

A counterpoint is New Zealand, which displays only one institutional veto player—national initiatives and referenda. As one of only three democracies in the world without a written constitution (along with the United Kingdom and Israel), it has flexibility to change the basic rules of the game when voters think it is necessary. Although it had a parliamentary upper house—the appointed Legislative Council of New Zealand—it was abolished in 1950 because it was not seen as contributing to the nation's well-being. Similarly, in 1993, New Zealand's single-district, first-past-the-post electoral system was changed by referendum to a mixed-member proportional system of representation, seen as a better way to reflect public preferences in a parliament that now consists of one chamber. New Zealand is a unitary, not a federal system; it has no significant tradition of judicial review, as does the United States; it is parliamentary, not strongly pluralist (Hayward 2015). Institutionally, it is system that could move quickly on climate change.

Yet New Zealand ranked 42nd on the CCPI, eight positions below the United States. In the most recent Yale-Columbia EPI, New Zealand ranked 11th, well above the United States. It happens that New Zealand has been led by a right-of-center, strongly pro-business and pro–economic growth party for several years. So it might be, as the wind power case illustrates, that structural factors matter but politics matters just as much. The lesson of both of these cases is that it is difficult to make general statements about the effects of specific institutional factors, although it is fair to say that change is more difficult where there are many veto points. If, however, public opinion does not support change, or brown sectors are powerful, being institutionally "nimble" may not matter that much.

What may be the most significant institutional strength for the United States in capacities for green growth in the coming decades is the effects of federalism. The quantitative research provides few clear answers on whether federal systems are better for ecological protection and innovation (Walti 2004). States like California, Massachusetts, Connecticut, Maryland, and New York, to name a few, have had the ability to innovate in climate energy. New Jersey, Massachusetts, and Minnesota have long been viewed as leaders in the area of pollution prevention, a major theme in the 1980s and 1990s (Rabe 2016). Many states were proactive in efforts to overcome limits in the aging Toxic Substances Control Act of 1976, and their efforts enabled a modernization of that law—a rare bipartisan action—in the summer of 2016 (Hulse 2016). Ecological protection, and as a consequence the potential for in green growth, tends to be facilitated by federalism.

One way of looking at structural factors is through a nation's policy capacities. The writing in comparative ecological policy differentiates three types of capacities—cognitive, legal-administrative, and integrating (Jänicke and Weidner 1997). *Cognitive* capacities describe knowledge for understanding, evaluating, and responding to ecological problems. They include scientific and technical capacities in such fields as chemistry, toxicology, earth sciences, ecology, and hydrology, as well as more solution-oriented capacities in economics, law, and policy analysis. *Administrative* capacities flow from the quality of the public sector, the ability to implement complex programs, low levels of corruption, a capable and uncorrupted civil service, and sound legal institutions. In both areas, as a wealthy and politically stable nation, the United States possesses well-developed capacities. Indeed, its scientific and technical capacity may be the best in the world, given its economic strengths, research universities and government labs, history of technology and business innovation, and its overall resources.

Still, these capacities should not be taken for granted. After all, one goal of a neo-liberal philosophy is cutting public spending, including energy and environmental technology research. Laura Diaz Anadon and John P. Holdren made this case for energy innovation in 2009:

> The United States ought to be the leader of the world in the energy technology that is needed. It has the largest economy, uses the most energy . . . has made the largest cumulative contribution to the atmospheric buildup of fossil carbon dioxide that is the dominant driver of climate change, has a large balance of payments stake in competitiveness in the global energy technology market as well as a large stake in the worldwide economic security benefits of meeting global energy needs in affordable and sustainable ways, and possesses by many measures the most capable scientific and engineering workforce in the world. The actual performance of this country in energy-technology innovation, however, has been falling short by almost every measure: in relation to the need, in relation to opportunities, in relation to what other countries are doing, and even in

the simple-minded but still somewhat instructive measure of investment in energy-technology innovation in absolute terms and as a proportion of GDP, compared to the past (Anadon and Holdren 2009, 89–90).

Indeed, when their article appeared, federal investments in energy research, development, and demonstration were "about the same in absolute terms as they were twenty-five years ago—and thus less than half as large as twenty-five years ago in relation to GDP" (90).

More recently, in 2015, the American Energy Innovation Council (AEIC) reported federal investment in clean energy research and development as just under 0.03% of GDP, some $5 billion annually—less than the annual spending on potato and tortilla chips. In comparison, China invested 0.11% of GDP, Norway 0.09%, Denmark 0.06%, and Finland 0.12%. The AEIC views the US level of investment as one-third of what is needed "to compete effectively in global energy markets, to diversify from foreign oil, and to mitigate environmental harms from energy production" (4).

Similarly, the trend in recent decades to defund, undermine, and delegitimize government at all levels will take a toll on administrative capacities. A continued diminution of technical and administrative capacities will have long-term implications for the quality of governance.

Another form of policy capacity that is worth considering in this analysis is what Jänicke and Weidner term *integrative* or *integrating* capacities (1997, 13). This is the ability at various levels of governance to conduct dialogue, develop consensus, evaluate solutions across policy sectors (e.g., economy or energy and ecology), and identify positive-sum solutions. Indeed, this is the advantage neo-corporatist systems appear to have over pluralist ones—the ability to attain high levels of ecological performance and, I would argue, to pursue a greener growth path.

Structural factors are relatively fixed, but some may be changed near term. In the next chapter, I consider mid-level institutional reform that may improve green growth capacities by expanding the basis for forming a political coalition and linking ecology–economy issues in positive ways. Following my objective of focusing on *what is possible*, constitutional change is off the table. Part of what is subject to change in coming decades is the political balance of power between brown and green economic sectors, so political factors come next.

## Political Factors

Democracies are complex mechanisms in which, if things are working well, public preferences are translated into policy. Politics is the process of understanding, shaping, reconciling, and responding to those preferences. Many critics are impatient with politics and its role in human affairs, particularly in the ability to respect ecological limits (e.g., Shearman and Smith 2007). Yet denying politics, democratic or otherwise, does not make it any less essential. Calls for a version of ecological autocracy still have to face the realities of politics, like it or not.

The best handle on political factors as they affect ecological capacities is John Kingdon's concept of the political stream, used in the next chapter to set out a strategy for green growth. The politics stream is "composed of such things as public mood, pressure group campaigns, election results, partisan or ideological distributions in Congress, and changes in administration" (1995, 145). The operations and outcomes from the political stream are defined and constrained by the structural factors discussed above. Obviously, parliamentary systems generate a different set of political dynamics than do presidential ones; federalism offers more points for access and innovation (as well as obstruction) than unitary ones. The research in Chapter 4 aims to untangle the effects of structural factors (institutions, economic composition) from political ones in general. Here, I untangle the effects of structural from political factors to evaluate capacities in the United States.

A review of elements of the political stream—the public mood, pressure groups, election results, partisan or ideological distributions in Congress, changes in administration—reveals how vulnerable progress toward ecological protection and green growth is to political factors. In the largest study of political attitudes it had ever conducted, the Pew Research Center found that "Republicans and Democrats are more divided along ideological lines—and partisan antipathy is deeper and more extensive—than at any point in the last two decades" (Pew Center 2014). Political polarization has grown dramatically, with 92% of Republicans to the right of the median Democrat, and 94% of Democrats to the left of the median Republican. Demonstrating the extent of the mutual antipathy, the survey found that 36% of Republicans and 27% of Democrats see the opposing party as "a threat to the nation's well-being." To the extent that a political center does exist, it is among the less politically engaged parts of the population.

Another indicator of the public mood is attitudes toward and confidence in government. If people do not trust institutions and leaders, they are unlikely to support collective action for ecological protection and green growth. Again, the picture is not positive for advocates of collective action and public goods. The dramatic decline in confidence in government since the 1960s is a subject of frequent commentary. Examining this issue in 2015, the Pew Research Center observed that "The public's trust in the federal government continues to be at historically low levels" (Pew Research 2015a). Asked if they trust the federal government to do "what is right" all or most of the time, those saying yes fell from a high of 77% in the late 1960s to 19%, with a major decline in the decade from the late 1960s to late 1970s, when confidence fell by more than half. Again, this is not an encouraging sign for collective problem solving.

Election results and changes in leadership also dramatically shape ecological capacities. Former EPA Administrator William Ruckelshaus (1998) once wrote about the "swings in the pendulum" that accompany changes in presidential administrations and influence environmental regulation. If anything, these swings have become more pronounced. From the 1970s and into the 1990s, ecological policy often was a consensus issue: there were disagreements over scope and stringency, but the need for action to protect public health and ecology generally was widely accepted. This relative consensus was reflected in votes on major laws, listed in Table 7.3. An example is the 1990 Clean Air Act Amendments, one of the most expansive regulatory laws in US history, where it passed 89–10 in the Senate and 401–25 in the House. A startling, recent exception was modernization of the Toxic Substances Control Act in 2016, an issue where there was a high level of business and (with exceptions) environmentalist consensus (enacted as the Frank R. Lautenberg Chemical Safety for the 21st Century Act).

Political polarization has grown in recent decades due to "the increasing alignment between party identification and political ideology, with Republicans becoming increasingly conservative and Democrats increasingly liberal" (Dunlap, McCright, and Yarosh 2016, 15). Within the US Congress, the trends

Table 7.3 CONGRESSIONAL VOTING ON MAJOR ENVIRONMENTAL LAWS

| Legislation | House Vote | Senate Vote |
|---|---|---|
| National Environmental Policy Act of 1969 | 372–15 | Unanimous |
| Clean Air Act of 1970 | 375–1 | 73–0 |
| Federal Water Pollution Control Act of 1972 | 247–23 | 52–12 |
| Endangered Species Act of 1973 | 355–4 | 92–0 |
| Toxic Substances Control Act of 1976 | 360–35 | 73–6 |
| Resource Conservation and Recovery Act of 1976 | 367–8 | 88–3 |
| Clean Air Act Amendments of 1977 | 326–49 | 73–7 |
| Superfund (CERCLA) of 1980 | 274–94 | Voice Vote |
| Hazardous and Solid Waste Amendments of 1984 | Voice Vote | Voice Vote |
| Water Quality Act of 1987 | 401–26 | 86–14 |
| Clean Air Act Amendments of 1990 | 401–25 | 89–10 |
| Lautenberg Chemical Safety Act of 2016 | 403–12 | Voice Vote |

SOURCE: Analysis by the Center for Environmental Policy, American University (based on data from www.congress.gov and www.govtrack.us)

toward greater polarization are unmistakable. In 1970s, the gap in the League of Conservation Voters congressional voting scores between the two parties was in the range of 20 to 25 points; by 2015 it had grown to some 85 points, making any sort of consensus or compromise on major ecological issues increasingly elusive.

The climate policy shifts from the Bush to the Obama administration in the last decade illustrate the contrasts. For political as well as ideological reasons, the Bush administration was unwilling to press the fossil fuel industry (among others) to reduce climate-related and other air emissions. It even relaxed air standards in many ways, such as changes in the complex New Source Review program requiring technology upgrades for existing sources undergoing major modifications and in proposing emissions trading for regulating mercury emissions from coal plants (a poor application of trading concepts that was later rejected by a federal court).

Differences between the Bush and Obama administrations specifically on climate change were even more dramatic. Despite claiming during the campaign that he would act on the climate issue, George W. Bush avoided doing much once in office. The exception was in supporting the Energy Policy Act of 2005 and Energy Independence and Security Act of 2007; both gave some support to energy efficiency and renewables, although falling well short of a comprehensive energy strategy (Rosenbaum 2015). The 2001–2009 period was one of inaction. A defining moment came in 2007 when the EPA declined California's request for a Clean Air Act waiver to set carbon standards for vehicles more stringent than the federal ones (Broder and Barringer 2007). To that point, all of California's general requests for mobile source waivers had been approved.

President Obama entered office with a commitment to climate action. He supported the Waxman-Markey bill and, once that failed, the EPA's use of authority from the *Massachusetts* ruling to reduce coal plant emissions. Still, it was not until his second term that President Obama initiated a range of policies for cutting emissions and pushing clean energy and efficiency (Landler and Broder 2013). Among these were strict vehicle fuel efficiency standards, to a European-style fleet average of 54.5 miles per gallon by 2025; renewable energy production on federal lands; stringent standards for new coal-fired power plants, also under the *Massachusetts* authority (although no new plants are expected to be built); the Clean Power Plan for reducing existing coal plant emissions by 32% by 2030; and a 2014 agreement with China where it committed to cutting emissions and expanding renewables. Two former EPA administrators under Republican presidents even endorsed Obama's plans (Ruckelshaus and Reilly 2016).

The effects of partisan differences on ecological protection and green growth are evident in the major party platforms adopted in the summer of 2016 during the presidential election. The Republican platform was based on the premise of inevitable ecology–economy conflicts, the virtues of markets, and the need for state-level policy control, as revealed in such statements as:

> We must also ensure that domestic policies do not compromise our global competitiveness through overregulation and undue interference in the marketplace (Republican National Committee, 17).

> States, not Washington bureaucrats, are best equipped to engage farmers and ranchers to develop sound farm oversight policies (18).

> Poverty, not wealth, is the greatest threat to the environment, while steady economic growth brings the technological advances which make environmental progress possible (21).

And, in an illustration of what John Dryzek calls "Prometheanism" (a view that growth will solve ecological problems) in his book on environmental discourses (2013), it offers the following:

> We firmly believe environmental problems are best solved by giving incentives for human ingenuity and the development of new technologies, not through top-down, command-and-control regulations that stifle economic growth and costs thousands of jobs (22).

On specifics, the platform calls for opening up public lands and the outer continental shelf to "responsible" oil exploration; handing over more control of land and water resources to states, including federal lands; encouraging renewable energy, but only through private capital; killing the Clean Power Plan and forbidding the EPA from regulating carbon; and allowing any marketable energy production. Environmentalists, it asserts, rest their appeals on "shoddy science, scare tactics, and centralized, command-and-control regulation" (21). Coal is an "abundant, clean, affordable, reliable domestic resource" (19). The Intergovernmental Panel on Climate Change—the body created in 1989 to establish consensus on climate science, is "a political mechanism, not an unbiased scientific institution" that should be relied upon (22).

The Democratic platform offers striking contrasts, describing climate change as "an urgent threat and a defining challenge of our time" and setting a goal of "running entirely on clean energy by mid-century" (Democratic Platform Committee 2016, 27). It adopts a green growth framing in such statements as: "Democrats reject the notion that we have to choose between protecting our planet and creating good-paying jobs. We can and will do both" (27). It calls for phasing down fossil fuel production on federal lands and prohibiting oil drilling in the Arctic and off the Atlantic coast. Although focused on energy and climate issues, the platform stresses issues of environmental justice, including lead in drinking water and protection of public land and water. On the specifics, it favors spending on public transit, eliminating fossil fuel subsidies, increasing infrastructure investment, and responsible hydraulic fracturing (controlling effects on water supplies and methane) with more state and local control over when and how it occurs.

Prevailing governing philosophies are part of Kingdon's political stream. Documenting the rise and influence of neo-liberal governance in recent decades, Judith Layzer has written that since the 1970s, "conservative activists have disseminated a compelling antiregulatory storyline to counter the environmentalist narrative, mobilized grassroots opposition to environmental regulations, and undertaken sophisticated legal challenges to the basis for and implementation of environmental laws." Over time, she adds, these actions "have imparted a legitimacy to a new antiregulatory rhetoric, one that emphasizes distrust of the federal bureaucracy, admiration for unfettered property rights and markets, skepticism about science, and disdain for environmental advocates" (2012, 4). Environmental policy has gone from a consensus issue in the 1970s to a far more partisan one since the 1990s. Indeed, neo-liberal emphasis on individualism, low taxation, limited government, and "unfettered markets" is antithetical to the capacities and policies that are needed for ecological protection and green growth. The alliance of this philosophy with the interests of fossil fuels and industrial agriculture constitutes a primary, although by no means the only, explanation for declining assessments of the US ecological performance in recent decades.

To be sure, factors other than ideological conflicts, hostility toward government action, and the rise of a neo-liberal governing philosophy explain the growing cleavages on ecological issues. To begin, the problems are not as obvious now as they were even a few decades ago. Ecological and environmental health policies have to a degree been victims of their own success. Despite the lingering problems, air quality has improved greatly in the United States, especially given population and economic growth. Still, major challenges remain in nonpoint source water pollution, impending shortages in water supplies in many parts of the country, threats to habitat and biodiversity, air toxics, impaired air quality due to fine particulates and ozone, and exposures to a range and quantity of chemicals whose toxicity is mostly undetermined. Climate change is an issue that has been difficult to establish as a health and ecological threat demanding action. Still, the notion that many ecological problems are "solved" or now are manageable has effects.

## GREEN GROWTH FRAMING IN US POLITICS

Green growth is used here to frame (or reframe, to be specific) presumed ecology–economy relationship as the basis of a change agenda. Previous chapters looked at the concept's uses in other countries and internationally. It has become an influential concept, often appearing as a competitor or successor to sustainable development. The questions for the rest of the chapter are: What effect has it had in the United States? Has the concept influenced political debates? Does it offer a means of reframing the zero-sum conflicts to which the United States especially appears to be prone?

Of course, the effects of green growth as a concept are not limited to that specific term. A variety of cognate concepts express the same core ideas. Among these, besides green economy, are smart growth, sustainable growth, the clean energy economy, and even pollution prevention. Each reflects an intention to link ecology and economics in positive ways. Smart growth, for example, is applied almost entirely by cities that aim to integrate ecological, economic, and often social goals. Pollution prevention is used in a production context, especially in referring to manufacturing (Geiser 2004). Clean energy and green energy are used to describe win–wins in renewable energy and efficiency.

Several trends and events combined to make the core idea of green growth— of finding positive relationships among ecological and economic goals— relevant to the United States. One was the simple need to break out of the old trap of assuming that zero-sum ecology–economy conflicts were unavoidable. The environmental decade of the 1970s challenged the notion that economic growth could be pursued without regard to ecological and health consequences. Ecologically unguided growth was rejected in favor of a somewhat more ecologically sensitive growth. Consistent with Dryzek's notion of problem-solving discourses (2013), the first epoch of policy in the United States and other developed countries consisted of incremental fine-tuning: the orchestra might be playing in a different key, but most of the music was the same. So rather than rethinking how electricity is generated, or how cities develop and use land, the strategy was to engage in selective interventions in various arenas, mostly in manufacturing, and mitigate the more obvious effects of pollution, waste, chemical use, and growth. All of this exemplifies Mazmanian and Kraft's first epoch (2009).

Looking back now, it is interesting that early statements by President Richard Nixon reveal hints of a green growth framing. In his 1970 State of the Union address, for example, as Judith Layzer describes it, he "decried the effects of unfettered economic growth and returned several times to two themes: that happiness was not to be found in personal economic wealth and that the economic indicators of government did not reflect citizens' well-being" (2012, 33). If such thinking had truly characterized his administration, the zero-sum mindset might have been replaced with one looking like that of ecological economics. Instead, Layzer continues, "there is overwhelming evidence that he [President Nixon] advocated on behalf of the environment out of political expedience, rather than conviction" (37). By 1971, President Nixon was stressing costs in policy debates, and he vetoed the 1972 Clean Water Act, although Congress later overrode it.

Some evidence of green growth ideas emanated from the center-left in the late 1970s, as illustrated in President Jimmy Carter's "Environmental Message to the Congress" in May 1977:

> I believe environmental protection is consistent with a sound econ-
> omy. Previous pollution control laws have generated many more jobs
> than they have cost. And other environmental measures whose time has
> come . . . will produce still more jobs, often where they are needed most.
> In any event, if we ignore the care of our environment, the day will even-
> tually come when our economy suffers for that neglect (available at http://
> www.presidency.ucsb.edu/ws/?pid=7561; accessed September 27, 2016).

What is notable is not just this green growth assertion of positive ecology–economy linkages—a negation of the zero-sum—but the view that economic well-being depends on ecological quality.

Two events sharpened the ecology–economy dichotomy in the 1970s—the energy crisis and the economic troubles that combined inflation with lagging growth. It was with the election of Ronald Reagan in 1980, however, that the environment as consensus issue was lost for good, and the roots of the cur-rent polarization on ecological and economic issues were fixed. Adopting a neo-liberal policy agenda stressing deregulation, smaller government, reliance on markets, and low tax rates, the Reagan administration aimed to roll back environmental programs across the board. This political polarization emerged again with the election of a conservative Republican majority and the rise of Newt Gingrich as House Speaker in 1994–1995. His "Contract with America" called for major reductions in regulation. A Democratic Senate and President blocked statutory change, but the House tried to gum up regulation with para-lyzing provisions on mandatory risk assessment and cost–benefit analysis that ultimately failed to pass (Kraft 2016).

With President Clinton came more efforts to reframe ecological and eco-nomic issues. This was partly a response to the conservative assault on regula-tion and the need to defuse claims of lost growth and jobs. On Earth Day 1993, he presented a classic green growth framing:

> First, we think you can't have a healthy economy without a healthy envi-
> ronment. We need not choose between breathing clean air and bringing
> home secure paychecks. The fact is, our environmental problems result
> not from robust growth but from reckless growth. The fact is that only a
> prosperous society can have the confidence and the means to protect its

environment. And the fact is healthy communities and environmentally sound products and services do best in today's economic competition. That's why our policies must protect our environment, promote economic growth, and provide millions of new high-skill, high-wage jobs (http://www.presidency.ucsb.edu/ws/?pid=46460; accessed September 27, 2016).

In a summary of accomplishments released in 1999, the administration asserted that "President Clinton's environmental strategy has given our nation the cleanest air and water in a generation and the strongest economy in the nation's history—*proving that you can both protect the environment and grow the economy*" (emphasis added).

The financial crisis, recession, and election of Barack Obama in 2008 sealed green growth as a (re)framing concept. A sure sign of its potency are the lengths to which opponents of climate action have gone to stress ecology–economy conflicts; for illustrations, see Box 7.1.

---

Box 7.1

### STATEMENTS CASTING THE CLEAN POWER PLAN AS A ZERO-SUM POLICY

*"the regulation could cost our country about a third of a trillion dollars in compliance costs and cause electricity price hikes in nearly every state."*
Kentucky Senator Mitch McConnell
http://www.kentucky.com/opinion/op-ed/article44558769.html

*"I urge leaders of both parties . . . who represent communities that will be devastated by this reckless policy, to stand against this administration's dangerous agenda of economic decline."*
Texas Senator Ted Cruz
https://www.tedcruz.org/news/cruz-statement-on-president-obamas-epa-regulations/

*"What it's going to do is kill our economy, and kill energy production in this country."*
Scott Pruitt, EPA Administrator and former Oklahoma Attorney General
http://www.cnn.com/2016/12/13/politics/kfile-scott-pruitt-climate-change-epa/

*The Administration is "pursuing an illegal plan that will drive up electricity costs and put people out of work."*
Coalition for Clean Coal Electricity
http://www.dw.com/en/about-dw/profile/s-30688

---

At the same time, the economic crisis made an integration of ecological and economic goals a political imperative. The result is a green growth framing, with claims of ecological–economic complementarities and synergies regularly emerging from the Obama administration. That green growth was emerging as a global concept, as discussed in Chapter 2, made these claims timely.

For example, in an op-ed piece in the *Wall Street Journal* in December 2010 (the midst of the recession) Lisa Jackson, Obama's first EPA Administrator, offered a green growth framing:

> Fortunately, the last 40 years show no evidence that environmental protection hinders economic growth. Neither the recent crisis nor any other period of economic turmoil was caused by environmental protection. In fact, a clean environment strengthens our economy (Jackson 2010).

Citing GDP growth of 207% since 1970 (the year the Clean Air Act was enacted), she observed:

> Instead of cutting productivity, we've cut pollution while the number of American cars, buildings and power plants has increased. Alleged 'job-killing' regulations have, according to the Commerce Department, sparked a homegrown environmental protection industry that employs more than 1.5 million Americans.

In a speech before the Council on Foreign Relations in January 2016, EPA Administrator Gina McCarthy—the second Obama appointee in that post— saw the challenge as continuing "to grow economically while still lowering air pollution that can harm human populations as well as the environment." Quoting her again later in the article, the *Washington Post* continues: "It can be done . . . and it can drive the new technologies you need to come to the point where you're not being forced to do it, but you're embracing it" (Warrick 2016). This positive conception of economic development and environmental technology is a core aspect of green growth thinking.

In remarks to the UN Climate Change Summit in 2014, President Obama said action on renewable energy and vehicle efficiency prove "there does not have to be a conflict between a sound environment and strong economic growth" (White House 2014). Before the Subcommittee on Energy and Power of the House Energy and Commerce Committee in 2013, Administrator Gina McCarthy stated: "Reducing carbon pollution is critically important to the protection of American's health and the environment upon which our economy depends." Carbon reductions are a "spark for business innovation, job creation, clean energy and broad economic growth. The United States' success over the last 40 years makes clear that environmental protection and economic growth go hand in hand" (EPA 2013). That these goals go "hand in hand" was a staple of EPA administrators' speeches for years, but the Obama administration took it to new heights.

The national elections in 2016 fundamentally transformed the political land-scape for green growth and ecological policies in general. Both the President and majorities in the Senate and House favored a continuation of a brown econ-omy based on the dominance of fossil fuels, resource exploitation, industrial agriculture, and a relative lack of regard for critical ecosystems. An early sign of this was the use of the Congressional Review Act to invalidate a recently issued rule requiring coal companies to restore damaged streams and surrounding areas to their original state, based on the argument that it protects coal mining jobs, despite contrary evidence (Tabuchi 2017). Most important, the case for inevitable ecology–economy conflicts again was dominant.

## CAPACITIES FOR GREEN GROWTH

Former George W. Bush administration Defense Secretary Donald Rumsfeld is rarely quoted in books on ecological policy; it was not a particular enthusiasm of his. Yet one of his better-known quotes is worth citing in discussing green growth capacities. He once remarked, on the practical realities of military action: "You go to war with the Army you have—not the Army you might wish you have" (Rumsfeld 2013). Similarly, for ecological protection and green growth, you take on the challenge with the institutions you have, not the ones you wish you had.

A look at the factors associated with ecological protection, and by inference with green growth, suggests several strengths and weaknesses for the United States. Among the strengths are the following:

- First-rate scientific and technological capabilities and wealth to expand and exploit them
- An accumulated *stock* of democracy and high levels of political stability and competence
- Relatively low corruption, although with an outsized role for money in elections
- An active and varied number of NGOs with impressive credentials and capabilities
- Many innovative subnational governments (state and local) committed to green growth

*but are they really u being used u I being enforced?*

- A comprehensive if not integrated set of laws and institutions for ecological protection
- An innovative business sector capable of green growth given the right rules of the game

Among the significant weaknesses, some of which are beyond the scope of this book, are the following:

*true*

- A political culture in which the state is viewed with suspicion and individualism is valued

*very!!!*

- Relatively high levels of economic inequality, which may undermine collective action
- A governing philosophy that devalues collective action and public goods across the board
- Relatively soft public opinion that tends to soften more in times of economic turmoil
- Large, politically powerful fossil fuel and industrial agriculture sectors that block change
- A large number of institutional veto players that make policy change difficult
- A number of imperfections in democratic effectiveness, accountability, and participation
- An adversarial, polarized, fragmented policy system that forces binary choices

Many factors could be added to the balance sheet. The above are the more significant ones, given the analysis in this book, and they illustrate challenges and options for the United States. Green growth is economically and technologically a distinct possibility (Green 2009). The issue is political feasibility. The next chapter argues that a green growth concept is well-suited to the United States. Indeed, it may be the only way to frame choices for recognizing the reality of ecological limits.

# Can Change Happen?

In September 2016, a report from the US Census Bureau delivered good news for the American public: household income for 2015 had grown by 5.2% in the previous year. As the *Washington Post* put it, "Middle-class Americans and the poor in 2015 enjoyed their best year of economic improvement in decades . . . a spike that broke a long streak of disappointment for American workers but did not fully repair the damage inflicted by the Great Recession" (Tankersley 2016). Median household income rose from an inflation-adjusted $53,700 in 2014 to $56,500 in 2015. This was the largest increase since the Bureau started tracking these numbers in 1968. The middle class were not the only beneficiaries. The poverty rate fell by 1.2%, the largest decline since 1968. Among the reasons for the positive trends were an improving job market (the unemployment rate had fallen to under 5%), low inflation, and rising wages, due in part to the adoption of a higher minimum wage in much of the country, although not nationally. The only wrinkle was that these gains had occurred in cities and suburbs and did not extend to rural areas.

Our discussion of green growth suggests many ways of looking at this news. For growth advocates, any sign of higher incomes is good. For anyone worried about economic inequality, here was a sign that, after years of being left out, at least *some* growth benefits were flowing to middle- and low-income groups. For proponents of ecological protection who see growth as a cause of climate change, habitat loss, water stress, and ecosystem degradation, this was not entirely good news; it offered evidence that growth pressures on the planet were firmly in place. For anyone concerned about political dysfunctionality, a worry was that incomes grew in cities and suburbs but not in rural areas; this was ominous given how economic and cultural divisions dominated the 2016 campaign, and voters split along urban–rural lines (Badger, Bui, and Pearce 2016).

To argue at the time that this positive news for middle- and low-income groups was bad for the planet would have been tone deaf politically and socially insensitive. On the other hand, to have argued that even more growth would have occurred without existing ecological policies would have been short-sighted and, as we have seen in this book, inconsistent with the evidence. While the long-term, ecological effects of growth are a legitimate concern, near-term effects are marginal, irrelevant, or mixed at worst, and depend far more on how growth occurs than the fact of growth itself. Moreover, the evidence from Chapter 5 suggests that sharing income more fairly can increase capacities for collective action, crucial for green growth and ecological protection.

Economies will continue to grow; voters elect leaders they think can deliver growth. The question is: Can we change the composition of growth and its meaning to make it reliably green?

This chapter considers green growth prospects in the United States. The logic of green growth—both as issue framing and policy agenda—is compelling only if there is a political path to making it happen. Forms of green growth are underway in the United States. Still, what is occurring falls short: it moves slowly and varies by state; it is not durable because it is not integrated into economic and political decision making. It is vulnerable to political change, which typically occurs for reasons unrelated to ecological policy. This vulnerability was strikingly apparent after the 2016 election.

This chapter considers the prospects for green growth from two perspectives. One draws upon theoretical models that have been influential in the field of public policy to determine what light they can shed on the prospects for change and ways of achieving it. My objective is not to apply these models in any depth, but to highlight their relevance and suggest lessons that may be drawn for future inquiry. The second perspective is to propose conditions under which a long-term, durable transition to green growth may occur. Most green growth assessments review policy and investment options but neglect processes and politics. The last part of the chapter envisions two plausible scenarios—a green and a brown—that could define the future of ecology–economy relationships.

## EXPLAINING POLICY CHANGE: THE RELEVANCE OF POLICY THEORY

Much of this book focuses on why some countries do better ecologically than others. There are no simple explanations. Political stability and economic success, which tend to go hand in hand, are part of the reason for differences among countries. Research and experience suggest that a strong science and technology base, reliable and independent judiciary, capable civil service, low levels of public and private corruption, democratic institutions with political and civil liberty, active NGOs, and a dynamic and innovative business sector all are positives.

As a stable and long-standing democracy with a high level of economic prosperity, the United States compares favorably with most any country in the world. I have suggested that federalism is an advantage, while separation of powers confers strengths and weaknesses. Still, it is hard to make broad generalizations on these and other institutional factors. Given the demands of a green economic transition, the limitations in integrating capacities that are characteristic of a pluralist, adversarial system like that in the United States are a challenge, as are aspects of the electoral system and political culture. The power of vested economic interests, in particular the fossil fuel sector, also presents barriers. Fossil fuels were critical in achieving the current quality of life, as their advocates like to point out, but clean and renewable energy holds the key to the future. Still, it is hard to shake the legacy of a past in which much of the country depends on fossil fuels.

Of course, explaining how, why, and when change occurs is a preoccupation of the public policy field (Kamarck 2013). Many quantitative and qualitative analyses have set out to answer such questions. This part of the chapter brings together two influential conceptual models for explaining policy change in an effort to assess the prospects for durable green growth in the United States and suggest how it may occur. Doing this involves many factors, most of which are discussed in previous chapters: public opinion, institutional rules of the game, policy capacities, electoral outcomes, interest groups, leaders' personalities and preferences, voting behavior, the nature of problems, and the slate of solutions, among others. With so many factors influencing policy change, it is hard to come up with easy explanations. The goal in policy studies is determining why and how change occurs—to go beyond a mere recitation of cases to patterns and lessons.

Certain conceptual models have been helpful in explaining policy change. Instrumental in shaping the course of policy studies was the writing on the limitations of the so-called rational policy model. This depicts policy change as guided by fully informed, goal-driven, and efficient decision makers seeking optimal outcomes. It assumes agreed-upon goals; clear policy options; timely, reliable data; and selection of options that maximize goals. Theorists argued this rational model not only was unrealistic in practice but not always worth emulating (Lindblom 1959).

Herbert Simon (1947) argued that we should aim not for a full or comprehensive but a *bounded* rationality to account for limited information, disagreement on goals, and constraints on human cognitive capacity. Charles Lindblom further distinguished *incremental* from *rational-comprehensive* policymaking (1959). Not only is the first more valid, he argues, it is often preferable in a world of complex choices, uneven information, and conflicting goals. Criticism of the rational model continued with the *garbage can* model of organizational choice, in which organizations are presented as "a collection of choices looking for problems, issues and feelings looking for decision situations in which they might be aired, solutions looking for issues to which they might be the answer, and decision makers looking for work" (Cohen, March, and Olsen 1972).

What these writers offer for our purposes are many theoretical insights into the politics of policymaking: it does not necessarily proceed in linear, rational ways; it is shaped by value and interest-based conflicts leading to disagreement over goals and how to achieve them; it is full of scientific, economic, and intertemporal uncertainty; and it is fluid and unpredictable. This work set a stage for two influential models of policy change: *multiple streams* theory (Kingdon 1995) and the *advocacy coalition framework* (Sabatier and Jenkins-Smith 1999). My goal here is not to apply these models in any detail but to consider their relevance to a political strategy. What do these theories offer in developing a political strategy for making a transition to green growth?

## Linking the Multiple Streams

Multiple streams theory builds explicitly on the garbage can model by emphasizing the fluidity and complexity of policymaking. It also links the world of ideas—of policy proposals, analyses, and solutions—with the workings of politics. It focuses on the front end of the policy process, on how agendas are set and alternatives identified. Policy change occurs as a result of the interactions among three streams. The *problem stream* is the list of issues requiring attention. Issues rise and fall on the agenda; their rise is influenced by feedback from various indicators, focusing events, crises, and trends. Problems fade because policymakers feel they are solved, their solutions are too costly, or other issues push them off the agenda. Something has to be perceived as a problem amenable to policy responses rather than as a condition that is not. An example is how opponents of climate action often concede the global climate is changing but as a result of normal variations in weather (a condition) rather than human activity (a problem). As Kingdon notes, "Getting people to see new problems, or to see old problems in one way rather than another, is a major conceptual and political accomplishment" (115).

The *policy stream* is the activity of policy communities, the "specialists in a given policy area" inside and outside of government (121). Made up of ideas, analyses, studies, alternatives, and solutions that are analyzed and debated by experts in these communities, this is the source of intellectual capital. Experts in an issue area may serve as "policy entrepreneurs" who develop, articulate, and advocate a solution to ecological problems (122). An example is emissions trading, which has been popular among economic and policy experts for decades and is now among the leading proposed solutions for many air, water, and climate issues (Tietenberg 2013).

The *political stream* flows independently of the others. As noted earlier, it is "composed of such things as public mood, pressure group campaigns, election results, partisan or ideological distributions in Congress, and changes in administration" (Kingdon 1995, 145). It is where choices are made and conflicts managed. It captures most of the political factors from the last chapter, although it is defined and constrained by structural factors. The political stream "flows along according to its own dynamics and its own rules" (162). The conditions for change exist when a "coupling" of the three streams occurs—when the political stream aligns with the recognition of problems in the problem stream, and the policy stream offers ideas and solutions. This creates a window that enables policy change, hence the *streams and windows* term often used to describe it.

What do the multiple streams offer for a green growth change strategy? The problem stream is a useful place to start. Without a doubt, the ecological problem stream has changed dramatically over the last five decades. Early concerns with major sources of air and water pollution remain, to be sure, and still are a threat to health and well-being everywhere, but in developing countries in particular. On top of these "first-generation" problems have come new challenges—nonpoint source pollution, water security, persistent and bio-accumulative toxics, radon, groundwater withdrawal and contamination, ecosystem degradation, and, of course, climate change (Fiorino 2001; Chertow and Esty 1997). Many indicators exist for tracking trends in these problems, although they are not as visible and sophisticated as the standard economic indicators. Some indicators are better than others; we know far more about air quality, for example, than chemicals. Still, it is fair to say our knowledge usually exceeds our ability to respond. The issue is not so much a lack of knowledge but *a collective inability to reach consensus and to act*. This surely is the case regarding climate, species and habitat, deforestation, urban air pollution, nonpoint water problems, and other issues.

It is not just the problems themselves that have changed; it is the sense of their reaching some kind of tipping point, in the complexity of the relationships among problems and in the formidable challenges to governance (Dovers 1996). Stresses on ecological systems push us closer to planetary boundaries, as Chapter 1 suggested. There is now more appreciation of the critical interactions among issues like energy and water, food and climate, or energy and health. Needs for integrating policy across political boundaries are more compelling. Most crucially, there is attention to thinking and acting systemically, as in restructuring energy, transport, and food systems or in focusing more on the sources rather than the manifestations of problems.

The policy stream as it relates to a green growth agenda is rich. Indeed, this is a source of strength in the literature: it organizes a formidable array of policy tools and strategies, supported by a great deal of analysis and evaluation, generated by a variety of experts. Chapter 6 described the richness of the policy stream. Many policy entrepreneurs push a green growth agenda, from city mayors to activists, from leadership states and cities to the OECD, World Bank, and UNEP.

Without a doubt, the political stream is a major barrier to a green economic transition in the United States and other countries. It is hard to put a finger on a concept like the "national mood," but the mood in the United States in the last few years has been one of dissatisfaction and anxiety, with major concerns about the direction of the country, the operation of major institutions, and economic insecurity. The sense of "us" versus "them" seems to be particularly strong and is reflected in national political contests. This aspect of the national mood surely was a major factor explaining the outcome of the 2016 election. All of this does not, to be sure, create a positive political environment for the collective action and attention to public goods needed for green growth.

As for other elements in the political stream, the prospects are not promising either. As discussed in Chapter 7, ideological conflicts in Congress and many state legislatures are high, and a political middle ground for building consensus on ecology–economy linkages often is absent (Binder 2003 and 2014). Ideological conflicts between the two parties on climate, air and water pollution, and resource development are so striking that a change in administrations alone may kill any hopes for green growth. Indeed, the 2016 election confirmed how transient ecological policy is; anything not hardwired into institutions and laws is vulnerable. Although the many veto players may impede a complete rollback, much of the Obama ecological agenda is in jeopardy, given the Republican takeover of the White House and control of Congress.

Multiple streams theory tells us that an opening in the problem or political stream creates windows in which new policies may be adopted and applied. Of course, with green growth we are talking about an array of related policies being adopted, not one in particular, so it is a slightly different challenge. At a specific level, the California water shortage reached a critical point at the same time that the right leadership (in the form of Governor Jerry Brown) was in a position to formulate a response (Moyer 2015). With an array of policy solutions developed by organizations like the Pacific Institute, it is fair to say the problem and political streams aligned, and the policy stream was able to provide needed answers (Christian-Smith and Gleick 2012).

Climate change presents a complicated picture in terms of the multiple streams. In recent decades, there has been steady accumulation of evidence on the near-certainty and profound impacts of a changing climate (IPCC 2014; Giddens 2011). With international organizations like the IPCC, and national agencies like National Oceanic and Atmospheric Administration and National Aeronautics and Space Administration doing research and analysis, feedback from the problem stream has been consistent enough to justify a response. As climate change moved up the agenda, new groups and interests joined the fray, a development having profound effects on energy policy (Lowry 2008).[1] The policy stream also has been active, not only with analysis but through actual experience with an array of solutions, as examined in Chapter 6.

It is in the political stream that climate policy has foundered. The national governing philosophy of one of the two major parties in the United States is hostile to collective action and public goods, as well as being tied politically to the fossil fuel industry and other pro-development, pro-growth interests. Any progress made in the last few years occurred despite and not because of that hostility. Opponents of climate action have pressed the issue in the terms of the problem stream—by arguing that climate instability is the result of natural cycles, not human activity. They use the policy stream by asserting that climate mitigation is too costly. Within the political stream, they take advantage of and encourage a national mood that has been skeptical of collective action and public goods, as the fierce opposition to the Affordable Care Act shows.

Thinking in terms of the multiple streams, one could argue that the problem stream is pointing clearly toward the need for action, and the policy stream offers a range of solutions—not only for climate change but for many other issues that could be addressed through green growth. A change strategy would need to focus on introducing the conditions in the political stream that would support a green growth agenda. At the end of the proverbial day, politics blocks change.

## Forming a Change Coalition

Another model used widely in policy research is the Advocacy Coalition Framework (ACF). It aims to explain all the stages of policymaking, even beyond those of agenda setting and formulation. Advocacy coalitions consist of "people from a variety of positions (elected and agency officials, interest group leaders, researchers) who (1) share a particular belief system—i.e., a set of basic values, causal assumptions, and problem perceptions—and who (2) show a non-trivial degree of coordinated activity over time" (Sabatier and Jenkins-Smith 1999, 138). These coalitions seek to alter policy by influencing legislative action (statutes and budgets), shaping public opinion, promoting leadership change, pursuing litigation, and promoting issue framings. Indeed, as this book argues, alternative issue framings may help in forming coalitions.

The unit of analysis in the ACF is not programs, laws, or institutions, but a "policy subsystem," the collection of people and organizations that specialize in and influence a defined issue area such as air quality, immigration, or children's health. Advocacy coalitions arise out of various policy subsystems to promote a point of view on issues. For any given issue, two or more advocacy coalitions may exist, often competing with each other. Although focused on the same issue area, two coalitions in the same subsystem may and often do compete, as in calling for more or less use of coal to generate electricity or in advocating contrasting water use policies.

The operations, strategies, and effectiveness of advocacy coalitions are shaped by two kinds of external factors—those that are fixed and hard to change (such as constitutional rules) and those that are dynamic and subject to change (like economic conditions and public opinion). These are identical to the structural and political factors distinguished in Chapter 7. Advocacy coalitions work within the constraints of the fixed factors in any given system—so that coalition strategies in parliamentary democracies differ from those in a separation-of-powers country, as do the chances of realizing a given policy goal. Coalitions compete in their ability to manipulate these variable factors: public opinion, elections, issue framings, or interest group influence.

The ACF differs from many other policy theories by emphasizing shared belief systems among coalition members and the role that technical and analytical information can play. Shared belief systems in an ACF exist at three levels (Sabatier and Jenkins-Smith 1999, 121–123). The most general are strongly held *deep core* beliefs; these are fundamental and normative on issues like freedom versus equality or security versus openness. They operate across policy domains and usually reflect standard left–right ideological contrasts. More specific to particular subsystems, and subject to change, are *policy core* beliefs, "assumed to be more readily adjusted in light of new data, new experience, or changing strategic considerations" (122). These define the typical contrasts in ecological debates: government's role in the economy, use of markets, trade-offs among economic and ecological goals, and national versus state roles. ACF assumes that policy core rather than deep core beliefs "are the fundamental glue of coalitions because they represent basic normative and empirical commitments within the domain of specialization of policy elites" (Sabatier and Jenkins-Smith 1999, 122). At a third level of generality are *secondary aspects* of belief systems; these are the more malleable beliefs on issues like policy instruments, budgetary allocations, allocation of institutional roles, and so on.

As for technical and analytic information, the ACF assumes that deep core beliefs are immune to such influences, while policy core and surely secondary beliefs are more open to them. One hypothesis underlying the ACF is that the natural sciences influence policy core beliefs more than the social sciences. Other assumptions of the ACF are that people trying to influence policy should be seen more as members of a coalition than in their formal organizational roles; scientists in coalitions are not necessarily neutral in their policy preferences; self-interest matters, but so do shared beliefs and problem perceptions; coalitions exist in many stages of development (from nascent to mature); and that coalitions influence policy at many levels of governance.

What does the ACF offer in thinking about the prospects for green growth? It may help to think of green growth as a collection of advocacy coalitions formed around specific issues, with climate–energy as the most relevant subsystem. Still other coalitions based on smart growth, water resources, sustainable farming and food, and green infrastructure define other subsystems that could make up an even larger green growth coalition. If people share elements of a belief system (basic values, causal assumptions, problem perceptions), and show "a non-trivial degree of coordination over time" (Sabatier and Jenkins-Smith 1999, 138), they could come together to form a broader green growth coalition. In this case, the deep core values holding the coalition together are a high regard for nature (at least in benefits to human well-being, if not its intrinsic value); concern for future generations; regard for collective over individual action; and concern for social equity and other liberal values.

The competing coalition, skeptical of green growth, shares such conservative values as individualism, competition, order, hierarchy, resistance to change, and justification of inequality (Lakoff 2002; Jost et al. 2003). There is a left–right basis to coalitions, as the ACF suggests.

At the level of policy core values, the broadly defined green growth coalition shares a belief in the inability of unregulated markets on their own to promote or protect well-being, in limits in ecosystems for absorbing unrestrained growth, in the economic value of ecological protection, and in state involvement in the economy. The competing coalition, committed to the status quo (given the current dominance of a largely brown economy), shares a different set of beliefs— that growth will generate the technologies and practices for reconciling growth and ecology, that markets nearly always deliver better outcomes for society, and that the state role should be highly limited. For issues like climate change, the coalitions differ in their regard for science, with the brown, anti-green coalition using skepticism about ecological signals to oppose change.

Does a third coalition exist, one that downplays simple growth and calls for a steady-state or even a de-growth trajectory? Simply put, it is hard to find a political coalition on any scale to support a deliberate shrinking of the economy and negative growth rates. The best examples are small policy subsystems that advocate a shared economy and related concepts (Alexander 2009 and 2012; Jackson 2011). These ideas have a merit, but they are small-scale and limited; few political leaders call for a smaller economy. Fair or not, the perception is that a shrinking economy leads to fewer jobs, less opportunity, more insecurity, and limited prospects. Even policies for limiting urban growth—Portland, Oregon being the best known—aim to control land use and sprawl, not economic growth per se (Portney 2013), although that may be a side effect.

Like multiple streams theory, the ACF offers many lessons. First is the need for a broad-based coalition for change. Moving from brown to green growth does not just happen: it involves political and policy change in many economic sectors as well as at multiple levels of governance. There should be two levels of coalition building. One is within the various ecological subsystems themselves, so that clean energy, water efficiency, climate action, smart growth, and smart farming, to name a few, are linked in a coherent coalition. The other is coalition building across policy sectors. Later I propose to expand green growth prospects by linking it with such policy goals as expanded job opportunities, increased economic equity, improved health, and so on.

This brief foray into policy theory tells us many things about the politics of green growth. The first is the need to understand the distinctive features of policy systems in envisioning a change strategy. Although some factors—public opinion, distributions of power, the level of economic development, and the quality of governance, to name a few—matter in any system, their effects on policymaking vary across different settings. Each of these policy theories was designed to explain how change happens in the United States; the basis for a political strategy could look very different in China and Brazil, or even in Canada or the United Kingdom. Second, they highlight the complexity of policy change, given all the factors that interact in unpredictable ways. The key is in finding patterns. Third, long-term fixed factors like federalism or separation of powers and short-term factors like the state of the economy should all be accounted for in any change strategy.

Green growth and similar framings of ecological issues are embraced most clearly by the center and left of center of the political spectrum. The *green* part of the concept is widely rejected from the right, which at this point includes almost all elected, national-level Republican officials. To concede that ecological and environmental health issues may and should interfere with an ideology of maximum possible, unguided growth is apparently unacceptable politically to the right. This is partly due to the core tenets of neo-liberal thinking, with the emphasis on small government, private goods, low tax rates, and unrestricted markets (although fossil fuel, grazing, and other subsidies are acceptable). It also is due, no doubt, to the close ties existing between the party and the fossil fuel industry, ones that are cemented by regional alliances.

The left of the political spectrum in the United States, beyond left of center, sometimes has been skeptical of the green growth concept. Many on the left suspect that concepts like green growth and economy are merely a rationale to justify a continued emphasis on economic growth over ecological and social goals. That is, we can talk about economic greening in a narrow sense— through more enlightened firms and more eco-efficiency—while still feeding the growth engine and its excessive consumption, wasteful lifestyles, poor land use, and fossil fuel economies. This skepticism however, may be a plus; it keeps us focused on the more transformational and perhaps achievable (but not radical) version of green growth rather than the narrower, technical one.

A durable green growth strategy will have to come from the center and expand. It will emerge as an alternative between ecologically destructive and short-sighted neo-liberalism and more conventional, confrontational ecological protection. This does not mean we should not rethink the social goal of simple, quantitative growth to measure well-being. My view of green growth involves such a rethinking. It also accepts that taking growth straight on— aiming to delegitimize it—will not work. It will not open up the political stream to needed change, nor will it create a foundation for the formation of a coherent, durable green growth advocacy coalition.

## TOWARD A POLITICAL STRATEGY

Policy theory is useful if it identifies directions for designing real-world politics that will facilitate a durable green growth strategy—one that is politically acceptable, economically feasible, and respects ecological and resource limits at local, regional, and global levels. Bear in mind that as green growth is defined here, we are not talking about wholesale, radical political and economic change, in the sense of moving toward some form of ecological authoritarianism or centrally planned economy. Nor are we limiting ourselves to mere incremental fine-tuning. Durable green growth depends not on radical change but on *a restructuring of policies and investments and an integration of ecological with economic strategies as* described in Chapter 6.

Given my focus on what is politically and economically possible within the next three decades or so, here are some ground rules for the discussion that follows. First, regarding a green growth strategy, I am limited to what may occur within the existing constitutional structure and political culture. The United States is not going to magically transform into a parliamentary democracy or unitary state nor become (in the foreseeable future) a non-pluralist, non-adversarial, integrated, consensual political system. For better or worse, the United States is not Denmark, Sweden, or Germany.

The discussion also is based on the assumption that the citizens of the United States—or for that matter of most any other country—will not suddenly adopt a full-bore ecological paradigm that makes a political shift to a green state easy. While we may hope that people around the world become more aware of the value of nature, preservation, and ecosystems to support the green side of the growth equation, and indeed I even assume so to some degree, a fundamental near-term shift in values is unlikely. Whatever appeal ecological protection has in in the abstract, we have to face the widespread belief—actively promoted by opponents of ecological protection—that near-term economic goals nearly always take priority over long-term ecological ones (Boston 2017).

On the positive, I assume it is possible to shape perceptions of ecological and economic issues and the relationships among them. With the right framing of the issues and a workable policy agenda, the emphasis on *growth* can be expanded to incorporate a concern for *green*. More broadly, what follows assumes some degree of economic and political change is possible. More specifically, it assumes institutional change is achievable, trends in economic inequality may be reversed over time, and more citizens are motivated to participate in the political process.

What follows is not a list of proposed policies, but a start on conditions that need to exist for a green growth transition to occur. It focuses on four conditions: forming a political coalition in favor of long-term, durable, green growth; making institutional reforms that lead to effective democracy; reducing economic inequality; and engaging actively in global, ecological problem solving. Although focused on the United States, most of them should apply to a degree to other countries, especially democracies.

Putting it the other way, among the principal barriers to a green transition in the United States are a lack of a political coalition on which to build the change process—a result largely of the inability to link ecological and economic issues in positive ways, institutional barriers to translating public preferences and values into outcomes and ecology–economy consensus, the effects of inequality on collective action for public goods, and far too little global engagement.

## Build a Political Coalition for Green Growth

The lessons that may be drawn from each of the policy models are that (1) the problem stream is changing and the policy stream is rich with solutions, but the political stream is in gridlock and often hostile to the *green* part of the equation; and (2) a dominant coalition favoring business as usual (meaning mostly brown growth with bursts of ecological change and progress nationally) that resists basic transformation has not been displaced by a green growth coalition.

All of this suggests a need to think about whether and how a political coalition in support of green rather than brown growth may be formed. Given the results of the 2016 election, the answers to this question matter now more than ever. Ecological policy played little role in the election, which is consistent with the environmental politics research in general. Ecological and health problems usually are secondary in determining election outcomes (List and Sturm 2006).

To advance an ecological agenda, economic concerns should be linked with ecological ones. The conventional zero-sum framing of ecology–economy issues makes this difficult. Advocating a hard anti-growth or de-growth framing of the issues makes a positive linking of ecological and economic goals next to impossible. Another foundation for a coalition to support green growth is linking ecological issues not only with economic vitality and security but also with energy, transportation, housing, food, public health, water security, and other issues.

How might such a coalition look? Many elements of a possible green growth advocacy coalition (or of smaller coalitions working toward the same end, as suggested in my review of theory) are plausible. Among them are working class voters looking to revive local economies; minority voters seeking similar opportunities as well a degree of environmental justice; young voters, especially urban ones, who exhibit strong support for ecological issues in general and climate action in particular; progressive business firms seeking strategic value in ecological innovation and leadership; and educated, mostly affluent, progressive voters sensitive to ecological protection and social equity. A green growth coalition thus might consist of the following:

> *Working class voters seeking to revive local economies.* Although opinion polls show reasonable support for the environment—more for health than ecology—economic concerns usually dominate. A lesson from the 2016 election is that support from midwestern industrial states is critical to any advocacy coalition for green growth. Linking clean energy and other green economic goals and sectors offers one path to a coalition. Instead of misleading voters into thinking that an earlier economy can be restored, leaders should make an appeal based on economic fairness and the need for a new economy.

> *Minority voters seeking economic and environmental justice.* Over the past nearly three decades, the disproportionate exposure of racial minorities to health risks, as well as a lack of access to many green amenities, has highlighted connections among economic equity, political access, and environmental justice. These concerns could be

linked to the economic opportunities from green growth, especially if joined to economic fairness.

*Younger citizens, especially in urban settings.* Younger people show strong support for ecological and other public goods, including climate (Chong 2015; Pew Research Center 2015b). Especially in cities, they exhibit lifestyle changes consistent with green growth (Brown and Vergragt 2015). Their values align better with the reality of ecological limits than those of their parents. The key, of course, is getting them to vote in high numbers.

*Progressive business firms that value ecological innovation.* A range of business firms now see value in ecological innovation and leadership. They recognize that water, ecosystem services, clean energy, eco-efficiency, and healthy workers are not a lag on but rather are conditions for economic success (Esty and Winston 2009; Reinhardt 2000). Engaging them effectively could be a vital building block for a coalition.

*Affluent voters who value ecological and social progress.* Patterns of political support from high- and low-income voters are changing; many high-income voters now support liberal candidates (Edsall 2015). Many also strongly support ecological values politically (Coan and Holman 2008; Konisky, Milyo, and Richardson 2008); economically, they are market-driving consumers for green products and services (Vona and Patriarca 2011).

Does policy theory tell us anything about the prospects of such a coalition emerging nationally? The ACF framework holds that a coherent political coalition should share a belief system and show a "non-trivial" degree of coordination among its elements. One could argue that dominant green growth coalitions may now exists in states like California, Connecticut, Vermont, and Massachusetts, to name a few. States that may be moving toward such a green coalition might include New York and Washington. In the renewable energy field, states like Iowa, Texas, and Arizona could, over time, create the relationships and influence for competing with the now-dominant brown growth coalition based on fossil fuels. In sum, in some states, shared belief systems and a degree of coordination is a basis for substantial policy shifts toward green growth. If the economic case exists and is made, other states with technology resources and needed leadership—perhaps Minnesota or Michigan—could see green coalitions form. At some point, they could constitute an advocacy coalition leading to a tipping point for change.

Demographic changes occurring in several states also could facilitate green growth. Although minority voters did not deliver a Democratic majority in 2016, in part because of low turnout, demographic trends could, over time, help to make a coalition emerge. For any of this to happen anytime soon, however, there is a need for institutional reform, which is taken up next.

What also may increase the chances for a new advocacy coalition are trends in clean and renewable energy. According to the International Energy Agency's (IEA) 2016 *World Energy Outlook*, annual global additions of renewable energy in the power generating sector now exceed those for coal, oil, and natural gas combined (IEA 2016). By 2040, the IEA estimates globally, renewables will account for 37% of power generation, driven mostly by government policies that have promoted major declines in the costs of wind and solar energy. In the United States, according to a report by the Department of Energy (2017), solar energy accounts for over 40% of employment in the electrical generating sector, compared to just over one-fifth from traditional fossil fuels (see DOE/EIA 2017 for US trends). By 2015, *Fortune* reports, there were "twice as many solar workers as coal miners" (Korosec 2015). Employment in energy efficiency has grown and will continue. These are promising ecological trends and evidence, again, of a political "tipping point" where clean and renewable energy competes for influence as an emerging green growth coalition.

## Deliver Institutional Reforms

There is a line of argument going around that democracies cannot meet the challenges posed by climate change and other forms of ecological degradation and health risks. Setting aside for the moment the question of whether we want to toss the benefits of democratic governance, there are many practical reasons why that cannot and should not happen, as discussed in Chapter 4. It is hard to imagine how such a drastic change in institutions and legitimacy might occur without widespread instability and conflict, neither of which is conducive to ecological progress. How would we expect an authoritarian but ecologically progressive regime to gain political support and legitimacy when we cannot even get agreement on a carbon tax? Are there many examples of authoritarian societies dealing well with ecological protection?

What is needed for ecological policy success and green growth is having more, not less democracy (Buitenzorgy and Mol 2011; Stehr 2015). By this I do not mean just more dialogue and debate, or that once people recognize their shared values they will come together for the sake of the ecological commons (Arias-Maldonado 2007). None of this hurts, of course; it is standard in sustainability writing to call for more community engagement and transparency (examples are Dryzek 1994 and 2013; Rydin and Pennington 2000). There is nothing wrong and much that is right about such arguments, but they will not on their own solve the problems of dominance by short-term and specialized interests, skewed political power due to inequality, and the failure of institutions and policymakers to create conditions needed for consensus and policy integration.

Promoting community engagement and building capacities for democratic dialogue and learning are worthy objectives. Especially in enhancing ecological values and promoting green growth at a national level, we need to think more broadly about what has to happen to bring about a durable green growth transition. The goals of the reforms considered here are to reflect public preferences more accurately; make compromise more acceptable and legitimate; and, of course, limit how short-term, special economic interests dominate over the general well-being.

As a start in using more rather than less democracy, four kinds of institutional reforms come to mind: increase political participation (i.e., voting) among minorities and the young; reform nominating processes to enable appeals to the political center rather than just the hard right or hard left; establish more politically neutral ways of drawing legislative districts; and (a standard issue in having more democracy) reduce the influence of money in politics. Each was implied by the analysis in the previous chapter; I see all as conditions for green growth.

Enhancing voting rates could increase the political power of citizens that the research suggests value public goods like ecological protection and economic fairness. For example, younger voters are inclined to see climate change as a problem requiring a governmental response. Yet, they participate in elections at lower rates than older voters. This is the case not only in presidential elections, which draw the most attention, but in congressional and state legislative voting. State legislative outcomes have a double effect: they enhance the power of ecological opponents and enable them to stack district line-drawing, a practice that works for either side but usually favors conservatives (although the courts have a say; see Wines 2016).

Other institutional barriers to a green growth transition, besides politically motivated redistricting, are the rules regarding money in politics (that is, campaign finance) and nominating processes that bring more hard right and left politicians into office and undermine incentives for compromise. Improving ecological protection—to develop common purpose on ecological and economic goals in society—is only one of many reasons for reform. Effectiveness in many other policy areas, even the legitimacy of democratic institutions, increasingly is at stake.

One policy reform—removing barriers to voting and generally increasing participation in the electoral process—illustrates the benefits for ecological protection as well as green growth prospects. Barriers to voting, such as strict identification laws, affect minorities and the young disproportionately. This is confirmed in empirical research finding that "strict identification laws have a differentially negative impact on the turnout of Hispanics, Blacks, Asian-Americans, and multi-racial Americans in primaries and general elections" (Hajnal, Lajevardi, and Nielson 2017, 1; for a short summary see Hajnal 2016). As of 2016, 34 states had voting identification laws, 11 of them strict. Most important, these restrictions were not ideologically neutral; the study concluded that "voter ID laws skew democracy toward those on the political right" (1).

That nonvoting—whether due to barriers like ID laws or other reasons—affects the capacity for ecological protection (and so green growth) is clear from research on nonvoters. In an analysis of who votes and the effects for policy, Jan Leighley and Jonathan Nagler (2014) find that voters differ from nonvoters in their policy preferences and are not representative of the overall public. Compared to voters, nonvoters are more liberal on economic policy, support more government involvement, and are more open to redistributive policies. In a summary of this and other studies, Sean McElwee concludes that "the median voter is more conservative than the electorate at large" (2014, 5). Voters are more likely to oppose unions, public health insurance, and federal assistance to schools. Although this research did not specifically address ecological policies, this support for public goods and action is likely to carry over from economic/social to ecological issues. McElwee cites research finding that, in a study of all 50 states, when the poor vote in high numbers inequality is lower, which addresses another of my conditions for change.

The solutions to these issues are complex, politically challenging, and (with nonvoting) require not just institutional reform but behavioral change. Certainly we are likely to gain a more effective democracy by removing barriers to voting, especially among the young and minorities, and by drawing more politically neutral legislative districts, reducing money's role, and reforming nominating processes—all of which may begin to restore the pragmatic, moderate center in American politics. It may even offer hope for overcoming the extreme polarization in Congress (Binder 2003 and 2014). Anyone who doubts the importance of such institutional factors need only look at the lineup of forces for and against at least a few of these institutional reforms (an example is the revealing analysis after the 2016 election in Waldman 2016).

Is it any surprise that proponents of voter suppression laws and opponents of campaign finance reform are also those who are standing in the way of a green economic transition?

## Reduce Economic Inequality

Economic inequality and its connection to ecological protection is a neglected issue. To the extent that inequality draws attention, it is on what are described in Chapter 5 as its effects on economic behavior—on how inequality promotes status consumption and positional goods. If economic inequality stimulates consumption for its own sake in a vicious cycle, the results are unlikely to be ecologically positive. Here is where social and ecological critiques of unabated growth converge, in the diminishing returns accruing from more growth—especially if benefits of that growth are allocated unequally. Happiness research is not always conclusive on growth and well-being, but it does suggest that the frequently assumed linear connections between higher incomes and a better quality of life are usually off the mark (Hirsch 1976; Graham 2011).

What may be more crucial in thinking of a green economic transition are the *political* effects of economic inequality (Stehr 2015; Uslaner 2002; Stiglitz 2012). Chapter 5 examined evidence on how inequality may undermine capacities to act collectively and value public goods. Empirical research on various countries suggests that more unequal societies have been less successful at reducing some forms of pollution and protecting habitat. These effects almost certainly vary at different levels of income and among political cultures, so they need to be explored further. Still, evidence on effects of inequality in promoting social mistrust, stressing what divides people more than what is shared, and casting economic and social relationships as more zero-sum than as a potential win–win deserves attention from researchers.

Reversing a decades-long trend toward inequality in the United States and, for that matter, in many other developed countries, is difficult. Public policy can play a role, to be sure, in changing tax policy, sustaining social safety nets, providing affordable health care, enacting reasonable minimum wage standards, improving educational quality and opportunity for low- and middle-income groups, and even something like a minimum guaranteed income. In the United States, state as well as federal policies may influence income inequality (Hatch and Rigby 2015). Many other causes of inequality are not a direct result of public policy and are less amenable to change. Much of it is attributed to technology and the need for higher levels of education and training in a new and an increasingly competitive global economy. Responding to this is even more challenging.

Of course, stressing a social issue like inequality plays to the hand of opponents. They cite it as evidence that progressives use issues of climate change, water quality, and habitat loss as a ruse for implementing a "radical" agenda they could not otherwise achieve. Still, green growth advocates may frame the issue positively, where the goal is not perfect equality or a radical redistribution of income but a *restoration of basic fairness, poverty reduction, a vibrant middle class, and a strong economy for the long haul.* It highlights the need for a strategy that reframes ecology–economy issues and puts them in a broader, strategic political context.

## Aggressively Push Global Action and Interdependency

Neither a national nor a global transition to green growth is unlikely without strong engagement by the United States, for two reasons. First, green growth globally becomes less likely if the United States is not an active part of it. Second, it will not occur in the United States if it does not occur elsewhere, especially in countries like China, India, Brazil, and Indonesia. On the first point, the United States is still the world's largest economy and, by most any measure, one of the most influential countries. The contrasting outcomes of the Copenhagen (2009) and Paris (2015) Conferences of the Parties regarding climate action are partly due to the larger role the United States played in Paris and the Obama administration's commitments. Its financial, scientific, and diplomatic capacities are crucial for achieving a green economic transition anytime soon.

Still, the United States may need the rest of the world even more, or enough of it to matter, for adopting and sustaining a green growth agenda at home. Despite the many positive relationships among ecological and economic goals, a green economic transition, like any process of change, involves risks. Although many of us argue that opponents of ecological protection exaggerate those risks, especially in acting on climate, the potential and perceived costs of change have to be addressed. Even the moderate critics of clean energy and climate action worry about higher production costs, lost manufacturing and job losses, consumer price increases, and other bad outcomes if the United States gets too far ahead of other countries.

David Victor puts this succinctly in a 2016 article shortly after the election, noting that "What the United States does at home will also eventually have an effect on the world, as few nations will go far in making costly reductions if other economic powerhouses are not doing the same" (Victor 2016). At a practical level, domestic and international politics move together, a reality Elizabeth DeSombre (2000) and others (Clapp and Dauvergne 2011) examine in detail. And we have evidence that when some countries act legislatively to mitigate climate change action by others is more likely, as a result of "peer pressure or intergovernmental learning" (Fankhauser, Gennaioli, and Collins 2016, 328).

That countries acting in concert for green growth is not only more feasible politically but less costly and disruptive is documented in the policy research.

A study from the Netherlands, for example, examined four scenarios for achieving a "sustainable economic structure" (essentially a green economy) in that country by 2030. In all four of their scenarios, "economic growth can be reconciled with a reduction in environmental pressure" (Dellink, Bennis, and Verbruggen 1999, 153). Some economic sectors lose in production share, notably food, chemicals, public utilities, transport, and agriculture—all major sources of ecological and health damages. Although there is some loss of growth under each of the four scenarios, losses (in GDP terms) are least under the "strong together" scenario, which incorporates a high degree of international cooperation.

Global cooperation for green growth reduces costs and risks for all by making domestic transitions more politically acceptable, limiting the collective action problem of free-riding, and reducing incentives for countries to undercut each other. Recall that even UNEP's green growth scenario involved slower growth rates in the first few years as economic adjustments took hold. Rather than a race to the bottom, we may see a "California effect": strong standards in one country or jurisdiction push others to keep up (Vogel 1995). In the European Union, high standards in the north improved policy in the south (Holzinger, Knill, and Sommerer 2011; Liefferink et al. 2009). Similarly, California's air, energy, and climate policies, even its chemical rules, spilled over into other states—a horizontally induced innovation.

This overall political strategy for green growth is summarized in Table 8.1.

## TWO VISIONS FOR THE NEAR FUTURE

This book concludes with two visions for a near-term future, aimed at what might occur by the 2040s. One vision is pessimistic and based largely on a continuation of business as usual, with perhaps some modest improvement in ecology–economy synergies. It assumes only marginal progress, in the United States and globally, on ecological issues like climate change, water scarcity, deforestation, habitat and species protection, and health issues like air and water pollution. Growth occurs, but it is more along the lines of ecologically sensitive (or maybe insensitive) than ecologically driven growth. The second vision is more optimistic. It imagines much higher levels of ecological performance made possible through the development of better governance capacities; more international cooperation, including that among richer and poorer ones; a major diminution in the economic and political power of historically brown economic sectors; and the adoption of the core elements of a green growth policy agenda. Many of the conditions outlined earlier to support green growth have been adopted to facilitate ecological and economic change.

## Table 8.1 ELEMENTS OF A POLITICS OF GREEN GROWTH

| | |
|---|---|
| **Build a Political Coalition** (an advocacy coalition built on a positive-sum framing) | • Working class voters seeking local development<br>• Minority voters seeking economic and ecological justice<br>• Younger citizens, especially in urban settings<br>• Progressive business firms that value ecological innovation<br>• Affluent voters who value ecological and social progress<br>• Work toward a green growth "tipping point" |
| **Deliver Institutional Reforms** (more and better democracy) | • Increase participation to better reflect public preferences<br>• Engage voters supporting public goods<br>• Establish politically neutral legislative districts<br>• Limit the influence of money in politics<br>• Generally promote legitimacy of and prospects for consensus |
| **Reduce Economic Inequality** (public goods/collective action) | • Reduce generalized mistrust in society<br>• Increase support for public goods and social fairness<br>• Increase sense of common purpose and shared values<br>• Enhance capacity for collective action<br>• Expand political participation |
| **Push Global Action and Interdependency** (all countries in it together) | • Bring US influence to bear globally<br>• Align global and domestic perspectives<br>• Strengthen the domestic case for green growth<br>• Promote a global "California" effect |

## Unguided or Misguided Growth (The Brown Economy)

In the pessimistic vision, the incorporation of ecological values and goals does not progress much beyond where we are now. The mindset of most countries is that of economic and ecological values being matched against each other incrementally in an old "minimize harm" model. Ecological issues remain at the margin of the business of states. Advocates of ecologically unguided or barely guided growth continue to frame ecological and economic issues in zero-sum terms; voters and policymakers confront a series of trade-offs with obvious complementarities and synergies being unrecognized or avoided. In this vision, ecological progress in the United States and most countries depends on the alternating shifts in political power, leading to continued patterns of ecological degradation that will undermine the ability to meet economic and social aspirations.

Globally, economic competition takes precedence over mutually beneficial cooperation, such as by integrating ecological goals into trade policy; global collective action on ecological issues takes a back seat. The drive for economic advantage takes priority. Not only does this the diminish options for green growth; it fuels domestic opposition in most countries for taking the perceived risks of transforming energy, agriculture, transportation, and manufacturing systems.

In the United States, the general polarization and dysfunction in governance continues at the national level, and protectors of the status quo and advocates of change are for the most part locked in conflict. One party still pushes for public goods like education, health care, environmental quality, social safety nets, infrastructure, and a strong public sector; the other promotes an agenda of low tax rates, deregulation, limited government, and maximum reliance on market forces. Neither the economy-versus-ecology nor the green growth framing is able to acquire dominance. Nationally, this political stalemate offers little in the way of policy stability or clarity to guide both public and private sector decision making. In terms of the policy theories discussed in this chapter, the political stream does not respond to the challenges from the problem stream to draw upon the richness of the analysis and solutions coming from the policy stream.

Similarly, despite a broadening of energy politics through climate issues and the obvious pressures on resources (like water quality and availability) and ecosystems (like the Chesapeake Bay or fisheries), an advocacy coalition for a new ecological policy based on green growth fails to emerge. Progress is halting, inconsistent, and uncertain—at best, too little, too late.

Because of these patterns of inconsistent and hard-to-predict policy shifts nationally, the private sector finds it difficult to make long-term decisions. Policy uncertainty makes choices about technologies and products difficult, and this has a chilling effect on needed investments. Solar and wind maintain a steady incremental climb in capacity, but missed opportunities (such as making dramatic gains in energy efficiency) and investor uncertainty keep the country reliant on fossil fuels, with coal still accounting for over one-third of power generation. Inconsistent growth, high inequality, global competition, and a failure to enact electoral reforms make the electorate more vulnerable to political appeals based on inevitable ecology–economy trade-offs. Change coalitions are temporary, fluid, and unreliable. Critical linkages among ecological, economic, transport, energy, agriculture, housing, and land use issues fail to be realized.

Of course, many states have made progress in adopting a green growth framing: building their economies around the protection of natural assets, generating jobs based on renewables and other technologies, investing in green infrastructure, accounting for the social costs of pollution, pricing resources like water fairly, and generally expanding beyond a simple growth conception of well-being. Others are locked in the old policy framing and fail to adapt to the opportunities.

In summary, unguided growth continues to stretch the limits of global, regional, and local ecosystems. The ecological, economic, and social benefits of collective action are unrealized.

## Ecologically Driven Growth (The Green Economy)

The second vision is more satisfying ecologically and economically. Internationally, climate change has served, as Anthony Giddens once suggested (2011), as the catalyst for a new era of cooperation on economic, ecological, and social issues. The 2015 Paris climate conference generated momentum. Climate politics has inspired broad, ecologically driven development.

Although the thoroughly green state envisioned in the governance research has not fully emerged, the progress and trends are promising. Voters in affluent economies are looking past a pure growth future to one founded on economic security, vitality, and fairness. Economic and social confidence among an expanded electorate creates a positive environment for positive-sum arguments; economic and political fairness in countries enhances the capacity to act collectively; the sense that all countries are in it together helps political leaders make a case for cooperation. This enables governments to move toward the political center, the space where positive linkages between ecological and economic issues and goals are most likely to be adopted and carried out.

The United States has made major strides at a national level in adopting a green growth issue-framing and policy agenda, for many reasons. One is the emergence of a political coalition in support of public goods like ecological quality, health care, and educational fairness. Another is progress in economic and political equity; this reduces social mistrust and facilitates consensus on goals. These trends, combined with electoral reforms that remove barriers to voting and other participation, bring out a different electorate. A third trend reflects the effects of federalism. Leadership states create successes that bring pressure to bear on elected officials in laggard states; successful policy innovations are copied; upward and downward pressures among state and federal levels create a virtuous circle of green economic and political change.

This virtuous circle is replicated globally. Global cooperation in linking ecological and economic goals allows leaders to justify national-level change; domestic issue framings and policies promote conditions needed for international agreements in support of greener growth. The wealthier countries see benefits in supporting a green economic transition as it occurs in emerging countries. The historical pattern of the Environmental Kuznets Curve, where countries endure a period of ecological degradation before turning the corner on at least some indicators, is broken. Voters in wealthy countries appreciate the value of promoting greener growth globally through financial assistance, sharing of technology, and other forms of green economic cooperation.

The expansion of green economic activity and the role of green sectors translates into a new distribution of political power nationally and in many states— perhaps a tipping point in the balance of political power. The clout of the wind and solar sectors increases, while fossil fuel interests like coal and oil are on the decline. Capable political leadership in the resource-heavy US states recognizes the need for economic innovation and diversification. The economic as well as ecological benefits of smart farming, land use planning, water and energy efficiency, habitat protection, and carbon neutrality are well established. Economic and ecological planning are more integrated; the positive synergies among ecological, transport, energy, housing, finance, forestry, land use, and other green economic policies are not only appreciated but incorporated into decision making. A revival of manufacturing, driven in part by green growth investments, is reversing the decades-long decline in economically pressed areas and reviving local economies.

In the terms of our policy models, the political stream is able to adapt to pressures from the problem stream and draw upon the richness of the ideas and solutions in the policy stream. The recognition of the linkages among ecological, economic, and social well-being supports the emergence of new advocacy coalitions. Historical patterns of unguided or barely ecologically sensitive growth are replaced by an era of ecologically driven governance built on green growth.

Of course, the first vision may be too pessimistic or the second too optimistic; or the actual trend could be toward a more muddled stalemate that satisfies neither set of goals. Three decades is a long time in politics; it is an even longer time in the exponential expansion of the stresses on local, regional, and global ecosystems and resources likely to occur under a business-as-usual scenario. The goal of policymakers and citizens should be to realize the more optimistic vision.

## TAKING STOCK, LOOKING AHEAD

Without a doubt, the 2016 elections were a setback for advocates of ecological protection and green growth. Not only are ecological policies at risk, but the conditions in this chapter for supporting a transition to green growth are unlikely to be advanced. Although it is hard to tell at this early stage of the administration, while this is being written, we can expect more rather than less inequality and greatly reduced engagement in global problem solving, especially compared to the Obama years. Unless courts stand in the way or drive the needed change, institutional reforms that better translate public preferences into policy and rebuild the political center are unlikely. If anything, the conditions outlined above will not improve and may even regress.

For the near term, the leadership in charting a green growth path will fall even more to the states. Federalism will prove to be even more of a virtue than it has been in the recent past. For the slightly longer term, there are positive signs: renewable energy is growing steadily, with wind and photovoltaic solar prices becoming competitive with fossil fuels; a generational shift in values appears to be underway; innovations in water technology and efficiency are becoming more available, if financing can be arranged; other countries may meet their obligations under the Paris climate agreement, pressuring the United States to return at some point.

That alternations in the cycles of political power can threaten progress on ecological protection makes a long-term shift to green growth more even compelling. Given the relevance and immediacy of threats to local, regional, and global ecosystems, progress from now on should be insulated as much as possible from short-term cycles in the balance of political power, most of which depend marginally on voter preferences on ecological issues. The more that ecological goals are integrated into economic structures and decision making, the more likely the earth's limits will be respected and economic and social aspirations fulfilled. Only by linking ecology with economy in positive ways is there a practical path to living a good life on a finite earth.

**CHAPTER 1**

1. Gross Domestic Product and per capita numbers are from the World Bank and stated in 2015 US dollars. http://data.worldbank.org/indicator/NY.GDP.MKTP.CD.
2. Although more recent additions to the OECD like Mexico and Turkey bring emerging economies into the membership as well.

**CHAPTER 3**

1. These numbers are in 2014 US dollars at purchasing price parity, which accounts for differences in purchasing power among countries.
2. That Daly worried about a global population of four billion shows how much the challenge has grown. The UN Department of Economic and Social Affairs projects the 2015 global population of 7.3 billion will to grow to 9.7 billion by 2050 and 11.2 billion by 2100. Half this growth will be concentrated in nine countries: India, Nigeria, Pakistan, the Democratic Republic of the Congo, Ethiopia, the United Republic of Tanzania, the United States, Indonesia, and Uganda. Available at: http://www.un.org/en/development/desa/news/population/2015-report.html.

**CHAPTER 5**

1. This was reported in several outlets but may be found here: https://www.forbes.com/forbes/welcome/?toURL=https://www.forbes.com/sites/timworstall/2011/12/14/six-waltons-have-more-wealth-than-the-bottom-30-of-americans/&refURL=https://www.google.com/&referrer=https://www.google.com/.

**CHAPTER 6**

1. Because my focus is on public governance, I do not consider possible changes in corporate governance. However, as evidence cited in the TEEB analysis on *Mainstreaming the Economics of Nature* documents, corporate ecological externalities involve "unaccounted costs to society of doing 'business as usual.'" For the top 3,000 listed companies only, these "amount to an estimated US $2.15 trillion, or 3.5 percent of GDP, every year . . ." This may require reforms that constitute "nothing short of a redesign of corporations themselves . . ." (2010, 11).

2.  For a useful resource on state renewable portfolio standards and other initiatives, see the material at https://www.c2es.org/us-states-regions/policy-maps/renewable-energy-standards. Especially since the 2016 elections, many states are emerging as energy policy leaders, and this role will become increasingly more important in the years to come.

3.  Taken from https://energy.gov/savings. A useful guide of federal tax incentives for clean energy may be found at: http://www.wri.org/publication/bottom-line-renewable-energy-tax-credits.

**CHAPTER 7**

1.  The Air, Energy, and Climate Index normalizes the four indicators by State Gross Product, so it provides a measure of the ecological impact within a state of producing a given unit of income. The indicators are based on federal agency data sources from the Departments of Transportation and Energy and the Environmental Protection Agency (see Fiorino and Frost 2016).

2.  On the Clean Power Plan, which many of us saw as a creative and innovative approach to energy policy, see https://www.c2es.org/federal/executive/epa/clean-power-plan. Another resource is the Union of Concerned Scientists: http://www.ucsusa.org/our-work/global-warming/reduce-emissions/what-is-the-clean-power-plan#.WLxDlW_yvIU.

3.  A leader in state litigation against the Clean Power Plan was Scott Pruitt, the Attorney-General of Oklahoma, who in 2017 became the EPA administrator. The lawsuits were consolidated as *West Virginia* v. *EPA*. Among the other states in the litigation were Alabama, Kansas, Texas, Florida, Missouri, Kentucky, and New Jersey. See Tsang and Wyatt (2017) for an analysis.

**CHAPTER 8**

1.  William Lowry (2008) makes an important point in his article on the interactions among energy and environmental policy issues. As the environmental aspects of energy policy, especially climate change, have become more contested, energy policy in the United States has moved from being a *distributive* to a *regulatory* policy issue, leading to more political conflict and partisan divides. I would extend this to observe that high levels of partisanship on climate change issues have in turn increased conflict on other environmental health and ecological issues.

Aamaas, Borgar, Jens Borken-Kleefeld, and Glen P. Peters. 2013. "The Climate Impact of Travel Behavior: A German Case Study with Illustrative Mitigation Options." *Environmental Science & Policy* 33: 273–282. doi: 10.1016/j.envsci.2013.06.009.

Abramowitz, Alan I. 2008. "Forecasting the 2008 Presidential Election with the Time-for-Change Model." *PS: Political Science and Politics* 41 (4): 691–695. doi: 10.1017/s1049096508081249.

Adler, Jonathan H. 2016. "Supreme Court Puts the Brakes on the EPA's Clean Power Plan." *Washington Post*, February 9. https://www.washingtonpost.com/news/volokh-conspiracy/wp/2016/02/09/supreme-court-puts-the-brakes-on-the-epas-clean-power-plan/. .

Agyeman, Julian, and Briony Angus. 2003. "The Role of Civic Environmentalism in the Pursuit of Sustainable Communities." *Journal of Environmental Planning and Management* 46 (3): 345–363. doi: 10.1080/0964056032000096901.

Alcott, Blake. 2008. "The Sufficiency Strategy: Would Rich-World Frugality Lower Environmental Impact?" *Ecological Economics* 64 (4): 770–786. doi: 10.1016/j.ecolecon.2007.04.015.

Alcott, Blake. 2010. "Impact Caps: Why Population, Affluence, and Technology Strategies Should Be Abandoned." *Journal of Cleaner Production* 18 (6): 552–560. doi: 10.1016/j.jclepro.2009.08.001.

Alexander, Samuel, ed. 2009. *Voluntary Simplicity: The Poetic Alternative to Consumer Culture*. Whanganui, New Zealand: Stead and Daughters.

Alexander, Samuel. 2012. "Planned Economic Contraction: The Emerging Case for Degrowth." *Environmental Politics* 21 (3): 349–368. doi: 10.1080/09644016.2012.671569.

American Council for an Energy-Efficient Economy (ACEEE). 2015. *The 2015 State Energy Efficiency Scorecard*. http://aceee.org/sites/default/files/publications/researchreports/u1509.pdf.

American Energy Innovation Council (AEIC). 2015. *Restoring American Energy Leadership: Report Card, Challenges, Opportunities*. Washington, DC: Bipartisan Policy Center. http://americanenergyinnovation.org/wp-content/uploads/2015/02/AEIC-Restoring-American-Energy-Innovation-Leadership-2015.pdf.

Anadon, Laura Diaz, and John P. Holdren. 2009. "Policy for Energy Technology Innovation." In *Acting in Time on Energy Policy*, edited by Kelly Simms Gallagher, 89–127. Washington, DC: Brookings Institution Press.

Andrews, Richard N.L. 1997. "Martin Jänicke and the 'Berlin School' of Environmental Policy Analysis: An American Perspective." In *Umweltpolitik und Staatsversagen*, edited by Lutz Metz and Helmut Weidner, 35–40. Berlin: Verlag.

Andrews, Richard N.L. 2006. *Managing the Environment, Managing Ourselves: A History of American Environmental Policy*. 2nd ed. New Haven, CT: Yale University Press.

Arias-Maldonado, Manuel. 2007. "An Imaginary Solution? The Green Defence of Deliberative Democracy." *Environmental Values* 16 (2): 233–252. doi: 10.3197/ 096327107780474573.

Ashkenas, Jeremy. 2016. "Nine New Findings about Inequality in the United States." *New York Times*, December 16. http://www.nytimes.com/interactive/2016/12/16/business/economy/nine-new-findings-about-income-inequality-piketty.html.

Bäckstrand, Karin. 2017. "Critical Loads: Negotiating What Nature Can Withstand." In *Conceptual Innovation in Environmental Policy*, edited by James Meadowcroft and Daniel J. Fiorino, 129–154. Cambridge, MA: MIT Press.

Badger, Emily, Quoctrung Bui, and Adam Pearce. 2016. "The Election Highlighted a Growing Rural-Urban Split." *New York Times*, November 11. https://www.nytimes.com/2016/11/12/upshot/this-election-highlighted-a-growing-rural-urban-split.html.

Baehler, Karen. 2017. "Environmental Justice: Making Policy, One Skirmish at a Time." In *Conceptual Innovation in Environmental Policy*, edited by James Meadowcroft and Daniel J. Fiorino, 233–258. Cambridge, MA: MIT Press.

Baek, Jungho, and Guankerwon Gweisah. 2013. "Does Income Inequality Harm the Environment? Empirical Evidence from the United States." *Energy Policy* 62: 1434–1437. doi: 10.1016/j.enpol.2013.07.097.

Baland, Jean-Marie, Pranab Bardhan, and Samuel Bowles, eds. 2007. *Inequality, Cooperation, and Environmental Sustainability*. New York: Russell Sage.

Barbier, Edward B. 2010. *A Global Green Deal: Rethinking the Economic Recovery*. Cambridge, UK: Cambridge University Press.

Bardhan, Pranab. 2005. *Scarcity, Conflicts and Cooperation: Essays in the Political and Institutional Economics of Development*. Cambridge, MA: MIT Press.

Barrett, Scott, and Kathryn Graddy. 2000. "Freedom, Growth, and the Environment." *Environment and Development Economics* 5 (4): 433–456. doi: 10.1017/ s1355770x00000267.

Bastien, Girard, and Peter de Haan. 2009. "GHG Reduction Potential of Changes in Consumption Patterns and Higher Quality Levels: Evidence from Swiss Household Consumption Survey." *Energy Policy* 37 (12): 5650–5661. doi: 10.1016/j.enpol.2009.08.026.

Battig, Michele B., and Thomas Bernauer. 2009. "National Institutions and Global Public Goods: Are Democracies More Cooperative in Climate Change Policy?" *International Organization* 63 (2): 281–308. doi: https://doi.org/10.1017/s0020818309090092.

Baumol, William J., Robert E. Litan, and Carl J. Schramm. 2007. *Good Capitalism, Bad Capitalism, and the Economics of Growth and Prosperity*. New Haven, CT: Yale University Press.

Beeson, Mark. 2010. "The Coming of Environmental Authoritarianism." *Environmental Politics* 19 (2): 276–294. doi: 10.1080/09644010903576918.

Bell, Michelle L., and Keita Ebisu. 2012. "Environmental Inequality in Exposures to Airborne Particulate Matter Compounds in the United States." *Environmental Health Perspectives* 120 (12): 1699–1704. doi: 10.1289/ehp.1205201.

Bellinger, David C. 2016. "Lead Contamination in Flint—An Abject Failure to Protect Public Health." *New England Journal of Medicine* 374 (12): 1101–1103. doi: 10.1056/nejmp1601013.

Berman, Eli, and Linda T.M. Bui. 2001. "Environmental Regulation and Labor Demand: Evidence from the South Coast Air Basin." *Journal of Public Economics* 79 (2): 265–295. doi: 10.1016/s0047-2727(99)00101-2.

Bernauer, Thomas, and Vally Koubi. 2009. "Effects of Political Institutions on Air Quality." *Ecological Economics* 68 (5): 1355–1365. doi: 10.1016/j.ecolecon.2008.09.003.

Bezdek, Roger H., Robert M. Wendling, and Paula DiPerna. 2008. "Environmental Protection, the Economy, and Jobs: National and Regional Analyses." *Journal of Environmental Management* 86 (1): 63–79. doi: 10.1016/j.jenvman.2006.11.028.

Bhattarai, Madhusudan, and Michael Hammig. 2001. "Institutions and the Environmental Kuznets Curve for Deforestation: A Crosscountry Analysis for Latin America, Africa and Asia." *World Development* 29 (6): 995–1010. doi: 10.1016/S0305-750X(01)00019-5.

Binder, Sarah A. 2003. *Stalemate: Causes and Consequences of Legislative Gridlock.* Washington, DC: Brookings Institution Press.

Binder, Sarah A. 2014. *Polarized We Govern?* Washington, DC: Brookings Institution. https://www.brookings.edu/wp-content/uploads/2016/06/BrookingsCEPM_Polarized_figReplacedTextRevTableRev.pdf.

Binder, Seth, and Eric Neumayer. 2005. "Environmental Pressure Group Strength and Air Pollution: An Empirical Analysis." *Ecological Economics* 55 (4): 527–538. doi: 10.1016/j.ecolecon.2004.12.009.

Bohmelt, Tobias, Thomas Bernauer, and Vally Koubi. 2015. "The Marginal Impact of ENGOs in Different Types of Democratic Systems." *European Political Science Review* 7 (1): 93–118. doi: 10.1017/s175577391400006x.

Booth, Douglas. 2004. *Hooked on Growth: Economic Addictions and the Environment.* Lanham, MD: Rowman and Littlefield.

Borzel, Tanga A. 2000. "Why There is No 'Southern' Problem: On Environmental Leaders and Laggards in the European Union." *Journal of European Public Policy* 7 (1): 141–162. doi: https://doi.org/10.1080/135017600343313.

Boston, Jonathan. 2011. "Biophysical Limits and Green Growth." *Policy Quarterly* 7 (4): 34–43.

Boston, Jonathan. 2017. *Governing for the Future: Designing Democratic Institutions for a Better Tomorrow.* Bingley, UK: Emerald.

Boyce, James K. 1994. "Inequality as a Cause of Environmental Degradation." *Ecological Economics,* 11 (3): 169–178. doi: 10.1016/0921-8009(94)90198-8.

Boyce, James K. 2007. "Is Inequality Bad for the Environment?" In *Equity and the Environment (Research in Social Problems and Public Policy, Volume 15),* edited by Robert Wilkinson and William Freudenburg, 267–288. Amsterdam: Elsevier.

Boyce, James K., Andrew R. Klemer, Paul H. Templet, and Cleve E. Willis. 1999. "Power Distribution, the Environment, and Public Health: A State-Level Analysis." *Ecological Economics* 29 (1): 127–140. doi: 10.1016/s0921-8009(98)00056-1.

Brand, Ulrich. 2012. "Green Economy—The Next Oxymoron? No Lessons Learned from Failures of Implementing Sustainable Development." *GAIA-Ecological Perspectives for Science and Society* 21 (1): 28–32. doi: 10.14512/gaia.21.1.9.

Bratt, Leon C., and Rudolf de Groot. 2012. "The Ecosystem Services Agenda: Bridging the Worlds of Natural Science and Economics, Conservation and Development, and Public and Private Policy." *Ecosystem Services* 1 (1): 4–15. doi: 10.1016/j.ecoser.2012.07.011.

Broder, John M. and Felicity Barringer. 2007. "E.P.A. Says 17 States Can't Set Emission Rules." *New York Times*, December 20. http://www.nytimes.com/2007/12/20/washington/20epa.html.

Brown, Halina, and Philip J. Vergragt. 2015. "From Consumerism to Well-Being: Toward a Cultural Transition?" *Journal of Cleaner Production* 132: 308–317. doi: 10.1016/j.jclepro.2015.04.107.

Buitenzorgy, Meilanie, and Arthur P.J. Mol. 2011. "Does Democracy Lead to a Better Environment? Deforestation and the Democratic Transition Peak." *Environmental and Resource Economics* 48 (1): 59–70. doi: 10.1007/s10640-010-9397-y.

Busch, Per-Olof, and Helge Jörgens. 2005. "International Patterns of Environmental Policy Change and Convergence." *European Environment* 15 (2): 80–101.

Carley, Sanya. 2011. "The Era of State Energy Policy Innovation: A Review of Policy Instruments." *Review of Policy Research* 28 (3): 265–294. doi: 10.1111/j.1541-1338.2011.00495.x.

Carson, Rachel. 1962. *Silent Spring*. Boston: Houghton Mifflin.

Cato, Molly Scott. 2009. *Green Economics: An Introduction to Theory, Policy, and Practice*. Abingdon, UK: Earthscan.

Center for Climate and Energy Solutions. 2009. "The American Clean Energy and Security Act (Waxman-Markey Bill)." http://www.c2es.org/federal/congress/111/acesa.

Chertow, Marian R., and Daniel C. Esty, eds. 1997. *Thinking Ecologically: The Next Generation of Environmental Policy*. New Haven, CT: Yale University Press.

Chetty, Raj, Nathaniel Hendren, Patrick Kline, Emmanuel Saez, and Nicholas Turner. 2014. *Is the United States Still a Land of Opportunity? Recent Trends in Intergenerational Mobility*. National Bureau of Economic Research (NBER Working Paper 19844).

Chong, Dennis. 2015. "Explaining Public Conflict and Consensus on the Climate." In *Changing Climate Policies: US Policies and Civic Action*, edited by Yael Wolinsky-Nahmias, 110–145. Washington, DC: CQ Press.

Christian-Smith, Juliet, and Peter H. Gleick. 2012. *A Twenty-First Century U.S. Water Policy*. Oxford: Oxford University Press.

Clapp, Jennifer, and Peter Dauvergne. 2011. *Paths to a Green World: The Political Economy of the Global Environment*. Cambridge, MA: MIT Press.

Coan, Travis G., and Mirya R. Holman. 2008. "Voting Green." *Social Science Quarterly* 89 (5): 1121–1135. doi: 10.1111/j.1540-6237.2008.00564.x.

Cohen, Michael D., James G. March, and Johan P. Olsen. 1972. "A Garbage Can Model of Organizational Choice." *Administrative Science Quarterly* 17 (1): 1–25. doi: 10.2307/2392088.

Cole, Matthew A., A.J. Rayner, and J.M Bates. 1997. "The Environmental Kuznets Curve: An Empirical Analysis." *Environment and Development Economics* 2 (4): 401–416. doi: 10.1017/S1355770X97000211.

Congleton, Roger D. 1992. "Political Institutions and Pollution Control." *The Review of Economics and Statistics* 74 (3): 412–421. doi: 10.2307/2109485.

Costanza, Robert. 1989. "What Is Ecological Economics?" *Ecological Economics* 1 (1): 1–7. doi: 10.1016/0921-8009(89)90020-7.

Costanza, Robert. 2006. "Nature: Ecosystems without Commodifying Them." *Nature* 443 (7113): 749. doi: 10.1038/443749b.

Crepaz, Marcus M.L. 1995. "Explaining National Variations of Air Pollution Levels: Political Institutions and Their Impact on Environmental Policy-Making." *Environmental Politics* 4 (3): 391–414. doi: 10.1080/09644019508414213.

Cushman, John H. 2015. "EPA's Clean Power Plan Will Create Quarter-Million Jobs." *Inside Climate News,* April 21. https://insideclimatenews.org/carbon-copy/21042015/epa-clean-power-plan-will-create-quarter-million-jobs.

Dadush, Uri, Kemal Dervis, Sarah P. Milsom, and Bennett Stancil. 2012. *Inequality in America: Facts, Trends, and International Perspectives.* Washington, DC: Brookings Institution Press.

Daly, Herman E. 1991. *Steady-State Economics.* 2nd ed. Washington, DC: Island Press.

Daly, Herman E. 1998. "Sustainable Growth: An Impossibility Theorem." In *Debating the Earth: The Environmental Politics Reader,* edited by John S. Dryzek and David Schlosberg, 285–289. Oxford: Oxford University Press.

Daly, Herman E, ed. 1973. *Toward a Steady-State Economy.* San Francisco: W.H. Freeman.

Daly, Lew, and Sean McElwee. 2014. "Forget the GDP: Some States Have Found a Better Way to Measure Our Progress." *The New Republic,* February 3. https://newrepublic.com/article/116461/gpi-better-gdp-measuring-united-states-progress.

Daniels, David P., Jon A. Krosnick, Michael P. Tichy, and Trevor Thompson. 2013. "Public Opinion on Environmental Policy in the United States." In *The Oxford Handbook of U.S. Environmental Policy,* edited by Sheldon Kamieniecki and Michael E. Kraft, 461–486. Oxford: Oxford University Press. doi: 10.1093/oxfordhb/9780199744671.013.0021.

Dasgupta, Susmita, Ashoka Mody, Subhendu Roy, and David Wheeler. 2001. "Environmental Regulation and Development: A Cross-Country Empirical Analysis." *Oxford Development Studies* 29 (2): 173–187. doi: 10.1080/13600810125568.

Dasgupta, Susmita, Kirk Hamilton, Kiran D. Pandey, and David Wheeler. 2006. "Environment During Growth: Accounting for Governance and Vulnerability." *World Development* 34 (9): 1597–1611. doi: 10.1016/j.worlddev.2005.12.008.

Davenport, Coral, Justin Gillis, Sewell Chan, and Melissa Eddy. 2015. "Inside the Paris Climate Deal." *New York Times,* December 12. https://www.nytimes.com/interactive/2015/12/12/world/paris-climate-change-deal-explainer.html.

Davies, J. Clarence, and Jan Mazurek. 1998. *Pollution Control in the United States: Evaluating the System.* Washington, DC: Resources for the Future.

D'Alessandro, Simone, Tommaso Luzzati, and Mario Morroni. 2010. "Energy Transition Towards Economic and Environmental Sustainability: Feasible Paths and Policy Implications." *Journal of Cleaner Production* 18 (4): 291–298. doi: 10.1016/j.jclepro.2009.10.015.

Death, Carl. 2016. "Green States in Africa: Beyond the Usual Suspects." *Environmental Politics* 25 (1): 116–135. doi: 10.1080/09644016.2015.1074380.

Dellink, Rob, Martijn Bennis, and Harmen Verbruggen. 1999. "Sustainable Economic Structures." *Ecological Economics* 29 (1): 141–159. doi: 10.1016/s0921-8009(98)00061-5.

Democratic Platform Committee. 2016. *2016 Democratic Platform*. https://www.dem-convention.com/wp-content/uploads/2016/07/Democratic-Party-Platform-7.21.16-no-lines.pdf. Accessed September 7, 2016).

Derthick, Martha. 2010. "Compensatory Federalism." In *Greenhouse Governance: Addressing Climate Change in America,* edited by Barry G. Rabe, 58–72. Washington, DC: Brookings Institution Press.

DeSombre, Elizabeth R. 2000. *Domestic Sources of International Environmental Policy: Industry, Environmentalists, and U.S. Power.* Cambridge, MA: MIT Press.

Dickinson, Elizabeth. 2011. "GDP: A Brief History." *Foreign Policy*, January 3. http://foreignpolicy.com/2011/01/03/gdp-a-brief-history/.

Dinda, Soumyananda. 2004. "Environmental Kuznets Curve Hypothesis: A Survey." *Ecological Economics* 49 (4): 431–455. doi: 10.1016/j.ecolecon.2004.02.011.

Dolsak, Nives. 2001. "Mitigating Global Climate Change: Why Are Some Countries More Committed Than Others?" *Policy Studies Journal* 29 (3): 414–436. doi: 10.1111/j.1541-0072.2001.tb02102.x.

Donohue, Thomas J. 2014. "4 Scary Threats from Government that Undermine Jobs, Growth, and Our Freedoms." U.S. Chamber of Commerce. https://www.uschamber.com/above-the-fold/4-scary-threats-government-undermine-jobs-growth-and-our-freedoms.

Dovers, Stephen R. 1996. "Sustainability: Demands on Policy." *Journal of Public Policy* 16 (3): 303–318. doi: 10.1017/S0143814X00007789.

Dryzek, John S. 1994. "Ecology and Discursive Democracy: Beyond Liberal Capitalism and the Administrative State." In *Is Capitalism Sustainable? Political Economy and the Politics of Ecology*, edited by Martin O'Connor, 176–197. New York: The Guildford Press.

Dryzek, John S. 2013. *The Politics of the Earth: Environmental Discourses*. 3rd ed. Oxford: Oxford University Press.

Dryzek, John S., Christian Hunold, David Schlosberg, David Downes, and Hans-Kristian Hernes. 2002. "Environmental Transformation of the State: The USA, Norway, Germany, and the UK." *Political Studies* 50 (4): 659–682. doi: 10.1111/1467-9248.00001.

Dryzek, John S., and Hayley Stevenson. 2011. "Global Democracy and Earth System Governance." *Ecological Economics* 70 (11): 1865–1874. doi: 10.1016/j.ecolecon.2011.01.021.

Dual Citizen. 2014. *The Global Green Economy Index: Measuring National Performance in the Green Economy*. 4th ed. http://dualcitizeninc.com/global-green-economy-index/.

Duit, Andreas, ed. 2014. *State and Environment: The Comparative Study of Environmental Governance*. Cambridge, MA: MIT Press.

Dulal, Hari Bansha, Roberto Foa, and Stephen Knowles. 2011. "Social Capital and Cross-Country Environmental Performance." *Journal of Environment and Development* 20 (2): 121–144. doi: 10.1177/1070496511405153.

Dunlap, Riley E., Aaron M. McCright, and Jerrod H. Yarosh. 2016. "The Political Divide on Climate Change: Partisan Polarization Widens in the U.S." *Environment: Science and Policy for Sustainable Development* 58 (5): 4–23.

Durant, Robert F. 2017. "Regulation-by-Revelation." In *Environmental Governance Reconsidered: Challenges, Choices, and Opportunities*, 2nd ed., edited by Robert F. Durant, Daniel J. Fiorino, and Rosemary O'Leary, 337–367. Cambridge, MA: MIT Press.

Durant, Robert F., Daniel J. Fiorino, and Rosemary O'Leary, eds. 2004. *Environmental Governance Reconsidered: Challenges, Choices, and Opportunities*. Cambridge, MA: MIT Press.

Durant, Robert F., Daniel J. Fiorino, and Rosemary O'Leary, eds. 2017. *Environmental Governance Reconsidered: Challenges, Choices, and Opportunities*. 2nd ed. Cambridge, MA: MIT Press.

Duwel, Andrea. 2010. "Democracy and the Environment: The Visibility Factor." https://papers.ssrn.com/sol3/papers.cfm?abstract_id=1582299.

Edsall, Thomas B. 2015. "How Did Democrats Become Favorites of the Rich?" *New York Times*, October 7. http://www.nytimes.com/2015/10/07/opinion/how-did-the-democrats-become-favorites-of-the-rich.html.

Edsall, Thomas B. 2016. "How Falling Behind the Joneses Fueled the Rise of Trump." *New York Times*, July 7. http://www.nytimes.com/2016/07/07/opinion/campaign-stops/how-falling-behind-the-joneses-fueled-the-rise-of-trump.html.

Eilperin, Juliet, and Steven Mufson. 2014. "Everything You Need to Know About the EPA's Proposed Rule on Coal Plants." *Washington Post*, June 2. https://www.washingtonpost.com/national/health-science/epa-will-propose-a-rule-to-cut-emissions-from-existing-coal-plants-by-up-to-30-percent/2014/06/02/f37f0a10-e81d-11e3-afc6-a1dd9407abcf_story.html.

Eriksson, Ralf, and Jan Otto Andersson. 2010. *Elements of Ecological Economics*. Abingdon, UK: Earthscan.

Eskeland, Gunnar S., and Ann E. Harrison. 2003. "Moving to Greener Pastures? Multinationals and the Pollution Haven Hypothesis." *Journal of Development Economics* 70 (1): 1–23. doi: 10.1016/s0304-3878(02)00084-6.

Esty, Daniel C., and Michael E. Porter. 2005. "National Environmental Performance: An Empirical Analysis of Policy Results and Determinants." *Environment and Development Economics* 10 (4): 391–434. doi: 10.1017/s1355770x05002275.

Esty, Daniel C., and Andrew Winston. 2009. *Green to Gold: How Smart Companies Use Environmental Strategies to Innovate, Create Value, and Build Competitive Advantage*. Hoboken, NJ: Wiley & Sons.

ETC Group. 2011. *Who Will Control the Green Economy?* http://www.etcgroup.org/content/who-will-control-green-economy-0.

Fankhauser, Sam, Caterina Gennaioli, and Murray Collins. 2016. "Do International Factors Influence the Passage of Climate Change Legislation?" *Climate Policy* 16 (3): 318–331. http://dx.doi.org/10.1080/14693062.2014.1000814.

Farley, Joshua. 2012. "Ecosystem Services: The Economic Debate." *Ecosystem Services* 1 (1): 40–49. doi: 10.1016/j.ecoser.2012.07.002.

Farzin, Y. Hossein, and Craig A. Bond. 2005. "Democracy and Environmental Quality." *Journal of Development Economics* 81 (1): 213–235. doi: 10.1016/j.jdeveco.2005.04.003.

Federal Coordination of Internationalismus. 2012. *After the Failure of the Green Economy: 10 Theses of a Critique of the Green Economy.* Last modified June 3, 2012. http://rio20.net/en/documentos/ten-theses-of-a-critique-of-the-green-economy/.

Federal Democratic Republic of Ethiopia (FDRE). 2011. *Ethiopia's Climate Resilient Green Economy.* http://www.undp.org/content/dam/ethiopia/docs/Ethiopia%20 CRGE.pdf.

Feindt, Peter H., Andreas Duit, and James Meadowcroft. 2016. "Greening Leviathan: the Rise of the Environmental State?" *Environmental Politics* 25 (1): 1–23.

Feiock, Richard C., and Christopher Stream. 2001. "Environmental Protection versus Economic Development: A False Trade-Off?" *Public Administration Review* 61 (3): 313–321. doi: 10.1111/0033-3352.00032.

Fiorino, Daniel J. 1990. "Can Problems Shape Priorities? The Case of Risk-Based Environmental Planning." *Public Administration Review* 50 (1): 82–90. doi: 10.2307/ 977298.

Fiorino, Daniel J. 1995. *Making Environmental Policy.* Los Angeles: University of California Press.

Fiorino, Daniel J. 2001. "Environmental Policy as Learning: A New View of an Old Landscape." *Public Administration Review* 61 (3): 322–334. doi: 10.1111/ 0033-3352.00033.

Fiorino, Daniel J. 2006. *The New Environmental Regulation.* Cambridge, MA: MIT Press.

Fiorino, Daniel J. 2010. "Sustainability as a Conceptual Focus for Public Administration." *Public Administration Review* 70 (Supplement): S78-S88. doi: https://doi.org/10.1111/ j.1540-6210.2010.02249.x.

Fiorino, Daniel J. 2011. "Explaining National Environmental Performance: Approaches, Evidence, and Implications." *Policy Sciences* 44 (4): 367–389. doi: 10.1007/ s11077-011-9140-8.

Fiorino, Daniel J. 2014a. "The Green Economy: Mythical or Meaningful?" *Policy Quarterly* 10 (1): 26–34.

Fiorino, Daniel J. 2014b. "Sustainable Cities and Governance: What Are the Connections?" In *Elgar Companion to Sustainable Cities: Strategies, Methods, and Outlook,* edited by Daniel A. Mazmanian and Hilda Blanco, 413–433. Cheltenham, UK: Edward Elgar.

Fiorino, Daniel J. 2014c. "Streams of Environmental Innovation: Four Decades of EPA Policy Reform." *Environmental Law* 44 (3): 723–760.

Fiorino, Daniel J. 2017. "The Green Economy." In *Conceptual Innovation in Environmental Policy,* edited by James Meadowcroft and Daniel J. Fiorino, 281–306. Cambridge, MA: MIT Press.

Fiorino, Daniel J., and Riordan Frost. 2016. "The State Air, Climate, and Energy Index." Paper presented at the Annual Research Conference of the Association for Public Policy Analysis and Management, Washington, DC, November 4.

Fisher, Dana R., and William R. Freudenberg. 2001. "Ecological Modernization and Its Critics: Assessing the Past and Looking Toward the Future." *Society and Natural Resources* 14 (8): 701–709. doi: 10.1080/08941920119315.

Fisher, Jonathan, and Timothy M. Smeeding. 2016. "Income Inequality." In *State of the Union: The Poverty and Inequality Report*, 32–38. Stanford Center on Poverty and Inequality. http://inequality.stanford.edu/sites/default/files/Pathways-SOTU-2016-Income-Inequality-3.pdf.

Fitzgerald, Joan. 2010. *Emerald Cities: Urban Sustainability and Economic Development.* Oxford: Oxford University Press.

Fredriksson, Per G., and Daniel L. Millimet. 2004. "Electoral Rules and Environmental Policy." *Economics Letters* 84 (2): 237–244. doi: 10.1016/j.econlet.2004.02.008.

Fredriksson, Per G., and Eric Neumayer. 2013. "Democracy and Climate Change Policies: Is History Important?" *Ecological Economics* 95: 11–19. doi: 10.1016/j.ecolecon.2013.08.002.

Fredriksson, Per G., and Jim R. Wollscheid. 2007. "Democratic Institutions versus Autocratic Regimes: The Case of Environmental Policy." *Public Choice* 130 (3): 381–393. doi: 10.1007/s11127-006-9093-1.

Freudenburg, William R. 2005. "Privileged Access, Privileged Accounts: Toward a Socially Structured Theory of Resources and Discourses." *Social Forces* 84 (1): 89–114.

Gallagher, Kelly Simms, and Joanna I. Lewis. 2016. "China's Quest for a Green Economy." In *Environmental Policy: New Directions for the Twenty-First Century,* edited by Norman J. Vig and Michael E. Kraft, 333–356. Washington, DC: CQ Press.

Gallagher, Kevin P., and Strom C. Thacker. 2008. "Democracy, Income, and Environmental Quality." University of Massachusetts, Political Economy Research Institute (PERI Working Paper 164). http://scholarworks.umass.edu/peri_working-papers/124/.

Gallego-Alvarez, Isabel, and Maria Jose Fernandez-Gomez. 2016. "Governance, Environmental, and Economic Factors: An International Analysis." *Environmental Governance and Policy* 26 (1): 29–44. doi: 10.1002/eet.1695.

Geiser, Ken. 2004. "Pollution Prevention." In *Environmental Governance Reconsidered,* edited by Robert F. Durant, Daniel J. Fiorino, and Rosemary O'Leary, 427–454. Cambridge, MA: MIT Press.

Germanwatch. 2016. *Climate Change Performance Index 2016.* https://germanwatch.org/en/11390.

Gibbs, David. 2000. "Ecological Modernisation, Regional Economic Development, and Regional Development Agencies." *Geoforum* 31 (1): 9–19. doi: 10.1016/s0016-7185(99)00040-8.

Giddens, Anthony. 1999. *The Third Way: The Renewal of Social Democracy.* Cambridge, UK: Polity Books.

Giddens, Anthony. 2011. *The Politics of Climate Change.* 2nd ed. Cambridge, UK: Polity Books.

Global Green Growth Institute. "About GGGI: Overview." http://gggi.org/about-gggi/background/organizational-overview/.

Goodstein, Eban. 1994. *Jobs and the Environment: The Myth of a National Trade-Off.* Washington, DC: Economic Policy Institute.

Gore, Al. 1993. *Earth in the Balance: Ecology and the Human Spirit.* New York: Plume.

Goulder, Lawrence H., and Andrew Schein. 2013. "Carbon Taxes vs. Cap and Trade: A Critical Review." *Climate Change Economics* 4 (3): 1350010. doi: 10.1142/s2010007813500103.

Graham, Carol. 2011. *The Pursuit of Happiness: An Economy of Well-Being.* Washington, DC: Brookings Institution Press.

GreenEconomyCoalition.2012. *TheGreenEconomyPocketbook:TheCaseforAction.*http://www.greeneconomycoalition.org/updates/green-economy-pocketbook-case-action.

Green Growth Knowledge Platform. 2013. *Moving Towards a Common Approach on Green Growth Indicators.* http://www.oecd.org/greengrowth/GGKP%20Moving%20towards%20a%20Common%20Approach%20on%20Green%20Growth%20Indicators%5B1%5D.pdf.

Green, Joshua. 2009. "The Elusive Green Economy." *The Atlantic,* July/August. http://www.theatlantic.com/magazine/archive/2009/07/the-elusive-green-economy/307554/.

Greenhouse, Linda. 2007. "Justices Say EPA has Power to Act on Harmful Gases." *New York Times,* April 3. http://www.nytimes.com/2007/04/03/washington/03scotus.html.

Greenstone, Michael, and Adam Looney. 2012. "Paying Too Much for Energy? The True Costs of Our Energy Sources." *Daedelus* 141 (2): 10–30. doi: 10.1162/daed_a_00143.

Grossman, Gene, and Alan Krueger. 1995. "Economic Growth and the Environment." *The Quarterly Journal of Economics* 110 (2): 353–377. doi: 10.2307/2118443.

Guber, Deborah Lynn, and Christopher J. Bosso. 2013. "Issue Framing, Agenda Setting, and Environmental Discourse." In *The Oxford Handbook of U.S. Environmental Policy,* edited by Sheldon Kamieniecki and Michael E. Kraft, 437–460. Oxford: Oxford University Press. doi: 10.1093/oxfordhb/9780199744671.013.0020.

Gunderson, Lance H. 2000. "Ecological Resilience—In Theory and Application." *Annual Review of Ecology and Systematics* 31 (1): 425–439. doi: https://doi.org/10.1146/annurev.ecolsys.31.1.425.

Gunningham, Neil, and Peter Grabosky. 1998. *Smart Regulation: Designing Environmental Policy.* Oxford: Oxford University Press.

Hajer, Maarten. 1995. *The Politics of Environmental Discourse: Ecological Modernization and the Policy Process.* Oxford: Oxford University Press.

Hajnal, Zoltan. 2016. "The Results on Voter ID Laws Are In—and It's Bad News for Ethnic and Racial Minorities." *Los Angeles Times,* September 8. http://www.latimes.com/opinion/op-ed/la-oe-hajnal-voter-id-research-20160908-snap-story.html.

Hajnal, Zoltan, Nazita Lajevardi, and Lindsay Nielson. 2017. "Voter Identification Laws and the Suppression of Minority Voters." *Journal of Politics* 79 (2): 363–379. doi: 10.1086/688343.

Hall, Peter A., and David Soskice. 2001. *Varieties of Capitalism: The Institutional Foundations of Comparative Advantage.* Oxford: Oxford University Press.

Hanusch, Frederic. 2016. "The Influence of the Quality of Democracy on Reactions to Climate Change: A Comparative Study of Climate Policies in Established Democracies." Paper presented at the European Consortium for Political Research General Conference, Prague, September 9. https://ecpr.eu/Events/PaperDetails.aspx?PaperID=30807&EventID=95.

Hardin, Garrett. 1968. "The Tragedy of the Commons." *Science* 162 (3859): 1243–1248. doi: 10.1126/science.162.3859.1243.

Harrington, Winston, Richard D. Morgenstern, and Thomas Sterner, eds. 2004. *Choosing Environmental Policy: Comparing Instruments and Outcomes in the United States and Europe.* Washington, DC: Resources for the Future.

Harrison, Kathryn, and Lisa McIntosh Sundstrom. 2010. *Global Commons, Domestic Decisions: The Comparative Politics of Climate Change.* Cambridge, MA: MIT Press.

Hatch, Megan E., and Elizabeth Rigby. 2015. "Laboratories of (In)equality? Redistributive Policy and Income Inequality in the American States." *Policy Studies Journal* 43 (2): 163–187. doi: 10.1111/psj.12094.

Hawken, Paul, Amory Lovins, and L. Hunter Lovins. 1999. *Natural Capitalism: Creating the Next Industrial Revolution.* Boston: Little, Brown and Company.

Hayward, Janine, ed. 2015. *New Zealand Government and Politics.* 6th ed. Oxford: Oxford University Press.

Heilbroner, Robert. 1974. *An Inquiry Into the Human Prospect.* New York: W.W. Norton & Company.

Hickman, Leo. 2010. "James Lovelock: Humans Are Too Stupid to Prevent Climate Change." Interview, *The Guardian*, March 29. Accessed July 16, 2016. https://www.theguardian.com/science/2010/mar/29/james-lovelock-climate-change.

Hirsch, Fred. 1976. *Social Limits to Growth.* Cambridge, MA: Harvard University Press.

Hochstetler, Kathryn. 2012. "Democracy and the Environment in Latin America and Eastern Europe." In *Comparative Environmental Politics*, edited by Paul Steinberg and Stacy VanDeveer, 199–230. Cambridge, MA: MIT Press.

Holland, Tim G., Garry D. Peterson, and Andrew Gonzalez. 2009. "A Cross-National Analysis of How Economic Inequality Predicts Biodiversity Loss." *Conservation Biology* 23 (5): 1304–1313. doi: 10.1111/j.1523-1739.2009.01207.x.

Holmberg, Susan. 2015. "Inequality Isn't Just Bad for the Economy—It's Toxic for the Environment." *Grist*, July 5. Accessed July 31, 2016. http://grist.org/politics/inequality-isnt-just-bad-for-the-economy-its-toxic-for-the-environment/.

Holzinger, Katharina. 2003. "The Problems of Collective Action: A New Approach." MPI Collective Goods Preprint No. 2003/2. doi: 10.2139/ssrn.399140.

Holzinger, Katharina, Christoph Knill, and Thomas Sommerer. 2011. "Is There Convergence of National Environmental Policies? An Analysis of Policy Outputs in 24 OECD Countries." *Environmental Politics* 20 (1): 20–41. doi: 10.1080/09644016.2011.538163.

Howlett, Michael. 2005. "What is a Policy Instrument? Tools, Mixes, and Implementation Styles." In *Designing Government: From Instruments to Governance*, edited by Pearl Eliadis, Margaret M. Hill, and Michael Howlett, 31–50. Montreal: McGill-Queen's University Press.

HSBC Global Research. 2009. *A Climate for Recovery: The Colour of Stimulus Goes Green.* http://globaldashboard.org/wp-content/uploads/2009/HSBC_Green_New_Deal.pdf.

Hsu, A. et al. 2016. *Environmental Performance Index.* New Haven, CT: Yale University. http://epi.yale.edu/reports/2016-report/.

Hulse, Carl. 2016. "Obama Set to Sign Bipartisan Update of the 1976 Toxic Substances Act." *New York Times,* June 22. https://www.nytimes.com/2016/06/23/us/obama-set-to-sign-bipartisan-update-of-1976-toxic-substance-law.html.

Hulse, Carl, and David M. Herszenhorn. 2010. "Democrats Call Off Climate Bill Effort." *New York Times,* July 22. www.nytimes.com/2010/07/23/us/politics/23cong.html.

Industrial Economics, Incorporated (IEC). 2015. *Assessment of the Economy-Wide Employment Impacts of EPA's Proposed Clean Power Plan.* Cambridge, MA: IEC.

Intergovernmental Panel on Climate Change (IPCC). 2014. *Climate Change 2014: Synthesis Report Summary for Policymakers.* https://www.ipcc.ch/pdf/assessment-report/ar5/syr/AR5_SYR_FINAL_SPM.pdf.

International Energy Agency (IEA). 2016. *World Energy Outlook 2016.* http://www.iea.org/newsroom/news/2016/november/world-energy-outlook-2016.html.

International Monetary Fund (IMF). 2015a. *Causes and Consequences of Economic Inequality: A Global Perspective.* International Monetary Fund Staff Discussion Note 15/13. https://www.imf.org/external/pubs/ft/sdn/2015/sdn1513.pdf.

International Monetary Fund (IMF). 2015b. *How Large Are Global Energy Subsidies?* International Monetary Fund Working Paper 15/105. Fiscal Affairs Department. https://www.imf.org/external/pubs/ft/wp/2015/wp15105.pdf.

Jackson, Lisa P. 2010. "The EPA Turns 40: 'Job-Killing' Environmental Standards Help Employ More Than 1.5 Million People." *Wall Street Journal,* December 2. https://www.wsj.com/articles/SB10001424052748704594804575648673952756954.

Jackson, Tim. 2011. *Prosperity without Growth: Economics for a Finite Planet.* Abingdon, UK: Earthscan.

Jacobson, Mark, and Mark A. Delucchi. 2009. "A Path to Sustainable Energy by 2030." *Scientific American* 301 (5): 58–65. doi: 10.1038/scientificamerican1109-58.

Jaffe, Adam B., Steven R. Peterson, Paul R. Portney, and Robert N. Stavins. 1995. "Environmental Regulation and the Competitiveness of U.S. Manufacturing: What Does the Evidence Tell Us?" *Journal of Economic Literature* 33 (1): 132–163. http://www.jstor.org/stable/2728912.

Jahn, Detlef. 1998. "Environmental Performance and Policy Regimes: Explaining Variations in 18 OECD Countries." *Policy Sciences* 31 (2): 107–131. doi: 10.1023/A:1004385005999.

Jänicke, Martin. 1996. "The Political System's Capacity for Environmental Policy." In *National Environmental Policies: A Comparative Study of Capacity-Building,* edited by Martin Jänicke and Helmut Weidner, 1–24. New York: Springer.

Jänicke, Martin. 2005. "Trend-Setters in Environmental Policy: The Character and Role of Pioneer Countries." *European Environment* 15 (2): 129–142. doi: 10.1002/eet.375.

Jänicke, Martin. 2008. "Ecological Modernisation: New Perspectives." *Journal of Cleaner Production* 16 (5): 557–565. doi: https://doi.org/10.1016/j.jclepro.2007.02.011.

Jänicke, Martin. 2012. "Green Growth: From a Growing Eco-Industry to Economic Sustainability." *Energy Policy* 48: 13–21. doi: 10.1016/j.enpol.2012.04.045.

Jänicke, Martin, and Helmut Weidner, eds. 1997. *National Environmental Policies: A Comparative Study of Capacity-Building*. New York: Springer.

Jeong, Moon-Gi, and Richard Feiock. 2006. "Impact Fees, Growth Management, and Development: A Contractual Approach to Local Policy and Governance." *Urban Affairs Review* 41 (6): 749–768. doi: 10.1177/1078087406287165.

Jones, Van. 2008. *The Green Collar Economy: How One Solution Can Fix Our Two Biggest Problems*. New York: HarperCollins.

Jordan, Andrew J. and Andrea Lenschow, eds. 2008. *Innovation in Environmental Policy? Integrating the Environment for Sustainability*. Cheltenham, UK: Edward Elgar.

Jordan, Andrew, Rudiger K.W. Wurzel, and Anthony R. Zito. 2003. "'New' Instruments of Environmental Governance: Patterns and Pathways of Change." *Environmental Politics* 12 (1): 1–24. doi: 10.1080/714000665.

Jorgenson, Dale W., and Peter J. Wilcoxen. 1990. "Environmental Regulation and U.S. Economic Growth." *Rand Journal of Economics* 21 (2): 314–340. doi: 10.2307/2555426.

Jost, John T., Jack Glaser, Arie Kruglanski, and Frank J. Sulloway. 2003. "Political Conservatism as Motivated Social Cognition." *Psychological Bulletin* 129 (3): 339–375. doi: 10.1037/0033-2909.129.3.339.

Kallis, Giorgos. 2011. "In Defence of Degrowth." *Ecological Economics* 70 (5): 873–880. doi: 10.1016/j.ecolecon.2010.12.007.

Kamarck, Elaine C. 2013. *How Change Happens—Or Doesn't: The Politics of US Public Policy*. Boulder, CO: Lynne Rienner.

Karapin, Roger. 2014. "Wind Power Development in Germany and the United States: Structural Factors, Multiple Stream Convergence, and Turning Points." In *State and Environment: The Comparative Study of Environmental Governance*, edited by Andreas Duit, 111–146. Cambridge, MA: MIT Press.

Karapin, Roger. 2016. *Political Opportunities for Climate Policy: California, New York, and the Federal Government*. Cambridge, UK: Cambridge University Press.

Katz, Cheryl. 2012. "Unequal Exposures: People in Poor, Non-White Neighborhoods Breathe More Hazardous Air." *Environmental Health News*, November 1. http://www.environmentalhealthnews.org/ehs/news/2012/unequal-exposures.

Keane, Brian F. 2012. *Green Is Good: Save Money, Make Money, and Help Your Community Profit from Clean Energy*. Guilford, CT: Lyons Press.

Kempf, Hubert, and Stephane Rossignol. 2007. "Is Inequality Harmful for the Environment in a Growing Economy?" *Economics & Politics* 19 (1): 53–71. doi: 10.1111/j.1468-0343.2007.00302.x.

Kennan, George F. 1947. "The Sources of Soviet Conduct." *Foreign Affairs* 25 (4): 566–582. doi: 10.2307/20030065.

Keynes, John Maynard. 1936. *The General Theory of Employment, Interest and Money*. London: Palgrave Macmillan.

Khor, Martin. 2011. *Risks and Uses of the Green Economy Concept in the Context of Sustainable Development, Poverty and Equity*. South Centre Research Paper 40.

http://www.southcentre.int/wp-content/uploads/2013/05/RP40_Green-Economy-Concept-Sustainable-Development-Poverty-and-Equity_EN.pdf.

Kingdon, John W. 1995. *Agendas, Alternatives, and Public Policies.* 2nd ed. New York: Harper Collins.

Klein, Naomi. 2014. *This Changes Everything: Capitalism vs. the Climate.* New York: Simon & Schuster.

Kolbert, Elizabeth. 2014. *The Sixth Extinction: An Unnatural History.* New York: Henry Holt and Company.

Konisky, David M. 2017. "Environmental Justice." In *Environmental Governance Reconsidered: Challenges, Choices, and Opportunities,* 2nd ed., edited by Robert F. Durant, Daniel J. Fiorino, and Rosemary O'Leary, 205–234. Cambridge, MA: MIT Press.

Konisky, David M., Jeffrey Milyo, and Lilliard E. Richardson, Jr. 2008. "Environmental Policy Attitudes: Issues, Geographical Scale, and Political Trust." *Social Science Quarterly* 89 (5): 1066–1085. doi: 10.1111/j.1540-6237.2008.00574.x.

Korosec, Kirsten. 2015. "In U.S., There Are Twice as Many Solar Workers as Coal Miners." *Fortune,* January 16. http://fortune.com/2015/01/16/solar-jobs-report-2014/.

Kraft, Michael E. 2015. *Environmental Policy and Politics.* 6th ed. Upper Saddle River, NJ: Pearson.

Kraft, Michael E. 2016. "Environmental Policy in Congress." In *Environmental Policy: New Directions for the Twenty-First Century,* 9th ed., edited by Norman J. Vig and Michael E. Kraft, 103–127. Washington, DC: CQ Press.

Kraft, Michael E. 2017. "Environmental Risk: New Approaches Needed to Address Twenty-First Century Challenges." In *Conceptual Innovation in Environmental Policy,* edited by James Meadowcroft and Daniel J. Fiorino, 103–128. Cambridge, MA: MIT Press.

Kraft, Michael E., Mark Stephan, and Troy D. Abel. 2011. *Coming Clean: Information Disclosure and Environmental Performance.* Cambridge, MA: MIT Press.

Krauthammer, Charles. 2009. "Charles Krauthammer on the New Socialism." *Washington Post,* December 11. http://www.washingtonpost.com/wp-dyn/content/article/2009/12/10/AR2009121003163.html.

Kubiszewski, Ida, Robert Costanza, Carol Franco, Philip Lawn, John Talberth, Tim Jackson, and Camille Aylmer. 2013. "Beyond GDP: Measuring and Achieving Global Genuine Progress." *Ecological Economics* 93: 57–68. doi: 10.1016/j.ecolecon.2013.04.019.

Kuznets, Simon. 1955. "Economic Growth and Income Inequality." *American Economic Review* 45 (1): 1–28. http://www.jstor.org/stable/1811581.

Lafferty, William M., and Eivind Hoven. 2003. "Environmental Policy Integration: Towards an Analytical Framework." *Environmental Politics* 12 (3): 1–22. doi: 10.1080/09644010412331308254.

Lafferty, William M., and James Meadowcroft, eds. 2000. *Implementing Sustainable Development: Strategies and Initiatives in High-Consumption Societies.* Oxford: Oxford University Press.

Lakoff, George A. 2002. *Moral Politics: How Liberals and Conservatives Think.* Chicago: University of Chicago Press.

Landler, Mark, and John M. Broder. 2013. "Obama Outlines Ambitious Plan to Cut Greenhouse Gases." *New York Times*, June 25. http://www.nytimes.com/2013/06/26/us/politics/obama-plan-to-cut-greenhouse-gases.html.

Lange, Philipp, Peter P.J. Driessen, Alexandra Sauer, Basil Bornemann, and Paul Burger. 2013. "Governing Towards Sustainability—Conceptualizing Modes of Governance." *Journal of Environmental Policy and Planning* 15 (3): 403–425. doi: 10.1080/1523908x.2013.769414.

Langhelle, Oluf. 2017. "Sustainable Development: Linking Environment and Development." In *Conceptual Innovation in Environmental Policy,* edited by James Meadowcroft and Daniel J. Fiorino, 181–206. Cambridge, MA: MIT Press.

Lawn, Philip, and Matthew Clarke. 2010. "The End of Economic Growth? A Contracting Threshold Hypothesis." *Ecological Economics* 69 (11): 2213–2223. doi: 10.1016/j.ecolecon.2010.06.007.

Layzer, Judith A. 2012. *Open for Business: Conservatives' Opposition to Environmental Regulation.* Cambridge, MA: MIT Press.

Layzer, Judith A., and Alexis Schulman. 2017. "Adaptive Management: Popular But Difficult to Implement." In *Conceptual Innovation in Environmental Policy*, edited by James Meadowcroft and Daniel J. Fiorino, 155–180. Cambridge, MA: MIT Press.

Leighley, Jan E, and Jonathan Nagler. 2014. *Who Votes Now? Demographics, Issues, Inequality, and Turnout in the United States.* Princeton, NJ: Princeton University Press.

Levinson, Arik. 2002. "The Ups and Downs of the Environmental Kuznets Curve." In *Recent Advances in Environmental Economics*, edited by John A. List and Aart de Zeeuw, 119–141. Cheltenham, UK: Edward Elgar.

Li, Quan, and Rafael Reuveny. 2006. "Democracy and Environmental Degradation." *International Studies Quarterly* 50 (4): 935–956. doi: 10.1111/j.1468-2478.2006.00432.x.

Liefferink, Duncan, Bas Arts, Jelmer Kamstra, and Jeroen Ooijevaar. 2009. "Leaders and Laggards in Environmental Performance: A Quantitative Analysis of Domestic Policy Outputs." *Journal of European Public Policy* 16 (5): 677–700. doi: 10.1080/13501760902983283.

Lindblom, Charles. 1959. "The Science of Muddling Through." *Public Administration Review* 19 (2): 79–88. doi: 10.2307/973677.

Lisciandra, Maurizio, and Carlo Migliardo. 2016. "An Empirical Study of the Impact of Corruption on Environmental Performance: Evidence from Panel Data." *Environmental and Resource Economics.* doi: 10.1007/s10640-016-0019-1.

List, John A., and Daniel Sturm. 2006. "How Elections Matter: Theory and Evidence from Environmental Policy." *Quarterly Journal of Economics* 121 (4): 1249–1281. doi: 10.1162/qjec.121.4.1249.

Lorente, Daniel B., and Agustin Alvarez-Herranz. 2016. "Economic Growth and Energy Regulation in the Environmental Kuznets Curve." *Environmental Science and Pollution Research* 23 (16): 16478–16494. doi: 10.1007/s11356-016-6773-3.

Lowry, William R. 2008. "Disentangling Energy Policy from Environmental Policy." *Social Science Quarterly* 89 (5): 1195–1211. doi: 10.1111/j.1540-6237.2008.00565.x.

Lubchenco, Jane. 1998. "Entering the Century of the Environment: A New Social Contract for Science." *Science* 279 (5350): 491–497. doi: 10.1126/science.279.5350.491.

Madden, Nathan J. 2014. "Green Means Stop: Veto Players and Their Impact on Climate-Change Policy Outputs." *Environmental Politics* 23 (4): 570–589. doi: 10.1080/09644016.2014.884301.

Magill, Bobby. 2016. "Lawsuit Aims to Overturn Obama's Clean Power Plan." *Scientific American*, April 4. http://www.scientificamerican.com/article/lawsuit-aims-to-overturn-obama-s-clean-power-plan/.

Magnani, Elisabetta. 2000. "The Environmental Kuznets Curve, Environmental Protection Policy, and Income Distribution." *Ecological Economics* 32 (3): 431–443. doi: 10.1016/s0921-8009(99)00115-9.

Mandarano, Lynn. 2011. "Clean Waters, Clean City: Sustainable Storm Water Management in Philadelphia." In *Sustainability in America's Cities: Creating the Green Metropolis*, edited by Matthew I. Slavin, 157–180. Washington, DC: Island Press.

Marcus, Ruth. 2012. "Bad Science around 'Job-Killing Regulations.'" *Washington Post*, April 24. https://www.washingtonpost.com/opinions/bad-science-around-job-killing-regulations/2012/04/24/gIQARQQTfT_story.html?utm_term=.f1edc0472865.

Matthews, John A. 2012. "Green Growth Strategies—Korean Initiatives." *Futures* 44 (8): 761–769. doi: 10.1016/j.futures.2012.06.002.

Matthews, Mary M. 2001. "Cleaning Up Their Acts: Shifts of Environment and Energy Policies in Pluralist and Corporatist States." *Policy Studies Journal* 29 (3): 478–498. doi: 10.1111/j.1541-0072.2001.tb02105.x.

Mazmanian, Daniel A., and Michael E. Kraft, eds. 2009. *Toward Sustainable Communities: Transition and Transformations in Environmental Policy*, 2nd ed. Cambridge, MA: MIT Press.

McCauley, Douglas J. 2006. "Selling Out on Nature." *Nature* 443 (7107): 27–28. doi: 10.1038/443027a.

McCauley, Kathy, Bruce Barron, and Morton Coleman. 2008. *Crossing the Aisle to Cleaner Air: How the Bipartisan 'Project 88' Transformed Environmental Policy*. Pittsburgh: University of Pittsburgh Institute of Politics. http://d-scholarship.pitt.edu/28739/1/Crossing%20the%20Aisle%20to%20Cleaner%20Air.pdf.

McElwee, Sean. 2014. *Why the Voting Gap Matters*. New York: Demos. http://www.demos.org/sites/default/files/publications/Voters&NonVoters.pdf.

Meadowcroft, James. 2005. "From Welfare State to Ecostate." In *The State and the Global Ecological Crisis*, edited by John Barry and Robyn Eckersley, 3–24. Cambridge, MA: MIT Press.

Meadowcroft, James. 2012. "Greening the State?" In *Comparative Environmental Politics*, edited by Paul Steinberg and Stacy VanDeveer, 63–88. Cambridge, MA: MIT Press.

Meadowcroft, James. 2017. "The Birth of the Environment and the Evolution of Environmental Governance." In *Conceptual Innovation in Environmental Policy*, edited by James Meadowcroft and Daniel J. Fiorino, 53–75. Cambridge, MA: MIT Press.

Meadowcroft, James, and Daniel J. Fiorino, eds. 2017. *Conceptual Innovation in Environmental Policy*. Cambridge, MA: MIT Press.

Meadows, Donella H., Dennis L. Meadows, and Jørgen Randers. 1992. *Beyond the Limits.* White River Junction, VT: Chelsea Green.

Meadows, Donella H., Dennis L. Meadows, Jørgen Randers, and William W. Behrens III. 1972. *The Limits to Growth: A Report for the Club of Rome's Project on the Predicament of Mankind.* New York: Universe Books.

Meadows, Donella, Jørgen Randers, and Dennis Meadows. 2004. *Limits to Growth: The 30-Year Update.* White River Junction, VT: Chelsea Green.

Midlarsky, Manus I. 2001. "Democracy and the Environment." In *Environmental Conflict*, edited by Paul F. Diehl and Nils Peter Gleditsch, 155–178. Boulder, CO: Westview Press.

Mikkelson, Gregory M., Andrew Gonzalez, and Garry D. Peterson. 2007. "Economic Inequality Predicts Biodiversity Loss." *Plos ONE* 2 (5): e444. doi: 10.1371/journal. pone.0000444.

Millennium Ecosystem Assessment. 2005. *Living Beyond Our Means: Natural Assets and Human Well-Being.* http://www.millenniumassessment.org/documents/document.429.aspx.pdf.

Milman, Oliver. 2016. "Republican Calls to Scrap EPA Met With Skepticism by Experts." *The Guardian*, February 26. https://www.theguardian.com/environment/2016/feb/26/republican-candidates-donald-trump-eliminate-epa-law-experts.

Mol, Arthur P.J., and David A. Sonnenfeld. 2000. "Ecological Modernisation around the World: An Introduction." *Environmental Politics* 9 (1): 1–14.

Morgenstern, Richard D., ed. 1997. *Economic Analyses at EPA: Assessing Regulatory Impact.* Washington, DC: Resources for the Future.

Morgenstern, Richard D., William A. Pizer, and Jhih-Shyang Shih. 2002. "Jobs versus the Environment: An Industry-level Perspective." *Journal of Environmental Economics and Management* 43 (3): 412–436. doi: 10.1006/jeem.2001.1191.

Moyer, Justin. 2015. "Jerry Brown Battles California Water Crisis Created by His Father, Gov. Pat Brown." *Washington Post*, April 2. https://www.washingtonpost.com/news/morning-mix/wp/2015/04/02/gov-jerry-brown-battling-california-water-crisis-created-by-his-father-gov-pat-brown/.

Muller, Nicholas Z., Robert Mendelsohn, and William Nordhaus. 2011. "Environmental Accounting for Pollution in the United States Economy." *American Economic Review* 101 (5): 1649–1675. doi: 10.1257/aer.101.5.1649.

Munasinghe, Mohan. 1999. "Is Environmental Degradation an Inevitable Consequence of Economic Growth: Tunneling Through the Environmental Kuznets Curve." *Ecological Economics* 29 (1): 89–109. doi: 10.1016/s0921-8009(98)00062-7.

Mundaca, Luis, and Jessika Luth Richter. 2015. "Assessing 'Green Energy Economy' Stimulus Packages: Evidence from the U.S. Programs Targeting Renewable Energy." *Renewable and Sustainable Energy Reviews* 42: 1174–1186. doi: 10.1016/j.rser.2014.10.060.

Murphy, Joseph. 2000. "Ecological Modernisation." *Geoforum* 31 (1): 1–8. doi: 10.1016/s0016-7185(99)00039-1.

Murray, Brian C. and Nicholas Rivers. 2015. "British Columbia's Revenue-Neutral Carbon Tax: A Review of the Latest 'Grand Experiment' in Environmental Policy." Nicholas Institute for Environmental Policy Solutions Working Paper 15-04.

Durham: NC: Duke University. https://nicholasinstitute.duke.edu/sites/default/files/publications/ni_wp_15-04_full.pdf.

Nagourney, Adam. 2017. "California Extends Climate Bill, Handing Gov. Jerry Brown a Victory." *New York Times*, July 17. https://www.nytimes.com/2017/07/17/climate/california-cap-and-trade-approved-jerry-brown.html.

National Research Council. 1983. *Risk Assessment in the Federal Government: Managing the Process*. Washington, DC: National Academies Press. doi: 10.17226/366.

National Research Council. 2010. *Hidden Costs of Energy: Unpriced Consequences of Energy Production and Use*. Washington, DC: National Academies Press. doi: https://doi.org/10.17226/12794.

National Research Council. 2011. *Sustainability and the U.S. EPA*. Washington, DC: National Academies Press. doi: 10.17226/13152.

Neumayer, Eric. 2002. "Do Democracies Exhibit Stronger International Environmental Commitment? A Cross-Country Analysis." *Journal of Peace Research* 39 (2): 139–164. doi: 10.1177/0022343302039002001.

Nelson, Arthur C., and David R. Peterman. 2000. "Does Growth Management Matter? The Effect of Growth Management on Economic Performance." *Journal of Planning Education and Research* 19 (3): 277–285. doi: 10.1177/0739456x0001900307.

Nijaki, Laurie Kaye. 2012. "Going Beyond Growth: The Green Economy as a Sustainable Development Strategy." In *The Next Economics: Global Cases in Energy, Environment and Climate Change*, edited by Woodrow W. Clark II, 251–274. New York: Springer.

Norgard, Jørgen Stig, John Peet, and Kristin Vala Ragnarsdottir, 2010. "The History of the Limits to Growth." *The Solutions Journal* 1 (2): 59–63. https://www.thesolutions-journal.com/article/the-history-of-the-limits-to-growth/.

Obydenkova, Anastassia, Zafar Nazarov, and Raufhon Salahodjaev. 2016. "The Process of Deforestation in Weak Democracies and the Role of Intelligence." *Environmental Research* 148: 484–490. doi: 10.1016/j.envres.2016.03.039.

O'Connor, Martin, ed. 1994. *Is Capitalism Sustainable? Political Economy and the Politics of Ecology*. New York: The Guildford Press.

Ophuls, William. 1977. *Ecology and the Politics of Scarcity: Prologue to a Political Theory of the Steady State*. San Francisco, CA: W.H. Freeman.

Ophuls, William, with A. Stephen Boyan, Jr. 1998. "The American Political Economy II: The Non-Politics of Laissez Faire." In *Debating the Earth*, edited by John S. Dryzek and David Schlosberg, 187–202. Oxford: Oxford University Press.

Oreskes, Naomi, and Erik M. Conway. 2010. *Merchants of Doubt: How a Handful of Scientists Obscured the Truth on Issues from Tobacco Smoke to Global Warming*. New York: Bloomsbury Press.

Organization for Economic Cooperation and Development (OECD). 2009. *Green Growth: Overcoming the Crisis and Beyond*. Paris: OECD Publishing. doi: 10.1787/9789264083639-en.

Organization for Economic Cooperation and Development (OECD). 2010. *Guidance on Sustainability Impact Assessment*. Paris: OECD Publishing. doi: 10.1787/9789264086913-en.

Organization for Economic Cooperation and Development (OECD). 2011. *Towards Green Growth*. Paris: OECD Publishing. doi: http://dx.doi.org/10.1787/9789264111318-en.

Organization for Economic Cooperation and Development (OECD). 2012. *Environmental Outlook to 2050: The Consequences of Inaction*. Paris: OECD Publishing. doi: 10.1787/9789264122246-en.

Organization for Economic Cooperation and Development (OECD). 2015. *In It Together: Why Less Inequality Benefits All*. Paris: OECD Publishing. doi: 10.1787/9789264235120-en.

Organization for Economic Cooperation and Development (OECD). 2016. *Income Inequality Update: Income Inequality Remains High in the Face of Weak Recovery*. https://www.oecd.org/social/OECD2016-Income-Inequality-Update.pdf.

Ostrom, Elinor. 1990. *Governing the Commons: The Evolution of Institutions for Collective Action*. Cambridge, UK: Cambridge University Press.

Ostrom, Elinor. 2000. "Collective Action and the Evolution of Social Norms." *The Journal of Economic Perspectives* 14 (3): 137–158. doi: 10.1257/jep.14.3.137.

Ozymy, Joshua, and Denis Rey. 2013. "Wild Spaces or Polluted Places: Contentious Policies, Consensus Institutions, and Environmental Performance in Industrialized Democracies." *Global Environmental Politics* 13 (4): 81–100. doi: 10.1162/glep_a_00199.

Pasurka, Carl. 2008. "Perspectives on Pollution Abatement and Competitiveness: Theory, Data, and Analyses." *Review of Environmental Economics and Policy* 2 (2): 194–218. doi: 10.1093/reep/ren009.

Pearce, David, and Edward B. Barbier. 2000. *Blueprint for a Sustainable Economy*. Abingdon, UK: Earthscan.

Pearce, David, Anil Markandya, and Edward Barbier. 1989. *Blueprint for a Green Economy*. Abingdon, UK: Earthscan.

Pellegrini, Lorenzo, and Reyer Gerlagh. 2006. "Corruption, Democracy, and Environmental Policy: An Empirical Contribution to the Debate." *Journal of Environment and Development* 15 (3): 332–354. doi: 10.1177/1070496506290960.

Perrings, Charles, and Alberto Ansuategi. 2000. "Sustainability, Growth and Development." *Journal of Economic Studies* 27 (1/2): 19–54. doi: 10.1108/eum0000000005309.

Pew Research Center. 2014. "Political Polarization in the American Public." Accessed September 3, 2016. http://www.people-press.org/2014/06/12/political-polarization-in-the-american-public/.

Pew Research Center. 2015a. "Beyond Distrust: How Americans View Their Government." Accessed September 3, 2016. http://www.people-press.org/2015/11/23/beyond-distrust-how-americans-view-their-government/.

Pew Research Center. 2015b. "Global Concern about Climate Change, Broad Support for Limiting Emissions." Accessed September 3, 2016. http://www.pewglobal.org/2015/11/05/global-concern-about-climate-change-broad-support-for-limiting-emissions/.

Pew Research Center. 2015c. "Women, More Than Men, Say Climate Change Will Harm Them Personally." Accessed August 2, 2016. http://www.pewresearch.org/fact-tank/2015/12/02/women-more-than-men-say-climate-change-will-harm-them-personally/.

Pollin, Robert, James Heintz, and Heidi Garret-Peltier. 2009. *The Economic Benefits of Investing in Clean Energy*. Washington, DC: Center for American Progress; Political Economy Research Institute. https://www.americanprogress.org/issues/green/reports/2009/06/18/6192/the-economic-benefits-of-investing-in-clean-energy/.

Pollin, Robert, Heidi Garrett-Peltier, James Heintz, and Bracken Hendricks. 2014. *Green Growth: A U.S. Program for Controlling Climate Change and Expanding Job Opportunities*. Washington, DC: Center for American Progress; Political Economy Research Institute. https://www.americanprogress.org/issues/green/report/2014/09/18/96404/green-growth/.

Poloni-Staudinger, Lori. 2008. "Are Consensus Democracies More Environmentally Effective?" *Environmental Politics* 17 (3): 410–430. doi: 10.1080/09644010802055634.

Porter, Eduardo. 2016. "Does a Carbon Tax Work? Ask British Columbia." *New York Times*, March 1. https://www.nytimes.com/2016/03/02/business/does-a-carbon-tax-work-ask-british-columbia.html.

Porter, Michael E., and Claas van der Linde. 1995. "Toward a New Conception of the Environment-Competitiveness Relationship." *Journal of Economic Perspectives* 9 (4): 97–118. doi: 10.1257/jep.9.4.97.

Portney, Kent. 2013. *Taking Sustainable Cities Seriously: Economic Development, Environment, and Quality of Life in American Cities*, 2nd ed. Cambridge, MA: MIT Press.

Portney, Paul R., and Robert N. Stavins, eds. 2000. *Public Policies for Environmental Protection*, 2nd ed. Washington, DC: Resources for the Future.

Povitkina, Marina. 2015. "Democracy, Bureaucratic Capacity and Environmental Quality." Quality of Government Institute, University of Gothenburg, Working Paper 2015:13. http://hdl.handle.net/2077/39891.

Provost, Claire. 2016. "Climate Change Could Drive 122m More People into Extreme Poverty by 2030." *The Guardian*, October 17. https://www.theguardian.com/global-development/2016/oct/17/climate-change-could-drive-122m-more-people-into-extreme-poverty-by-2030-un-united-nations-report.

Przeworski, Adam, Michael E. Alvarez, Jose Antonio Cheibub, and Fernando Limongi. 1995. *Democracy and Development: Political Institutions and Well-Being in the World, 1950–1990*. Cambridge, UK: Cambridge University Press.

Putnam, Robert D. 2007. "E Pluribus Unum: Diversity and Community in the Twenty-first Century." *Scandinavian Political Studies* 30 (2): 137–174. doi: 10.1111/j.1467-9477.2007.00176.x.

PWC. 2015. *The World in 2050: Will the Shift in Global Economic Power Continue?* https://www.pwc.com/gx/en/issues/the-economy/assets/world-in-2050-february-2015.pdf.

Rabe, Barry G. 2004. *Statehouse and Greenhouse: The Emerging Politics of American Climate Change Policy*. Washington, DC: Brookings Institution Press.

Rabe, Barry G. ed. 2010. *Greenhouse Governance: Addressing Climate Change in America*. Washington, DC: Brookings Institution Press.

Rabe, Barry G. 2016. "Racing to the Top, the Bottom, or the Middle of the Pack? The Evolving State Government Role in Environmental Protection." In *Environmental Policy: New Directions for the Twenty-First Century*, 9th ed., edited by Norman J. Vig and Michael E. Kraft, 33–57. Washington, DC: CQ Press.

Ravallion, Martin, Mark Heil, and Jyotsna Jalan. 2000. "Carbon Emissions and Income Inequality." *Oxford Economic Papers* 52 (4): 651–669. http://www.jstor.org/stable/3488662.

Recchia, Steven P. 2002. "International Environmental Treaty Engagement in 19 Democracies." *Policy Studies Journal* 30 (4): 470–494. doi: 10.1111/j.1541-0072.2002.tb02159.x.

Reich, Robert B. 2011. *Aftershock: The Next Economy and America's Future.* New York: Vintage Books.

Reid, Walter. 2006. "Nature: The Many Benefits of Ecosystem Services." *Nature* 443 (7113): 749. doi: 10.1038/443749a.

Reinhardt, Forest. 2000. *Down to Earth: Applying Business Principles to Environmental Management.* Cambridge, MA: Harvard Business School Press.

Reisner, Marc. 1986. *Cadillac Desert: The American West and Its Disappearing Water.* New York: Viking Penguin.

Republican National Committee. 2016. *Republican Platform 2016.* https://prod-static-ngop-pbl.s3.amazonaws.com/media/documents/DRAFT_12_FINAL[1]-ben_1468872234.pdf.

Ringquist, Evan J. 2005. "Assessing Evidence of Environmental Inequities: A Meta-Analysis." *Journal of Policy Analysis and Management* 24 (2): 223–247. doi: 10.1002/pam.20088.

Ringquist, Evan J. 2006. "Environmental Justice: Normative Concerns, Empirical Evidence, and Government Action." In *Environmental Policy,* 6th ed., edited by Norman J. Vig and Michael E. Kraft, 239–263. Washington, DC: CQ Press.

Ringquist, Evan J., Milena I. Neshkova, and Joseph Aamidor. 2013. "Campaign Promises, Democratic Governance, and Environmental Policy in the U.S. Congress." *Policy Studies Journal* 41 (2): 365–387. doi: 10.1111/psj.12021.

Rockstrom, J., et al. 2009. "Planetary Boundaries: Exploring the Safe Operating Space for Humanity." *Ecology and Society* 14 (2): 32. http://www.ecologyandsociety.org/vol14/iss2/art32/.

Rosenbaum, Walter A. 2015. *American Energy: The Politics of 21st Century Policy.* Washington, DC: CQ Press.

Rosenbaum, Walter A. 2017. *Environmental Politics and Policy,* 10th ed. Washington, DC: CQ Press.

Rothstein, Bo, and Eric M. Uslaner. 2005. "All for All: Equality, Corruption, and Social Trust." *World Politics* 58 (1): 41–72. doi: 10.1353/wp.2006.0022.

Ruckelshaus, William D. 1998. "Stepping Stones." *The Environmental Forum* 15 (2): 30–36.

Ruckelshaus, William D., and William K. Reilly. 2016. "Why Obama Is Right on Clean Energy." *New York Times,* September 25. http://www.nytimes.com/2016/09/26/opinion/why-obama-is-right-on-clean-energy.html.

Rumsfeld, Donald. 2013. *Rumsfeld's Rules: Leadership Lessons in Business, Politics, War, and Life.* New York: Broadside Books.

Rydin, Yvonne, and Mark Pennington. 2000. "Public Participation and Local Environmental Planning: The Collective Action Problem and the Potential of Social Capital." *Local Environment* 5 (2): 153–169. doi: 10.1080/13549830050009328.

Sabatier, Paul A., ed. 1999. *Theories of the Policy Process*. Boulder, CO: Westview Press.

Sabatier, Paul A., and Hank Jenkins-Smith. 1999. "The Advocacy Coalition Framework: An Assessment." In *Theories of the Policy Process*, edited by Paul A. Sabatier, 117–166. Boulder, CO: Westview Press.

Sachs, Jeffrey D. 2006. *The End of Poverty: Economic Possibilities for Our Time*. New York: Penguin.

Sagoff, Mark. 1988. *The Economy of the Earth*. Cambridge, UK: Cambridge University Press.

Saha, Devashree, and Robert G. Paterson. 2008. "Local Efforts to Promote the 'Three Es' of Sustainable Development: Survey in Medium to Large Cities in the United States." *Journal of Planning Education and Research* 28 (1): 21–37. doi: 10.1177/0739456x08321803.

Schlossberg, Tatiana. 2017. "What to Know About Trump's Order to Dismantle the Clean Power Plan." *New York Times*, March 27. https://www.nytimes.com/2017/03/27/science/what-to-know-about-trumps-order-to-dismantle-the-clean-power-plan.html

Schmalensee, Richard. 2012. "From 'Green Growth' to Sound Policies: An Overview." *Energy Economics* 34 (S1): S2-S6. doi: 10.1016/j.eneco.2012.08.041.

Schreurs, Miranda. A. 2002. *Environmental Politics in Japan, Germany, and the United States*. Cambridge, UK: Cambridge University Press.

Scruggs, Lyle. 1998. "Political and Economic Inequality and the Environment." *Ecological Economics* 26 (3): 259–275. doi: 10.1016/s0921-8009(97)00118-3.

Scruggs, Lyle. 2003. *Sustaining Abundance: Environmental Performance in Industrial Democracies*. Cambridge, UK: Cambridge University Press.

Selman, Mindy, Suzie Greenhalgh, Evan Branosky, Cy Jones, and Jenny Guiling. 2009. *Water Quality Trading Programs: An International Overview*. Washington, DC: World Resources Institute. http://www.wri.org/publication/water-quality-trading-programs-international-overview.

Shapiro, Isaac. 2011. *The Combined Effect of the Obama EPA Rules*. Washington, DC: Economic Policy Institute. http://www.epi.org/publication/combined-effect-obama-epa-rules/.

Shapiro, Isaac, and John Irons. 2011. *Regulation, Employment, and the Economy: Fears of Job Loss Are Overblown*. Washington, DC: Economic Policy Institute. http://www.epi.org/publication/regulation_employment_and_the_economy_fears_of_job_loss_are_overblown/.

Shearman, David, and Joseph Wayne Smith. 2007. *The Climate Change Challenge and the Failure of Democracy*. Westport, CT: Praeger.

Siaroff, Alan. 1999. "Corporatism in 24 Industrial Democracies: Meaning and Measurement." *European Journal of Political Research* 36 (2): 175–205. doi: 10.1111/1475-6765.00467.

Simon, Herbert A. 1997. *Administrative Behavior: A Study of Decision-Making Processes in Administrative Organizations*, 4th ed. New York: The Free Press.

Slavin, Matthew I., ed. 2011. *Sustainability in America's Cities: Creating the Green Metropolis*. Washington, DC: Island Press.

Sommeiller, Estelle, Mark Price, and Ellis Wazeter. 2016. *Income Inequality in the U.S. by State, Metropolitan Area, and County.* Washington, DC: Economic Policy Institute. http://www.epi.org/files/pdf/107100.pdf.

Sommerer, Thomas, and Sijeong Lim. 2016. "The Environmental State as Model for the World? An Analysis of Policy Repertoires in 37 Countries." *Environmental Politics* 25 (1): 92–115. doi: 10.1080/09644016.2015.1081719.

Stavins, Robert N., ed. 2005. *Economics of the Environment: Selected Readings*, 5th ed. New York: W.W. Norton & Company.

Stehr, Nico. 2015. "Climate Change: Democracy is Not an Inconvenience." *Nature* 525 (7570): 449–450. doi: 10.1038/525449a.

Stehr, Nico. 2016. "Exceptional Circumstances: Does Climate Change Trump Democracy?" *Issues in Science and Technology* 32 (2). http://issues.org/32-2/exceptional-circumstances-does-climate-change-trump-democracy/.

Stern, David I. 2004. "The Rise and Fall of the Environmental Kuznets Curve." *World Development* 32 (8): 1419–1439. doi: 10.1016/j.worlddev.2004.03.004.

Stern, David, Michael Common, and Edward Barbier. 1996. "Economic Growth and Environmental Degradation: The Environmental Kuznets Curve and Sustainable Development." *World Development* 24 (7): 1151–1160. doi: 10.1016/0305-750x(96)00032-0.

Stern, Nicholas. 2007. *The Economics of Climate Change: The Stern Review.* Cambridge, UK: Cambridge University Press.

Stiglitz, Joseph E. 2012. *The Price of Inequality: How Today's Divided Society Endangers Our Future.* New York: W.W. Norton & Company.

Stone, Chad. 2015. "Designing Rebates to Protect Low-Income Households under a Carbon Tax." *Resources* 190: 31–35. http://www.rff.org/research/publications/designing-rebates-protect-low-income-households-under-carbon-tax.

Sulemana, Iddisah, Harvey S. James, and James S. Rikoon. 2015. "Environmental Kuznets Curves for Air Pollution in Developed and Developing Countries: Exploring Turning Points and the Role of Institutional Quality." Paper presented at the Annual Mid-America Environmental Engineering Conference, Columbia, Missouri, October 23–24.

Sumner, Jenny, Lori Bird, and Hillary Dobos. 2011. "Carbon Taxes: A Review of Experience and Policy Design Considerations." *Journal of Climate Policy* 11 (2): 922–943. doi: 10.3763/cpol.2010.0093.

Tabuchi, Hiroko. 2017. "Republicans Move to Block Rule on Coal Mining Near Streams." *New York Times*, February 2. https://www.nytimes.com/2017/02/02/business/energy-environment/senate-coal-regulations.html.

Tan, Xiaomei. 2006. "Environment, Governance, and GDP: Discovering their Connections." *International Journal of Sustainable Development* 9 (4): 311–335. doi: 10.1504/ijsd.2006.014218.

Tankersley, Jim. 2016. "Middle Class Incomes Had Their Fastest Growth on Record Last Year." *Washington Post*, September 13. https://www.washingtonpost.com/news/wonk/wp/2016/09/13/the-middle-class-and-the-poor-just-had-the-best-year-since-the-end-of-the-great-recession/.

ten Brink, Patrick, Leonardo Mazza, Tomas Badura, Marianne Kettunen, and Sirini Withana. 2012. *Nature and Its Role in the Transition to a Green Economy*. http://www. teebweb.org/publication/nature-and-its-role-in-a-green-economy/.

The Economics of Ecosystems and Biodiversity (TEEB). 2010. *Mainstreaming the Economics of Nature: A Synthesis of the Approach, Conclusions and Recommendations of TEEB*. http://www.teebweb.org/publication/mainstreaming-the-economics-of-nature-a-synthesis-of-the-approach-conclusions-and-recommendations-of-teeb/.

Thomas, Ward. 2009. "Do Environmental Regulations Impede Economic Growth? A Case Study of the Metal Finishing Industry in the South Coast Basin of Southern California." *Economic Development Quarterly* 23 (4): 329–341. doi: 10.1177/0891242409343184.

Tietenberg, Tom H. 2013. "Reflections—Carbon Pricing in Practice." *Review of Environmental Economics and Policy* 7 (2): 313–329. doi: 10.1093/reep/ret008.

Timiraos, Nick, and Laura Meckler. 2016. "Democratic Economists Say Bernie Sanders's Math Doesn't Add Up." *Wall Street Journal*, February 16. http://www.wsj.com/articles/democratic-economists-say-bernie-sanders-math-doesnt-add-up-1455726507.

Tokic, Damir. 2012. "The Economic and Financial Dimensions of Degrowth." *Ecological Economics* 84: 49–56. doi: 10.1016/j.ecolecon.2012.09.011.

Torras, Mariano. 2005. "Income and Power Inequality as Determinants of Environmental and Health Outcomes: Some Findings." *Social Science Quarterly* 86 (S1): 1354-1376. doi: 10.1111/j.0038-4941.2005.00350.x.

Torras, Mariano, and James Boyce. 1998. "Income, Inequality, and Pollution: A Reassessment of the Environmental Kuznets Curve." *Ecological Economics* 25 (2): 147–160. doi: 10.1016/s0921-8009(97)00177-8.

Tsang, Linda, and Alexandra M. Wyatt. 2017. *Clean Power Plan: Legal Background and Pending Litigation in West Virginia v. EPA*. Washington, DC: Congressional Research Service. https://www.hsdl.org/?view&did=799441.

Turner, Graham M. 2008. "A Comparison of The Limits to Growth with 30 Years of Reality." *Global Environmental Change* 18 (3): 397–411. doi: 10.1016/j.gloenvcha.2008.05.001.

Turok, Ivan, and Jacqueline Borel-Saladin. 2013. "Promises and Pitfalls of the Green Economy." In *World Social Science Report 2013: Changing Global Environments*, 289–294. Paris: UNESCO; ISSC; OECD. doi: 10.1787/9789264203419-en.

Uekotter, Frank. 2014. *The Greenest Nation? A New History of German Environmentalism*. Cambridge, MA: MIT Press.

United Nations (UN). 2010. *Objectives and Themes of the United Nations Conference on Sustainable Development*. https://ggim.un.org/docs/meetings/Forum2011/A-Conf_216-PC-7.pdf.

United Nations Environment Programme (UNEP). 2008. *Payments for Ecosystem Services: Getting Started*. http://hdl.handle.net/20.500.11822/9150.

United Nations Environment Programme (UNEP). 2011. *Towards A Green Economy: Pathways to Sustainable Development and Poverty Eradication—A Synthesis for Policy Makers*. https://sustainabledevelopment.un.org/content/documents/126GER_synthesis_en.pdf.

United States Department of Energy (DOE). 2017. *Annual Energy Outlook 2017.* Energy Information Administration (EIA). http://www.eia.gov/outlooks/aeo/pdf/0383(2017).pdf.

United States Department of Energy (DOE). 2017. *U.S. Energy and Employment Report.* https://www.energy.gov/sites/prod/files/2016/03/f30/U.S.%20Energy%20and%20Employment%20Report.pdf.

United States Environmental Protection Agency (EPA). 1997. *The Benefits and Costs of the Clean Air Act, 1970–1990—Retrospective Study.* https://www.epa.gov/clean-air-act-overview/benefits-and-costs-clean-air-act-1970-1990-retrospective-study.

United States Environmental Protection Agency (EPA). 2010. *Guidelines for Preparing Economic Analyses.* http://yosemite.epa.gov/ee/epa/eerm.nsf/vwAN/EE-0568-51.pdf/$file/EE-0568-51.pdf.

United States Environmental Protection Agency (EPA). 2010. *The Benefits and Costs of the Clean Air Act from 1990–2020.* https://www.epa.gov/sites/production/files/2015-07/documents/summaryreport.pdf.

United States Environmental Protection Agency (EPA). 2013. *The Importance of Water to the United States Economy: Synthesis Report.* http://bafuture.org/sites/default/files/key-topics/attachments/Importance-of-water-synthesis-report.pdf.

United States Environmental Protection Agency (EPA). 2015. *Clean Power Plan by the Numbers.* https://www.epa.gov/cleanpowerplan/fact-sheet-clean-power-plan-numbers.

United States Environmental Protection Agency (EPA). 2016. *Report on the Environment.* https://cfpub.epa.gov/roe/index.cfm.

United States Global Change Research Program. 2014. *National Climate Assessment.* http://nca2014.globalchange.gov/report.

Uslaner, Eric. 2002. *The Moral Foundations of Trust.* Cambridge, UK: Cambridge University Press.

van den Bergh, Jeroen C.J.M. 2001. "Ecological Economics: Themes, Approaches, and Differences with Environmental Economics." *Regional Environmental Change* 2 (1): 13–23. doi: 10.1007/s101130000020.

van den Bergh, Jeroen C.J.M. 2010. "Relax About GDP Growth: Implications for Climate Crisis Policies." *Journal of Cleaner Production* 18 (6): 540–543.

van den Bergh, Jeroen C.J.M. 2011. "Environment Versus Growth—A Criticism of 'Degrowth' and a Plea for 'A-Growth'." *Ecological Economics* 70 (5): 881–890. doi: 10.1016/j.ecolecon.2010.09.035.

Vergragt, Philip J. 2017. "Sustainable Consumption: An Important but Ambiguous Concept." In *Conceptual Innovation in Environmental Policy,* edited by James Meadowcroft and Daniel J. Fiorino, 307–334. Cambridge, MA: MIT Press.

Victor, David. 2016. "What to Expect from Trump on Energy Policy." Brookings. https://www.brookings.edu/blog/planetpolicy/2016/11/17/what-to-expect-from-trump-on-energy-policy/.

Victor, Peter. 2008. *Managing Without Growth: Slower by Design, Not Disaster.* Cheltenham, UK: Edward Elgar.

Vogel, David. 1993. "Representing Diffuse Interests in Environmental Policymaking." In *Do Institutions Matter? Government Capabilities in the United States and Abroad,* edited by R. Kent Weaver and Bert A. Rockman, 237–271. Washington, DC: Brookings Institution Press.

Vogel, David. 1995. *Trading Up: Consumer and Environmental Regulation in a Global Economy.* Cambridge, MA: Harvard University Press.

Vona, Francesco, and Fabrizio Patriarca. 2011. "Income Inequality and the Development of Environmental Technologies." *Ecological Economics* 70 (11): 2201–2213. doi: 10.1016/j.ecolecon.2011.06.027.

von Weizsacker, Ernst Ulrich, Karlson Hargroves, Michael H. Smith, Cheryl Desha, and Peter Stasinopoulos. 2009. *Factor Five: Transforming the Global Economy through 80% Improvements in Resource Productivity.* Abingdon, UK: Earthscan.

Wagner, Gernot, and Martin L. Weitzman. 2015. *Climate Shock: The Economic Consequences of a Hotter Planet.* Princeton, NJ: Princeton University Press.

Waldman, Paul. 2016. "Republicans are Now Vowing Total War. And the Consequences Could Be Immense." *Washington Post*, November 4. https://www.washingtonpost.com/blogs/plum-line/wp/2016/11/03/republicans-are-now-vowing-total-war-and-the-consequences-could-be-immense/.

Walti, Sonja. 2004. "How Multilevel Structures Affect Environmental Policy in Industrial Countries." *European Journal of Political Research* 43 (4): 599–634. doi: 10.1111/j.1475-6765.2004.00167.x.

Ward, Hugh. 2008. "Liberal Democracy and Sustainability." *Environmental Politics* 17 (3): 386–409. doi: 10.1080/09644010802055626.

Warrick, Joby. 2016. "EPA Chief: Obama Administration Will Seek to Lock in Climate Gains in 2016." *Washington Post*, January 7. https://www.washingtonpost.com/national/health-science/epa-chief-obama-administration-will-seek-to-lock-in-climate-gains-in-2016/2016/01/07/016fc1f4-b4ce-11e5-9388-466021d971de_story.html.

Weaver, R. Kent, and Bert A. Rockman, eds. 1993. *Do Institutions Matter? Government Capabilities in the United States and Abroad.* Washington, DC: Brookings Institution Press.

Webber, Michael E. 2016. *Thirst for Power: Energy, Water, and Human Survival.* New Haven, CT: Yale University Press.

Weidner, Helmut. 2002. "Capacity Building for Ecological Modernization: Lessons from Cross-National Research." *American Behavioral Scientist* 45 (9): 1340–1368. doi: 10.1177/0002764202045009004.

White House, Office of the Press Secretary. 2014. "Remarks by the President at U.N. Climate Change Summit." https://obamawhitehouse.archives.gov/the-press-office/2014/09/23/remarks-president-un-climate-change-summit.

Wilkinson, Richard, and Kate Pickett. 2009. *The Spirit Level: Why Equality is Better for Everyone.* London: Penguin.

Will, George. 2015. "'Sustainability' Gone Mad on College Campuses." *Washington Post*, April 15. https://www.washingtonpost.com/opinions/sustainability-gone-mad/2015/04/15/f4331bd2-e2da-11e4-905f-cc896d379a32_story.html.

Willamette Partnership, World Resources Institute, and the National Network on Water Quality Trading. 2015. *Building a Water Quality Trading Program: Options and Considerations.* http://willamettepartnership.org/wp-content/uploads/2015/06/BuildingaWQTProgram-NNWQT.pdf.

Williams III, Roberton C., Dallas Burtraw, and Richard D. Morgenstern. 2015. "The Impacts of a US Carbon Tax across Income Groups and States." *Resources* 190: 25–29. http://www.rff.org/research/publications/impacts-us-carbon-tax-across-income-groups-and-states.

Wines, Michael. 2016. "Judges Find Wisconsin Redistricting Unfairly Favored Republicans." *New York Times*, November 21. http://www.nytimes.com/2016/11/21/us/wisconsin-redistricting-found-to-unfairly-favor-republicans.html.

Winslow, Margrethe. 2005. "Is Democracy Good for the Environment?" *Journal of Environmental Planning and Management* 48 (5): 771–783. doi: 10.1080/09640560500183074.

World Bank. 2012. *Inclusive Growth: The Pathway to Sustainable Development.* https://openknowledge.worldbank.org/handle/10986/6058.

World Bank. 2014. *State and Trends of Carbon Pricing 2014.* https://openknowledge.worldbank.org/handle/10986/18415.

World Bank. 2016. *Shock Waves: Managing the Impacts of Climate Change on Poverty.* https://openknowledge.worldbank.org/handle/10986/22787.

World Business Council for Sustainable Development (WBCSD). 2012. *Vision 2050: The New Agenda for Business.* http://www.wbcsd.org/Overview/About-us/Vision2050/Resources/Vision-2050-The-new-agenda-for-business.

World Commission on Environment and Development. 1987. *Our Common Future.* Oxford: Oxford University Press.

Worldwatch Institute. 2015. *State of the World 2015: Confronting Hidden Threats to Sustainability.* Washington, DC: Island Press.

Tables, figures, and boxes are indicated by an italic *t*, *f*, and *b* following the page number.